TRADITIONALISTS, MUSLIMS, AND CHRISTIANS IN AFRICA

TRADITIONALISTS, MUSLIMS, AND CHRISTIANS IN AFRICA

Interreligious Encounters and Dialogue

Prince Sorie Conteh

CAMBRIA
PRESS

AMHERST, NEW YORK

Requests for permission should be directed to:
permissions@cambriapress.com, or mailed to:
Cambria Press
20 Northpointe Parkway, Suite 188
Amherst, NY 14228

Library of Congress Cataloging-in-Publication Data

Conteh, Prince Sorie.
    Traditionalists, Muslims, and Christians in Africa: interreligious encounters and dialogue / Prince Sorie Conteh.
        p. cm.
    Includes bibliographical references (p.) and index.
    ISBN 978-1-60497-596-3 (alk. paper)
    1. Sierra Leone—Religion. 2. Religions—Relations. I. Title.

BL2470.S55C66 2009
201'.509664—dc22

2008055425

To Mrs. Esther Epp
in appreciation of her continued love and support
and her relentless encouragement for this project

TABLE OF CONTENTS

PREFACE

This multifaceted book is a result of library research and fieldwork undertaken in 2002, 2005, and 2006 in Sierra Leone, West Africa, where the main subjects of this study reside. It seeks to provide a book for students, teachers, scholars, religious leaders, missionaries, and those interested in interfaith cooperation and dialogue, especially among all three of Africa's major living religions—African Traditional[1] Religion[2] (ATR), Christianity, and Islam.

Most of the extant books and courses about interreligious encounters and dialogue deal primarily with the interaction between two or more of the major world religions: Christianity, Islam, Judaism, Hinduism, Buddhism, and Sikhism. This book fills a gap in the study of interreligious dialogue in Africa by taking into consideration the place and relevance of ATR in interreligious dialogue and cooperation in Sierra Leone.

It provides the reader with basic knowledge of ATR, Islam, and Christianity in their Sierra Leonean contexts, and of interfaith encounter and dialogue among the three major faith traditions in Africa. As such, it provides for the first time a historical, chronological, and comparative study of interreligious encounters and dialogue among Traditionalists, Muslims, and Christians in Sierra Leone. It proceeds to investigate the reasons for the exclusion of ATR from interreligious dialogue/cooperation and its relevance and place in the socioreligious landscape of Sierra Leone and the rest of the world, and to discuss possible ways for ATR's inclusion in the ongoing interfaith dialogue and cooperation in Sierra Leone.

FIELDWORK

Fieldwork was first undertaken from April to June 2002 for my doctoral dissertation in theology.[3] It brought together Limba Christians, Limba Traditionalists, and Christian Limbas for the first time to provide a broader understanding of Limba religion, as well as to discover the effects of Limba religiosity and of the tenacity with which the Limba hold to their culture and religion on the National Pentecostal Limba Church (NPLC) for over three decades.[4] The dissertation discussed at length the encounter between Christianity and Limba Traditional Religion and made recommendations for a fruitful dialogue between them.[5]

Further fieldwork, undertaken in May and June 2005, broadened the discussion on interfaith dialogue to include Traditionalists from four additional ethnic groups, and Muslim and Christian practitioners from all ethnic groups in the country. African Traditionalists from the Mende, Temne, Limba, Krio, and Kono were interviewed[6] to provide, where necessary, updates to existing documented information, and to fill gaps in the extant literature on the topics discussed in chapter 2. Both fieldwork experiences also provided the information in the first segment of chapter 7.

A final piece of fieldwork was undertaken in May and June of 2006 in order to complete the 2005 field research by gaining further contemporary understanding of the ongoing interreligious encounters. In this project, Christians and Muslims were interviewed—along with personnel of the Christian[7] and Muslim[8] national secretariats in Freetown, the Project for Christian-Muslim Relations in Africa (PROCMURA), and the Inter-Religious Council of Sierra Leone (IRCSL)—to find ways in which Sierra Leone Traditionalists could be included in the ongoing interfaith cooperation and dialogue between Muslims and Christians.[9] Information gathered from this project is discussed in the second and third segments of chapter 6.

Endnotes

1. Some scholars are still of the opinion that the adjective 'traditional' should be dropped in ATR in favour of using simply African Religion (AR). I have no problem using either ATR or AR. However, I feel more comfortable with the former. I have yet to discover in the English language where the word 'traditional' implies any derogatory meaning. If 'traditional' has become unacceptable, does it logically follow that any word used to describe a 'traditional' religion will eventually become derogatory? 'Traditional' was chosen over 'primitive' specifically because it was not derogatory. If we refer to ATR as simply 'African Religion', how will we then differentiate between ATR and the broader context of AR, which encompasses all religious expression (of any origin) in Africa?

2. The sound arguments of some scholars about the use of the singular 'Religion' instead of 'Religions' in reference to ATR may have laid to rest the debate regarding the appropriateness of these terms. The two outstanding arguments in favour of the homogeneity of ATR have come from Idowu (1973, 104) and Magesa (1997, 14–18). Idowu argued that African people have a common racial origin and therefore all African culture and religious beliefs have evolved from a common source, which he described as 'negritude', an expression of their common Africanness. Magesa argued that AR is one in its essence. There is a 'basic worldview' that is fundamentally the same throughout Africa. The varieties that exist within ATR cannot be taken to mean a diversity of fundamental belief. Parrinder (1962, 11), writing earlier, observed, over four decades, that homogeneity is apparent in ATR. In similar vein, Taylor stated,

   > There is not one homogeneous system of belief throughout Africa... Nevertheless anyone who has read a number of anthropological works dealing with different parts of Africa must be struck not only by the remarkable number of features that are common but by the emergence of a basic world-view which fundamentally is everywhere the same. (1963, 27)

3. The dissertation, entitled *Fundamental Concepts of Limba Traditional Religion and Its Effects on Limba Christianity and Vice Versa in Sierra Leone in the Past Three Decades*, was completed in 2004.

4. See DTh dissertation (2004, 281) for profiles of interviewees and consultants.
5. My first fieldwork experience also motivated an article, 'Discussing the Trinity with African Traditionalists' (2005), in which I made a solid case for the inclusion and involvement of African Traditionalists in interfaith dialogue.
6. Due to time constraints, the research was limited to five groups of traditionalists chosen because of the size of the groups and the availability of written information on these groups. The Mende, Temne, Limba, and Krio are the four major ethnic groups in Sierra Leone. In that regard, any work on ethnicity must include them. I included the Kono because of the availability of documented information.
7. These include the Council of Churches in Sierra Leone, the Evangelical Fellowship of Sierra Leone, Pentecostal Churches in Sierra Leone, and the Catholic Church in Sierra Leone.
8. These include the Federation of Sierra Leone Islamic Organisations, Federation of Muslim Women Associations of Sierra Leone, Muslim Brotherhood Islamic Mission, Sierra Leone Muslim Congress, Sierra Leone Muslim Missionary Union, Supreme Islamic Council, and United Council of Islam.
9. See appendix A for profiles of interviewees and consultants.

ACKNOWLEDGMENTS

I am grateful to many people whose help and support were vital in the writing of this book. I would like to recognise them and I hope I do not forget anyone. My thanks go to the members of Carleton United Church, Niagara Presbytery, for allowing me to complete this work while ministering with them.

I am indebted to Prof. G. J. A. Lubbe for his academic guidance and inspiration. Thanks to all the incredible people I interviewed and consulted who are listed in appendix A. Special thanks to the Rev. Moses Khanu for providing information and research materials on interreligious dialogue and cooperation in Sierra Leone. My thanks go to Connie Consonni, pastoral assistant at St. Alfred's Catholic Parish in St. Catharines, Ontario, for providing information and materials on Catholicism, Vatican II, and Catholic-related documents.

Thanks and appreciation to Rev. Dr. Hans Ucko (formerly of the Program on Interreligious Dialogue Cooperation), World Council of Churches (WCC), and Msgr. Chidi Denis Isizoh, Traditional Religions desk at the Pontifical Council for Interreligious Dialogue (PCID), Vatican, for providing relevant information and research books and materials on interreligious dialogue and cooperation. Thanks to my wife, Mrs. Peggy Conteh Wallace, for her moral and academic support.

LIST OF ABBREVIATIONS

AACC	All Africa Conference of Churches
AIC	African indigenous/independent churches
AME	African Methodist Episcopal
AOG	Assemblies of God
APC	All People's Congress
AR	African Religion
ATR	African Traditional Religion
AU	African Union
AWC	American Wesleyan Church
BICMURA	*Bulletin on Islam and Christian-Muslim Relations in Africa*
BMS	Baptist Missionary Society
CCSL	Council of Churches in Sierra Leone
CMS	Church Missionary Society
CWR	Council for World Religions
ECOWAS	Economic Organisation of West African States
IRCSL	Inter-Religious Council of Sierra Leone

IRP Series	Inter-Religious Publications Series
LEV	Liberia Editrice Vaticana
LXX	Septuagint
MCA	Missionary Church Association
MCSL	Methodist Church, Sierra Leone
NPLC	National Pentecostal Limba Church
NT	New Testament
OIRRD	Office on Inter-Religious Relations and Dialogue
OT	Old Testament
PCID	Pontifical Council for Interreligious Dialogue
PROCMURA	Project for Christian-Muslim Relations in Africa
RCC	Roman Catholic Church
RME	Religious and Moral Education
RUF	Revolutionary United Front
SAC	Société Africaine de Culture
SDA	Seventh Day Adventists
SLIR	Sierra Leone Indigenous Religion
SLPP	Sierra Leone People's Party
SSBA	Special Synod of Bishops of Africa
TRC	Truth and Reconciliation Commission
UCC	United Church of Canada
UMC	United Methodist Church
UN	United Nations
WAM	West African Methodist
WCC	World Council of Churches
WCRP	World Conference on Religion and Peace

TRADITIONALISTS, MUSLIMS, AND CHRISTIANS IN AFRICA

CHAPTER 1

INTRODUCTION

This book, *Traditionalists, Muslims, and Christians in Africa: Interreligious Encounters and Dialogue*, is about interreligious encounters among ATR, Islam, and Christianity in sub-Saharan Africa,[1] with special focus on Sierra Leone.

The primal religion of the indigenes of sub-Saharan Africa is ATR. These indigenes opened up their countries to accommodate foreigners of different backgrounds and walks of life who continue to introduce new social values and religions. Islam first landed on the east coast of Africa in the seventh century (Mbiti 1989a, 237), and later arrived in Sierra Leone in the eleventh century (Parsons 1964, 226). There is evidence that missionaries from Alexandria brought Christianity to Ethiopia by the middle of the fourth century (Groves 1948). However, in modern times, Christianity was brought to sub-Saharan Africa in the sixteenth century by the Portuguese. By 1541, the Portuguese were already in Ethiopia (Nthamburi 1995, 50), and a century later, they arrived in Sierra Leone (Fyle 1981; Alie 1990, 101–111).

Contrary to the claim by some scholars that Islam and Christianity are indigenous to Africa (Booth 1977, 297; Rieber 1977, 255; Mbiti 1989a, 223), a majority of Sierra Leone Traditionalists still consider Islam and Christianity to be 'immigrant religions' (Khanu 2001, 17–53; Alie 1990, 110) brought by foreigners, some of whom were interested in adventure and trade in Sierra Leone (Fyle 1981, 27; Alie 1990, 43, 101). It is an established fact that these faiths have, for many years, impacted African peoples, particularly invading their traditional religion and culture. However, in the Sierra Leonean context, neither their length of stay nor their impact on the religious landscape makes them indigenous.

The advent of these immigrant religions was the beginning of a long history of coexistence among practitioners of ATR, Islam, and Christianity in the region. In most countries, this relationship has been cordial.[2] However, this peaceful coexistence does not imply equality.

As in all experiences of encounter and coexistence, there have been challenges as well as benefits. People living side by side meet and interact personally and communally on a regular basis. They share common resources and communal benefits. The social and cultural interaction and cooperation involved in this dialogue of life are what compel us to fully understand the worldviews of our neighbours and to seek out better relationships with them. In the history of this culture of dialogue and cooperation, ATR, the host religion, which has played and continues to play a vital role in the assimilation of Christianity and Islam, seems to have been marginalised and stereotyped.

The estimated religious statistics in Sierra Leone are as follows: Muslim, 50 percent; Traditionalist, 30 percent; Christian, 15 percent; and other faiths, 5 percent. Each of these religious traditions constitutes an important phenomenon and affects the future of the nation. In that respect, a programme must be developed for the constructive engagement of Traditionalists, Christians, and Muslims in the emerging post-war Sierra Leone.

In the Truth and Reconciliation Commission (TRC) of the Sierra Leone Act, explicit reference is made 'to the assistance from traditional and religious leaders in facilitating reconciliation'. The commission's final report—volume 3b, chapter 7, paragraph 39, on the subject 'Traditional values and methods informing reconciliation'—portrays the importance and indispensable contribution of African traditional values in society and public life by stating, among other things, that 'the reconciliation process cannot move forward without the participation of the religious and traditional leaders'.

Therefore, neglecting or relegating ATR to an inferior position may cost Sierra Leoneans 'an essential component in the indigenous religious heritage', which constitutes 'a vital factor in the religious motivation and perception of Africans' (Sanneh 1983, 86). In the spirit of justice, relations among these religious parties demand serious study and action.

In view of the long history of coexistence among the peoples of these faith traditions and the important role played by ATR and its practitioners in the transformation of society and culture, as well as the impact thereof[3] on Christianity and Islam, this book aims to answer the following questions:

- Why have Muslim and Christian leaders long marginalised ATR, its practices, and practitioners from interfaith dialogue and cooperation in Sierra Leone?
- What is lacking in ATR that continues to prevent practitioners of Christianity and Islam from officially involving Traditionalists in the socioreligious development of the country?

In view of the aforementioned, this study will later investigate the reasons for the exclusion of ATR from interreligious dialogue, the relevance and place of traditional religion in interreligious encounters, and ways in which ATR might possibly be included in Sierra Leone interfaith dialogue and cooperation.

The rest of this chapter provides past and present academic context relating to interreligious encounters and dialogue among the three faith traditions under study. This is followed by a social history of Sierra Leone and is concluded with an outline of the rest of the book.

PAST AND PRESENT ACADEMIC CONTEXT

Very little has been written on interreligious encounters and dialogue among ATR, Christianity, and Islam in Africa. The majority of existing literary accounts of interreligious encounters are of those between Christianity and Islam, and between Christianity and ATR.

McKenzie's book *Inter-Religious Encounters in West Africa* is one of the very few works that addressed interfaith interactions among all three belief systems under study. It examined one of the earliest interreligious encounters among ATR, Christianity, and Islam in West Africa.

Although the book records interreligious interactions that occurred several centuries ago, its contribution is a foundational resource for this study and for the general spectrum of interfaith encounter and dialogue. It gave comprehensive accounts of the exclusivist and flexible approaches of a conservative African Christian, Ajayi Crowther—who later became an Anglican priest and eventually a bishop—in interreligious encounters, mainly in Sierra Leone and some regions of Nigeria. ATR, Islam, and Christianity were 'linked together by Crowther for good or ill—since it was clear that in the lives of the people as a whole they were also inextricably interwoven' (1976, 46).

Although Crowther was born into a multireligious society, he could not withstand the existence of non-Christian religious traditions. This makes it hard to consider some of his methods of interreligious encounters as a paradigm for today's interfaith relation and cooperation, but we can certainly learn from them.

Sanneh's 1983 book *West African Christianity* is another work on early interreligious encounters among ATR, Islam, and Christianity. Chapter 4 of the book provided an early history of the coming and expansion of Christianity, especially Protestant Christianity, into West Africa in the nineteenth century through Sierra Leone, which was the chosen location for the Nova Scotians, the Maroons, and the Recaptives (i.e., slaves that were recaptured and freed), including Ajayi Crowther. These groups later came to be known as the Settlers.

Sanneh gave Ajayi Crowther a place of recognition for his work in interreligious encounters in West Africa. He started by providing a brief chronicle of his religious background, early life, achievements, and later life (1983, 75–76). This was followed by a brief sketch of the four major religious groups among the early settlers in Sierra Leone, and how the Christianity of these settlers interacted with African traditional religiosity. Although the settlers were Christians and were living in Christian communities, they tenaciously held on to their traditional religious customs and practices. Their dual religiosity, of course, provoked interreligious fracas with missionaries and church leaders.

Crowther's views on non-Christian faith traditions, like those of the missionaries of his time, were uncompromising (Sanneh 1983, 76). Rev. James Johnson and Crowther were involved in several encounters with staunch Traditionalists. Their constant criticism of ATR resulted in confrontations with practitioners who were determined to defend their worldviews. Beyond the interreligious encounters, there are helpful points about the importance and contribution of ATR to the two foreign faiths. ATR, we must note, has penetrated Christianity and Islam and 'endowed them with a tolerant, absorptive capacity' (1987).

Sanneh's eighth chapter contained glimpses of interreligious encounters among Christianity, Islam, and ATR. It supplies basic information first about the encounter of Christianity and Islam. After providing brief histories of the early advents of the two faiths, the reader is introduced to Dr. Edward Blyden, an agent in Sierra Leone, who was a noted sympathiser of Islam, and Bishop Bowen, who was determined to positively use the common ground that existed between Christianity and Islam. Dr. Blyden's campaign and work for the place of Islam, and a better relationship between Christianity and Islam, earned him widespread respect.

The chapter concluded with Islam and Christianity encountering traditional religions (1983, 227–241). A sharp contrast can be seen between the attitudes of these two outside faiths towards ATR. Islam was far more tolerant to traditional religion than was Christianity. Many Muslims even adopted elements of ATR into their own religious practices. The Christian attitude towards ATR, as perpetrated by Crowther, was predominately negative. However, Rev. Johnson's approach was more favourable to Traditionalists. In several ways, 'the historic meeting of different religions in Africa should help to provide a positive framework for cross-religious influences' (87).

Another work that is relevant for this study is that of Blyden ([1887] 1994). The book, which is commonly referred to as Blyden's *magnum opus*, is primarily about the influence of Christianity and Islam on the Africans, especially those in Sierra Leone and Liberia, in the nineteenth century. Blyden traced the means by which the two foreign faiths came to Africa, and their attitudes towards African culture and religion. He portrayed Islam as being more accommodating to, and sharing more affinity with, the African. Its original tradition was modified in Africa 'by shaping many of its traditional customs to suit the milder and more conciliatory disposition' of the Africans ([1887] 1994, 14). Islam was helpful in guiding Africans to overcome the traditional polytheistic worship. Muslims have done more to improve the socioculture of Africa and to promote the achievements and religiosity of Africans.

Unlike Islam, Christianity is less tolerant of African culture and beliefs, and tends to degrade them ([1887] 1994, 30–53). The teachings of Christianity are exclusive and uncompromising. Although a Christian himself, Blyden was very sympathetic to Islam and worked hard to gain for Islam the respect and recognition it deserved. Blyden's work also provided the reader with knowledge of the efforts made, and the achievements gained, by Africans in public services and in promoting African values.

Sanneh's 1996 book *Piety and Power* is relevant at a time when the world is very aware of the importance of exploring new and creative methods for engagement in interfaith dialogue, especially between Muslims and Christians. It is an analysis of Christianity and Islam in West Africa. Muslim-Christian encounters and relationships are not new in Africa, but constitute a vital phenomenon that affects not only Muslims and Christians, but people of other religious faiths. Africa has been helpful in mediating 'between the world of Islam and that of the West, and in so doing has itself received the imprints of the two influences while adding its own accent' (1996, 3). The added African accent shows how Africans hold tenaciously to their indigenous beliefs.

In chapter 4 of his work, Sanneh provided analysis of the 1888 debate on Islam and Christianity, which was prompted by Edward Blyden's aforementioned book ([1887] 1994). The subject of the debate was, 'Is Christianity or Islam best suited to promote the true interests of the Negro race?' This appears to have been the first organised interreligious debate in Freetown, Sierra Leone. This debate, as the subject implies, was intended to examine which one of these two foreign faiths most suitably promoted African interest and identity. The debate, like the book that prompted it, testified to Blyden's passion for interreligious understanding and cooperation. It portrayed the engagement of the three religious traditions under study.

Sanneh's analysis of this debate is very helpful for interfaith debate and dialogue today. He discussed the debate, the manner and style of its proceedings, its issues, its meaning and relevance for our contemporary religious landscape, and the religious rules of engagement. This discussion makes the book crucial to our study.

The essays in Olupona (1991) reflect the issues and themes discussed at a conference hosted by the Council for World Religions (CWR) in Nairobi, Kenya, 10–14 September 1987, on 'The place of African Traditional Religion in contemporary Africa'. The CWR conference was called in response to the struggle ATR continues to face with the degradation it suffers from Islam and Christianity. It brought together scholars and religious leaders from the three faith backgrounds to engage in dialogue, share ideas, and discuss issues of common concern. Although these essays, unlike the aforementioned works, do not specifically featured Sierra Leone, the relevance of this book for our study should not be underemphasised. It promises to be helpful in several ways, as follows:

- It examines the constitution, structure, and significance of ATR as a dynamic, changing tradition.

- It analyses and interprets important aspects of African religion and explores its possible contributions to national development and the modernisation process.
- It takes into consideration the impact of social change on African religion today.

Some of the individual essays are worth noting:

Abimbola's essay, 'The Place of African Traditional Religion in Contemporary Africa: The Yoruba Example' (1991, 51–58), argues that in spite of their influence, Christianity and Islam have been unable to penetrate the traditional religion of the Yoruba people.

Mbon's work, 'African Traditional Socio-Religious Ethics and National Development: The Nigeria Case' (1991, 101–109), is reminiscent of the findings of the TRC in Sierra Leone that African social ethics are capable of promoting impressive socioeconomic development in contemporary African societies.

Awolalu's paper, 'The Encounter Between African Traditional Religion and Other Religions in Nigeria' (1991, 111–118), gives readers an account of the advent and interaction of Islam and Christianity with ATR in Northern Nigeria. Awolalu traced the different encounters of Islam and Christianity with ATR. Like Blyden, Awolalu showed that Islam has proven more tolerant of ATR than was Christianity.

Mulago's essay, 'African Traditional Religion and Christianity' (1991, 119–134), argues that ATR has been a vital religious force in Africa and has had a long relationship with Christianity.

The book edited by Olupona and Nyang (1993) comprises chapters written in honour of John Mbiti's enormous contribution and pioneer work in African scholarship. The religious plurality, which is prevalent in Africa, makes this work relevant to this study. The book is divided into five sections. The first two deal with matters concerning African religion and theology. The next two deal with ATR and other religious faiths. The last section presents responses to John Mbiti's work. The following two essays are among those worth considering.

In 'Traditional African Healing System Versus Western Medicine in Southern Ghana: An Encounter' (1993, 95–107), Appiah-Kubi deals with the question of healing processes in Ghana. It discusses concepts and approaches to patient care and healing by western medicine and traditional healers. This is vital to our study because medicine is the only area I have discovered in which Sierra Leonean Traditionalists are encouraged on a national level, as evidenced by the formation of an association of medical doctors and traditional healers.

In 'Africa and Christianity: Domestication of Christian Values in the African Church' (1993, 179–196), Byaruhanga-Akiiki discusses some areas in which Christianity and ATR share similar values or parallel concepts. It also presents valid cautionary notes when dealing with Traditionalists in order to avoid the mistakes of missionary Christianity.

The publication by Oke (2005) contains papers from the first International Congress of Dialogue on Civilizations, Religion and Cultures in West Africa, which was held in Abuja, Nigeria, in December 2003, organised by the UNESCO Interreligious Dialogue Programme. The objective 'was to examine, through the lenses of Interreligious dialogue, such specific topics as sustainable development, situations of conflict or tension, and the HIV/AIDS pandemic' (2005, 27). The papers proposed actions that should be considered 'if cultural and spiritual diversity is to benefit multicultural societies rather than hamper them' (2005, 27).

The paper 'Managing Conflicts in the African Context: The Role of Religious Leaders' (2005, 29–34), by Isizoh, is about the role that the leaders of Africa's three major religions—ATR, Christianity, and Islam—can play to prevent or resolve conflicts. He noted the mediation of the IRCSL between the government and the rebels during the civil war. This is followed by a list of interreligious councils in West Africa. 'Religious leaders', he stated, 'can get involved in resolving conflicts by acting on behalf of the marginalised and as the voice of the voiceless' (2005, 33).

Adegbite, a Muslim scholar, presented a paper entitled 'The Role of Religious Leaders in Conflict Resolution' (2005, 35–36). He suggested that religious diversity does not destroy the potency of religions. A careful look at the teachings of different religions reveals that there are many values they share in common (35). In order to produce a better understanding of and regard for other religions, he proposed that all practitioners 'must be taught the elements of their own religion as well as those of other faiths in their community' (36).

In the essay 'How to Improve the Relationship Between Islam, Christianity and Traditional African Religion' (2005, 37–38), Abimbola argued that, if they were serious about religious, ethnic, and cultural harmony and peace, it was essential 'for the leadership of Islam and Christianity in Africa to accept the validity of Traditional African Religion' (37). In his view, all the faiths of the world are valid. He pleaded with Christians and Muslims to put into practice the tolerance and respect they preach by tolerating and respecting other religious faiths.

Ajayi delivered a paper on 'Promoting Religious Tolerance and Co-Operation in the West African Region: The Example of Religious Plurality and Tolerance Among the Yoruba of South-Western Nigeria' (2005, 43–47). The paper examines the example of peaceful coexistence among Traditionalists, Christians, and Muslims in Yoruba land. He attributed the interreligious tolerance and cooperation in Yoruba land to the tolerance inherited from ATR, 'whose accommodation and tolerance paved the way for Islam and Christianity' (44). There is no place where 'tolerance and peaceful coexistence is exhibited more than in the accommodation and mutual coexistence of Traditional Religion, Islam and Christianity in Yoruba land' (45).

SOCIOHISTORY OF SIERRA LEONE

Sierra Leone is located in West Africa. It is bounded on the northwest and northeast by the Republic of Guinea, on the south by Liberia, and on the west and southwest by the Atlantic Ocean. It occupies a total area 27,925 square miles and is fairly circular in shape; the distance from north to south is 210 miles, and from west to east is approximately 204 miles (Alie 1990, 1). There are two main seasons in the country: the dry, from mid-November to April, and the wet, from May to early November. Sierra Leone became an independent state within the British Commonwealth on 27 April 1961, and subsequently attained republican status on 19 April 1971. The capital city is Freetown, and there are four national administrative divisions: the Eastern, Northern, and Southern Provinces, and the Western Area (Fyle 1981, 3).

There are seventeen ethnic groups within Sierra Leone:[4] Mende are found in the Southern and Eastern Provinces; Temne, Limba, Kuranko, Loko, Fula, Mandigo (or Mandika), Soso, and Yalunka inhabit the Northern Province; Krio and Kru are found in the Western Area; Kono inhabit the Eastern Province; and Kissi live further inland in the Eastern Province. Sherbro/Bullom, Vai, Krim, and Gola are found along the north and south coast.

As a former British colony, Sierra Leone retains English as the official language used primarily by the literate minority, while Krio is the lingua franca. According to the National Census and Central Statistic offices in Freetown, the estimated population of Sierra Leone (as of July 2008) is 6,294,774.

Common Cultural Straits

With the notable exception of the Krio,[5] most of Sierra Leone's people groups are subsistence farmers. A comparatively small number in city centres are engaged in commercial businesses, such as the buying and selling of goods. Some craftspeople, such as blacksmiths, sculptors, and leather workers, produce and sell goods. Many master blacksmiths are Krio.

The African is a communal being. This is why the extended family system is one of the aspects of African culture that has remained largely unaltered by the impact of Westernisation. In most Sierra Leonean cultures, the basic unit is the household. This unit comprises a husband, a wife or wives (in the case of the Mende, Temne, Limba, Kono, and Muslim Krio),[6] their children, 'and frequently also blood and affinal relatives—for example, junior brothers and their wives, and unmarried sisters—as well as dependants' (Alie 1990, 20). Whether in a monogamous or polygamous home, the household is usually under the charge of the husband or a responsible adult male. Two decades ago, the husband, as head of the home, was considered to be the sole breadwinner, and everyone in the home depended on him to provide for their needs. In the hinterland, it was, in turn, the assumed responsibility of the wife/wives to help on the farm, prepare meals, nurse infants, and nurture and instruct the children in the norms of the society.

In the absence of grown-up children capable of doing chores, the cleaning, laundry, and gathering of firewood fall on the wife—or on the junior wives if there is more than one wife in the home. In the Western Area, the wife/wives assume similar responsibilities (with the exception of working on the farm), and women who work outside of the home take maternity leave in order to raise their children.

Today, as a result of social and economic changes, some gender roles have been altered. As well as general living expenses, families now have to pay head and income taxes, and children who show academic promise have to be sent to college or university after secondary school. As these expenses increased, in many cases, one income was not enough to make ends meet. In rural regions, produce from the farm often was not enough to meet the financial demands of the household. For many of those with jobs, in both rural and urban areas, a single salary was often not enough to pay the monthly bills and to provide other necessities. In the hinterland, most married women became involved in small-scale businesses to supplement their husbands' farming income. In the urban areas, non-educated women also engaged in petty trading, while educated women either took jobs in offices or began their own businesses. Thus, breadwinning has become a responsibility that is shared between husband and wife, often with the wife managing the finances of the home.

Although breadwinning is now a task shared between husband and wife, traditionally, the husband is still seen as the provider. Even if the wife's income is greater than that of the husband, it is still seen as the responsibility of the husband to provide the family with necessities. For this reason, if the husband requires his wife's assistance in providing for the family, he should be very kind and polite to her because if the family is not provided for, society will hold only the husband accountable for the failure to provide, regardless of his wife's financial status.

This change in gender roles has positively affected the lives of many women and has made a significant impact on the status of women in Sierra Leone. Some women have taken over as much as 70 percent of the household responsibilities, and this has earned them immense respect and appreciation from their families and society associates.

In most Sierra Leonean cultures, the elderly are accorded a great deal of respect (Alie 1990, 23; Fyle 1981, 64). The young must respect not only the elders of his or her family, but also those of the society. In general, older people are addressed by a title of respect and not by their ordinary names.

OUTLINE

Following this chapter is part 1, 'That We May Know One Another', which contains chapter 2, 'Sierra Leone Indigenous Religion and Culture'; chapter 3, 'Islam in Sierra Leone'; and chapter 4, 'Christianity in Sierra Leone'. Part 2, 'Meetings and Partings', comprises the fifth chapter, 'Comparative Analysis of ATR With Islam and With Christianity'. Part 3, 'Then, Now, and Why', is composed of chapter 6, 'Historical and Contemporary Interreligious Dialogue and Cooperation, and Reasons for the Exclusion of ATR'. Part 4, 'The Challenge', contains the seventh chapter, 'The Place and Recognition of ATR in Interreligious Cooperation'. Chapter 8, 'Concluding Remarks', recapitulates the whole study and concludes with my final thoughts.

ENDNOTES

1. The term 'sub-Saharan Africa' is used in reference to the countries in Africa that are not part of North Africa, in other words, countries south of the Sahara. In the early eighth century, sub-Saharan West Africa was known by the Arabs who went to evangelise the region as *Bilad as Sudan* ('The land of the Blacks'). Later, in the nineteenth century, the whole of sub-Saharan Africa was commonly referred to as 'Black Africa' or 'the Dark continent' by Westerners. This was to some extent due to the skin colour of the indigenes, and because much had not been fully discovered or investigated about Africa by Arabs and Westerners. These terms are viewed as derogatory and pejorative, and are further considered misleading because black Africans are also indigenous to much of North Africa. Westerners are not the only ones who are guilty of using the term. Today some Africans refer to the region as 'Black Africa' as well (Ikenga-Metuh 1987, ix). Sub-Saharan Africa, especially East Africa, has been suggested as the birthplace of the human race (Mbiti 1991, 2). There are evidences of early forms of human found in Ethiopia, Tanzania, and Kenya. There are forty-two countries in the sub-Saharan African mainland, and six island nations: CENTRAL AFRICA: Democratic Republic of Congo; Republic of Congo; Central African Republic; Rwanda; Burundi. EAST AFRICA: Kenya; Tanzania; Uganda; Djibouti; Eritrea; Ethiopia; Somalia (excluding Somaliland); Sudan. SOUTHERN AFRICA: Angola; Botswana; Lesotho; Malawi; Mozambique; Namibia; South Africa; Swaziland; Zambia; Zimbabwe. WEST AFRICA: Benin; Burkina Faso; Cameroon; Chad; Cote d'Ivore; Equatorial Guinea; Gabon; The Gambia; Ghana; Guinea; Guinea-Bissau; Liberia; Mali; Mauritania; Niger; Nigeria; Senegal; Sierra Leone; Togo. AFRICAN ISLAND NATIONS: Cape Verde and Sao Tome and Principe (West Africa); Comoros, Madagascar, and Mauritus (Southern Africa); Seychelles (East Africa). It should be noted that Mauritius is generally not considered to be a sub-Saharan African island because the ethnic makeup of the country is predominately East Indian, Chinese, and French.
2. In Nigeria, the cynical manipulation of religion by the federal government has led to a combative dimension in Christian-Muslim relations since the 1980s (see Olupona 1991, 9).
3. Although Christianity and Islam are the religious traditions to which most Africans have converted over the century, many of these converts are influenced by ATR in their religious thoughts and expressions. They tenaciously retain elements of their traditional religious origins.

4. Fyle (1981, 3) excludes the Kru and puts the number at sixteen. For many decades now, the Mende, Temne, Limba, and Krio have been considered the leading groups in Sierra Leone culture. The main news on the national radio station is read in the languages of these four groups. Also, in the current 6-3-3-4 educational system—6 years at primary school, 3 years at junior secondary school, 3 years at senior secondary school, and 4 years tertiary education—courses in the Mende, Temne, Limba, and Krio cultures and languages are offered in the country's schools, colleges, and university. In the primary and secondary school levels, students are required to study one of these four ethnic groups.

5. Freetown peninsula was planned as an agricultural settlement for the ex-slaves, but poor soil in the peninsula frustrated farming efforts and did not make that come true (Wyse 1989, 5). This might be the reason why the Krio did not become farmers like the other groups in Sierra Leone. Commerce/trading provided an alternative for Krio men and women (Wyse 1989, 5; Fyle 1981, 72; Alie 1990, 80, 82).

6. In spite of the occasional difficulty inherent in having many wives, men in the hinterland traditionally like to marry many wives if at all possible. The reasons given for polygamy are both economic and social. A man's wealth is measured by the number of wives and children that he has. The understanding is that a man with more wives must maintain a larger farm and build more houses than a man with fewer wives. It is also believed that each wife brings more wisdom to the husband. A man with one wife has only one outside source of information and guidance, a man with many wives will have many sources and, therefore, a distinct advantage. Polygamy is practised only rarely in Freetown because the higher cost of living in an urban environment makes it very difficult for a man to support more than one wife.

PART I

THAT WE MAY KNOW ONE ANOTHER

One main principle of interreligious dialogue I discovered during my first fieldwork experience in Sierra Leone in 2002 is that to establish fruitful dialogue, the participants must be acquainted with their own values, social and religiocultural, as well as those of the other party. Most interreligious conflicts emanate from ignorance and prejudice. An informed understanding of one's perspective and experience and that of one's neighbour is a crucial component of living in community. In that regard, this portion of the book contains information about the three religious traditions under study. Chapter 2, 'Sierra Leone Indigenous Religion (SLIR) and Culture', deals with the religious worldviews and practices of five Sierra Leonean ethnic groups. Chapter 3, 'Islam in Sierra Leone', and chapter 4, 'Christianity in Sierra Leone', survey the historical arrival and growth of Islam and Christianity in Sierra Leone, their basic tenets, and their encounters with traditional religion.

CHAPTER 2

SIERRA LEONE INDIGENOUS RELIGION (SLIR) AND CULTURE

This chapter attempts to offer a comprehensive and comparative systematic study of Sierra Leone indigenous religious beliefs and practices. The fundamental religious tenets of the five ethnic groups in Sierra Leone mentioned in the preface are discussed. This not only provides an understanding of the religiosity of these groups, but also serves as a major source for discovering the relevance and place of traditional religion. It thereby equips readers, to some extent, for a comparative analysis with Christianity and Islam, and helps to draw contours for an understanding of the differences between these three religious traditions, making recommendations for better interfaith dialogue and cooperation.

ATR, referred to in this study as SLIR,[1] is the indigenous religion of the people of Sierra Leone.[2] As such, it could be said that SLIR, like most African indigenous religion, 'emerged from the sustaining faith held by the forebears of the present generation', and is 'being practised today in various forms and intensities' (Awolalu 1991, 111) in the country.

Traditional religion is a way of life that intertwines with the secular. There is no sharp dividing line between the sacred and the mundane, because the latter is a vehicle of the former.

In spite of the changes indigenous religion in Sierra Leone has undergone due to external and internal influences[3]—the intrusion of comparatively new religions and the complexities of modernisation—the presuppositions of ATR still pervade the whole life of the Traditionalists and continue to be an integral part of their culture, even after they have become Muslim or Christian. ATR continues to play an important role in shaping the character of Sierra Leonean societies. Yet, as in other modern African cultures, it 'continues to suffer from lack of acceptance and inadequate understanding of its central tenets and essence' (Olupona 1991, 1) in the hands of nonpractitioners.

Through social-functionalist and comparative thematic approaches, this chapter discusses systematically the fundamental beliefs and practices of the five cultural groups by first identifying their sources, which is followed by the components upon which this chapter is built.

SOURCES OF SLIR

SLIR, like all other AR, is not a 'religion of the book'. There are no scriptures to serve as repertoires of the tenets, teachings, and practices of the faith. However, there are devices for the preservation and transmission of its tenets and traditions. The main identifiable sources in SLIR can be categorised as oral tradition and art forms.

Oral Tradition
Many of the tenets of SLIR are transmitted orally through myths/stories, proverbs, oaths, dreams, prayers, blessings, and curses (Parsons 1964; Finnegan 1967; Harris and Sawyerr 1968; Gittins 1987; Ottenberg 1996).

African Mythology
African myths provide 'a "sacred history" of the people'. They tell how some things came into being, and about supernatural beings. They are

'stories, the product of fertile imagination, sometimes simple, often containing profound truths. Myths are not meant to be taken too literally'; however, most of them 'express serious beliefs in "human being, eternity, and God"' (Parrinder 1967, 16). They are the stories of a people's origin and religion. They express 'the history, the culture, and the inner experience of the African', which further portray the wishes and fears of the African people as they grope to understand the unknown by dissecting and remoulding it to fit their frame of reference (Koech 1977, 117). Myths serve as 'a language depicting truths or realities for which history does not provide a full explanation' (Mbiti 1991, 59). They should be seen as a crucial component of socioculture. They are the way a society expresses their traditions and heritage in their own language and worldview. Myths provide the fuel that maintains the systems that govern African societies (Thomas 2005, 143).

The purpose of mythology is more than explanatory. Koech explained the purposes of African mythology in context as follows:

- African mythology acts as a socialising agent. It is used to nourish and continue the traditions of the elders or ancestors. The morals, norms, conventions, customs, and manners are part of the myth.
- Education is another function of the myth—teaching people, especially the youngsters, the meaning of the universe and those things which belong to it.
- The myth provides emotional and psychological easement by pointing towards the redeeming features in what appears to be a bad situation.
- The African myth is entertainment, and may become a part of drama, art, and of skill. The African mythologist, or his students, seeks to employ all forms of theatrical skill and to put to use every faculty in his delivery. (1977, 118)

In SLIR, myths and stories are interchangeable, depending on the area and the understanding of the people.

Proverbs

Proverbs are rich sources of African wisdom and philosophy. They enshrine wisdom, beliefs, and accumulated experiences of past and present generations (Ikenga-Metuh 1987, 32). Proverbs may be secular or religious. Religious proverbs contain beliefs, worldviews, ethics, and cautions about human activities or relations. In most African traditional cultures, the use of proverbs is a common feature of African religion. The 'entire worldview of the people' is 'rooted within proverbs and wise saying', and many of these 'proverbs govern religious and social behaviour' (Thomas 2005, 109). African societies have 'succeeded in developing complicated and beautiful webs of proverbs for all conceivable circumstances' (Oguejiofor 2006, 84). African proverbs

> cover every department of human endeavour and human relation, and thus there is hardly any African imbued to any measure with the culture of his people who has not a good stock of proverbs for ready application, though, like in all things expertise and refinement in their use vary widely. (Oguejiofor 2006, 84)

There are thousands of African proverbs that researchers/students could arrange into large collections, analyse, and categorise according to theme.

Ethno-Philosophy and Sage Philosophy

Ethno-philosophy is the expression of African worldviews in shared beliefs, values, and assumptions through myths, proverbs, songs, folktales, and rituals. Sage philosophy is the individual expression of ethnophilosophy, whereby the beliefs and wisdom of respected individuals in the community are considered vital and at par with the council of the ancestors.[4]

Other Oral Traditions

Oaths, dreams, prayers, blessings, and curses contain a great deal of information about religious beliefs. In Sierra Leone, during initiation ceremonies, secret society members commonly swear oaths to conceal certain information from nonmembers. An infraction of a secret society oath is believed to result in severe punishment from the society's patron spirit. Dreams are believed to be a vital means through which the supernatural communicates with the living. Prayers are crucial in a Traditionalist's relationship with the supernatural. Blessings are pronounced on people and individuals in the name of God. People who feel they have been taken advantage of use the name of God to curse those who have offended them with ill health, disaster, and bad luck.

Forms of Art

Hocking (1912, 13), almost a century ago, posited that religion is the 'mother of the arts'. This observation is still relevant. African art has for centuries been used to interpret life in every aspect. Art was used in 'religious life, which was not separated from other parts of life, to give spiritual meaning and function to objects used in ceremonies of individual or the community. It was used to illustrate proverbs and express the wisdom of the people'. Thus, African art provides a sacred literature, which gives beauty and solemnity to the face of humankind (Parrinder 1969, 13).

Arts continue to be a fertile source of cultural expression in Sierra Leone. Visual arts, in the form of sculptures, charms, amulets, swears,[5] shrines, native cloth,[6] and musical instruments—as well as performance art, in the form of songs, music, and dance—not only play a vital role in traditional life, but are also invaluable sources of SLIR (see Parson 1964, 200; Fyle 1981, 8–9; Ottenberg 1983, 1984, 1988a, 1988b, 1989, 1996, 2004; Ali 1990, 4, 23). Bascom, writing about sculptures, says,

> Most African sculptures appear to have been associated with religion, which pervades most aspects of African life. The religious genres include, votive figures, which adorned shrines, reliquary figures, charms, figures, stools used in initiation to the cults, the apparatus for divination, dance staff, musical instruments and a variety of other paraphernalia. (1973, 11)

A popular religious sculpture in Sierra Leone is the *nomoli*, which originated from the Kissi and Bullom ethnic groups (Fyle 1981, 8) and is now also associated with the Mende people. *Nomoli* are made of soapstone or wood,[7] and are believed to possess supernatural powers (Fyle 1981, 8; Alie 1990, 23). They are kept in a temporary shrine and regularly fed with little portions of cooked rice. Small whips are kept by their side and are used to ceremonially flog the *nomoli* as they are told to bring plenty of rice (Ali 1990, 23). *Nomoli* are also kept in homes as guardian spirits or angels (Ali 1990, 23; Fyle 1981, 8). At times, a *nomoli* is fashioned after an ancestor and kept in a shrine where sacrifices are made to it annually as a form of ancestral veneration (Fyle 1981, 8). Sculptures portraying the head of an ancestor are sometimes buried on the farm for successful harvest. Such figures among the Mende are often referred to as 'rice gods' (Parrinder 1967, 30). Diviners also use sculptures for various purposes.

Among the Mende, Temne, Limba, and Kono, sculptures of women and elaborate wooden masks symbolise the guardian spirit or represent the ancestors of the *Sande* and *Bondo* secret societies, which prepare girls for adulthood (cf. Parrinder 1967, 13, 119). Similarly, the men in these ethnic groups also have masks that represent the spirit of their respective *Poro* societies.

Oral tradition and the various forms of art in Sierra Leone allow a person to glean an understanding of the Traditionalists, and are crucial sources for an informed knowledge of ATR.

COMPONENTS OF **SLIR**

The components of ATR are basically the same among the various ethnic groups in Sierra Leone with slight differences. ATR generally consists of a belief in the supernatural—and the practices by which the Traditionalists relate to the supernatural—in religious objects, in sacred places, in sacred institutions (secret societies), and in sacred specialists. Each of the ethnic groups under study has categorised its belief in the supernatural according to a scale of preference.[8] At the top of the scale for all these groups is the Supreme Being. Next in rank for the Mende and the Krio are ancestral spirits, followed by nonancestral spirits. The Temne and Kono place lesser deities/gods, and the Limba place angels, next, followed by the ancestral spirits and nonancestral spirits. The practices employed by Sierra Leoneans include those showing reverence to these supernatural beings, through worship and sacrifice, and those intended to control supernatural forces. These components address both the sacred and functional aspects of religion.

While the various African cultures, and resultantly various scholars, hold differing views on the interrelationship of these elements,[9] they form an identifiable core. By this core, we are able to identify ATR as the institutionalised beliefs, teachings, and practices of various African societies in relation to the supernatural, in the context of their respective societies and experiences.

The Supreme Being

Sierra Leone Traditionalists hold as an integral part of their worldview a belief in a Supreme Being. Like other African Traditionalists,[10] the belief in the existence of God is prevalent among Traditionalists in Sierra Leone (Sawyerr 1970, 1–12).[11] God is simply known to be in existence. The Supreme Being 'is no stranger' (Mbiti 1989a, 29),[12] and he looms large in the consciousness of the people. The notions of and beliefs about God—as they are expressed in his names, attributes, and activities, and through the worship he receives—reflect the Sierra Leone Traditionalists' awareness of God. Let us identify these notions and beliefs.

Names of God

Sierra Leoneans in general attach great importance to names. In most African cultures, names function not merely as 'identification marks' applied to people (Ikenga-Metuh 1981, 19), but they 'often express qualities for which the owners are conspicuous' (Smith 1950, 4). Usually, a name either portrays or denotes a defining characteristic of its bearer. A name, in the Sierra Leone traditional worldview, is often an indication of a person's character, nature, or rank, or an expression of some peculiar quality. It denotes essence, identity, and power. It is likely upon these premises that Sierra Leone Traditionalists base their understanding of God's character and attributes.[13]

Among the Mende, the Supreme Being is commonly called *Ngewoh* (Harris 1950, 278; Parrinder 1962, 33; Harris and Sawyerr 1968, 5; Gittins 1987, 46; Yambasu 2002, 61). However, the origin of the name *Ngewoh* is unclear (Harris and Sawyerr 1968, 6). Some say the name is likely derived from the words 'sky' and 'long ago', a combination that means '[i]n the sky, from long ago' (Harris 1950, 278; Harris and Sawyerr 1968, 6)[14] or 'the sky is great' (Sawyerr 1970, 4). The more satisfactory derivation of the name is found in a 'withdrawal story'[15] about God, who once lived among humankind and, due to the persistent demands of the people, decided to leave and went to stay above, from which the name 'sky' was derived (Harris 1950, 278–279; Harris and Sawyerr 1968, 6–7; cf. Yambasu 2002, 61).

The Temne refer to the Supreme Being as *Kuru Masaba* (Turay 1967, 50–51; Sawyerr 1970, 3; Fyle 1981, 8; Alie 1990, 22; National Curriculum Development Centre [NCDC] 1993, 204). The first part of this name, *Kuru* ('God'), seems cognate with *Kur*, which suggests 'old age' (Sawyerr 1970, 4). *Kuru* also means 'sky' (Sawyerr 1970, 4), but it literally means 'the abode of God' (Turay 1967, 50). To differentiate this *Kuru* from other equally potent beings, the borrowed ending, *Masaba* ('almighty'), from the Mandigo language *maŋsa ba* ('the big king') (Turay 1967, 50–51),[16] was added to the word *Kuru*, resulting in the combination, *Kuru Masaba* ('God Almighty' or 'God the big king') (Turay 1967, 50).

The common name the Limba use for the Supreme Being is *Kanu Masala*. The first word, '*Kanu*', is believed to have come from the Biriwa and Safroko Limba peoples (Finnegan 1967, 107; cf. Ottenberg 1988a, 441). Two theories exist about the origin and meaning of the name *Kanu*. As with the Mende, the first Limba theory is a 'withdrawal story' about a caring king (God) who once lived with his subjects and who fled because of the increasing demands of his people. When the eventual search and plea of the people did not get the invisible king to return, the subjects therefore called him '*Kanu*' ('the one we all continue to search for'). The second theory is theological. It is based on the etymology of the word *Kanu*.[17] The name *Kanu* is a lengthened word for *Kan*, which means the sun. Literally, the name *Kanu* means 'like the sun'. God is likened to the sun, which is above.[18] The Limba are careful to specify that they do not worship the sun as a deity.[19] The likening of God to the sun is, rather, a way of explaining their perception of the nature and activity of God using a familiar human experience. If, then, the sun is not a manifestation of *Kanu*, it is, instead, used as a type. Hence the literal meaning of *Kanu* is 'like the sun'.

There are three theories about the origin of the word *Masala*[20] (the other half of the Limba name for the Supreme Being). One theory is that the word *Masala* is a Limbanised form of the word *Allah* (the name of the Muslim God). Another theory is that *Masala* is borrowed from either the Kuranko[21] word *Mansa* ('chief'). The final theory is that *Masala* is a 'Limbanised' form of the Temne word *Masaba* ('almighty'),[22] which, as we have already noted, is borrowed from the Mandigo word *mansa ba* ('the big king'). This is perhaps the most probable origin; the generally accepted meaning of *Masala* is 'supreme'.

Among the Krio people, the Supreme Being is referred to as either *Papa God* ('Father God') or *Daddy God* ('God our Dad').[23] Although the linguistic origin of the name is most obviously English, this does not necessarily mean that the concept of God as parent is necessarily Christian. It may also be authentically African Traditionalist, as the concept appears elsewhere in Sierra Leone and elsewhere in Africa.[24] The Mende have a few explicit references to God as father (Harris and Sawyerr 1968, 10). He is considered as a 'Father-Protector'. He is the father of humankind, 'upon whom anyone may call in times of personal distress; to whom the poor', abused, marginalised, and defenceless all turn as a final resort (Sawyerr 1970, 62). Before the Mende encountered Christian missionaries, God was regarded an ungendered deity. On account of their interactions with the missionaries, most Mende came to consider God as a male deity (Yambasu 2002, 63). This may also be true about the Limba, who also see God as a male figure who is now often referred to as 'Our Father'.

The Kono people use two words as names of God, the older of which is *Meketa* ('remain-to-meet'). God is thought to be the one who existed long ago before any one met him: 'he is the one who remains, does not die, each generation finds him living'. As such, he is the Everlasting One (Parsons 1964, 163; 1950, 260; Sawyerr 1970, 5). The contemporary word is *Yataa* ('you-he-met'). *Yataa* is the one whom you meet everywhere. He is the Great One who is above and over all (Parsons 1964, 163; 1950, 261; Sawyerr 1970, 4).

God Lives Above

There is a strong belief among all these groups that the Supreme Being lives above in the sky.[25] As we have already discovered in the case of the Mende and the Temne, the name of God is sometimes the same as the word for the sky. Among the Mende, God is also said to have gone up to the sky and became known as *Leve* ('up', 'high') (Sawyer 1970, 85). The Temne believe that God abides 'in the sky' (Turay 1967, 50; cf. Gbla 1993, 23). The Limba believe that 'God Supreme' lives above the sky just like the sun, and in that regard, he is also referred to as 'God above'.

The Krio usually talk about 'Father God up in heaven'. Among the Kono, 'the Great God, is above us far away in the sky' (Parsons 1950, 262). When birds soar high up in the sky, the Kono use the expression, 'it went up very far, it entered in God', which implies 'that God is high above the sky' (Parsons 1964, 165). As already noted, the Mende and the Limba have mythico-religious stories about God's withdrawal from his people to go and live above.[26]

The belief that God lives above in the sky, out of reach of people, suggests that '[h]e is obviously a transcendent Being' (Sawyerr 1970, 9). The transcendence of God portrays his supremacy over any other spiritual being (Parsons 1964, 163; Finnegan 1965, 107). Although God is conceived of as being physically out of reach, he is accessible through worship, natural manifestations, and his establishment of and participation in human activities. God may be transcendent; nevertheless, his name is constantly invoked in prayers or when a hope or wish is expressed (Harris and Sawyerr 1968, 9), or to take part in people's affairs (Sawyerr

1970, 4–5; Parsons 1950, 269). As such, God is both transcendent and immanent.[27] The Mende say God is not 'far off', although he lives in the sky (Yambasu 2002, 62).

According to Mbiti, God's transcendence

> is a difficult attribute to grasp, and one which must be balanced with God's immanence. The two attributes are paradoxically complimentary: God is 'far' (transcendent), and men cannot reach him; but God is also 'near' (immanent), and he comes close to man. (1970a, 12)

However, the association of God with the sky—and the fact that although God is far away from humankind, he is still reachable—are two vital components of the African concept of God (Sawyerr 1970, ix). The Limba believe that the Supreme Being is not only transcendent in terms of time and space, but he also transcends human understanding. He is conceived of as being incomprehensible.

It is no longer a fact that all Limba Traditionalists believe only in a single high God who lives in the sky, as suggested by Finnegan (1965, 107). Some juxtapose their belief in 'God above' with a belief in a 'God below'. 'God below' is not perceived of as a personal being, but is used as a general category to describe any evil spirit.[28] In other words, there is a Supreme God who lives in the sky and who is considered to be the good God, and there is a God who resides on earth, who is held responsible for all the evil and mischievous occurrences in the universe. There are stories that make references to both God above and God below: for example, 'Kanu gave food to the Limba' (Finnegan 1967, 235–238) and 'Kanu above and Kanu below' (274–276).

God's Intrinsic Attributes

Omnipotence

God is the one to whom absolute power and might are attributed. The African God is 'a God of Power…the ultimate source of all power' (Sawyerr 1970, 5). In the Sierra Leone traditional worldview, the omnipotence of God has far-reaching implications. It is seen as the source and the basis upon which other attributes and activities of God are discussed. It is because of God's omnipotence that he can be present everywhere, is all-knowing and all-seeing, and can carry out his activities as he chooses.

God's overriding power surpasses that of any being, natural or supernatural. He has no equal. God is who he is, and can do what he chooses because of his omnipotence. He is considered the ultimate cause of a person's fortunes or misfortunes in life and death, the determiner of the number of children born in a household and of all events. In that regard, ultimate responsibility for everything that happens from birth until death is attributed to God. However, this does not mean that God is held responsible for the perpetration of evil or for unfortunate happenings; it simply infers that God has allowed these situations to occur.

The Mende regard God as the one with ultimate and supreme authority and power, from whom everything derives, and without whose aid and permission nothing good or bad can happen (Harris and Sawyerr 1968, 2, 11). As such, everything that occurs does so only with the express permission of *Ngewoh* (Sawyerr 1970, 67; Yambasu 2002, 62). It is for this reason that you frequently hear the expression, 'God's willing', or, 'under God's protection, may it be so' (Harris and Sawyerr 1968, 10). There are several proverbial expressions of submissiveness to God's authority: 'it is God', meaning God permitted it; 'everything is God'; and 'nothing happens but with God's consent' (Harris 1950, 280). The Temne speak of 'God of power' as the only being with unimaginable power who can therefore do whatever he chooses.

There are two ascriptions used by the Limba to describe the omnipotence of God: 'the Powerful One' and 'the Great One/the Almighty'. In the Limba worldview, people live and exist 'by the grace of God'; therefore, every plan is made and every human achievement is reached 'by the grace of Kanu'. No human effort will ever succeed 'if God does not agree'.[29] There are also other proverbial phrases that the Limba use to express God's supremacy, such as, 'It is God's doing' or 'I will leave everything in the hands of God'.

Similarly, the Kono like to say, 'It is in God's hands'; 'I left it to God'—that is, to get revenge; or 'God will pay him'—that is, the one who may have wronged the person (Parsons 1964, 165). There is a cause behind every problem or disaster that befalls humankind. When something out of the ordinary happens, the Limba often say, 'Not for nothing', which means that there is something responsible for the problem. The Kono dependence on God's supremacy is further expressed through blessings such as, 'May God lengthen your life', 'May God add to your life', or 'May God make you well' (163).

Omnipresence
The Temne and Limba believe that 'God is everywhere'. As already noted, the name of God among the Kono means 'the one whom you meet everywhere' (Parsons 1950, 261; 1964, 165). God is not only the 'Preexisted One', but also the one whose presence pervades the earth. In general, the Traditionalists believe that God manifests himself to them during times of worship and religious gatherings. God's presence is strongly assumed at all major sacrifices. The omnipresence of God is also connected with natural occurrences, such as thunder and lightning.[30]

Omniscience
God's omniscience means that his wisdom and knowledge are limitless, and that even if we may know some things, it is only God who knows all. No one else, apart from God, 'is worthy of, or is given, the attribute of omniscience' (Mbiti 1970a, 3). Often it is because of our imperfect and incomplete knowledge that we affirm God's omniscience. There is a common view in West Africa, which may have originated from Nigeria, that says, 'No one knows tomorrow'. You can make your plans ahead, but from a human point of view, you cannot tell exactly how things will turn out; in the final analysis, only God knows.

Among the Mende, God's omniscience is acknowledged in a general way (Gittins 1987, 49). The Limba refer to God as 'the One Who Knows All'. The Kono say, 'God knows how' (Parsons 1964, 164). For the Traditionalists, God's ability to know everything further implies that he knows what is right and suitable for humankind.

All-Seeing
God not only knows, but he also sees, for nothing is hidden from him. According to the Mende, because God lives above, he sees everything (Harris and Sawyerr 1968, 11). The Kono believe that 'God sees whatever we do', and they therefore say, 'May God see this person' (1964, 165). The Limba, when they have been wronged and are unable to discover the person who has wronged them, say, 'God sees you, you will meet him', which idiomatically means, 'I did not see you doing the act but God saw you and you will meet him in judgment'. This concept echoes the African belief that 'wrong-doers cannot escape the judgment of God' (Mbiti 1989a, 31).

Activities of God
Creator
Like most Africans,[31] Sierra Leoneans attribute the creation of the universe to the Supreme Being. There is no one with such power to have created the world except God. The Mende believe that God created the universe and humankind, including animate and inanimate existence (Harris and Sawyerr 1968, 5; Sawyerr 1970, 66–67; Gittins 1987, 46; Parrinder 1962, 33). Similarly, among the Temne, God is believed to have created the earth (Gbla 1993, 59). The Temne further assert that 'God created us all'. God is known to the Limba as 'the One who made the Universe', and he is referred to as 'the One who made humankind/ us' and as 'our Owner'.[32] On account of possibly being the earliest ethnic group in Sierra Leone, some Limba in the hinterland still claim that they were God's primary creation, followed by the other cultural groups in the country.[33] In the Kono worldview, God created humankind first, followed by the rest of creation (Parsons 1964, 165).

There are several creation myths and stories. In the two Mende stories (Harris and Sawyerr 1968, 6; Sawyerr 1970, 66–67), the first story shows God creating *ex nihilo* ('creation out of nothing'),[34] and in the second, God is seen as fixing, ordering, and making things. There is a story about God as the creator and caretaker of the Limba (Finnegan

1967, 238–239). From the Limba perspective, creation is not so much 'creation from nothing' as 'fixing or ordering' (Finnegan 1965, 107). The Kono believe that when God first made the world, it never became really dark or cold, and they have a story about the coming of darkness (Parrinder 1967, 28–29).

As creator, God in the Mende worldview is the Supreme Ruler of the universe. So often, prayers, wishes, and blessings are followed by the exclamation, 'Under the sovereign governance of *Ngewoh*'. God as creator is the ultimate cause and justification of all things, including animate and inanimate things, and everything seen and unseen. The belief that God is the creator implies that God exists and that he is 'the fount and apex of all existence' (Sawyerr 1968, 12).

God as Ruler

The concept of God the creator as the supreme ruler of the world is prevalent in Africa.[35] In Sierra Leone, the notion of sovereignty is of particular significance in the peoples' attitude towards God. Among the Mende, Limba, Temne, and Kono, God's role as ruler is of course understood to be analogous to that of a chief. As a chief, God is always thought of as one with immense authority and wisdom, and as one who performs the functions of a judge and maintains justice and equity. It is by the chief's authority that the people in his jurisdiction are able to carry on their day-to-day affairs or maintain their respective position. As such, the Traditionalists find it difficult to conceive of social life and maintain daily living without the chief.

As protector and judge of both the good and the bad, God is 'the great chief God' (Yambasu 2002, 63). In some prayers, God is referred to as 'the One Chief' (Harris 1950, 278; Harris and Sawyerr 1968, 6) or 'the Great Chief' (Sawyerr 1970, 5). God is the chief who created humankind (Harris and Sawyerr 1968, 6), the chief who has the last say in a dispute (Harris and Sawyerr 1968, 6; Yambasu 2002, 63), and the chief who has no fault (Harris and Sawyerr 1968, 6).

Because of God's outstanding power and his ability to rule well and to dispense justice without prejudice, the Limba refer to God as 'chief', 'the Only Chief', and 'the Great Chief'. God is the chief to whom the marginalised and the victims of injustice turn in times of distress. When taken advantage of, the Limba—as well as the Krio—are quick to say, 'I leave my case with God'. God, 'the Great Chief' (Parsons 1964, 165), is the one the Kono depend on for justice.

The Worship of God

Earlier, in discussing the transcendence and immanence of God, it was stated that God is conceived as being physically out of reach; he is accessible through worship and through his establishment of and participation in human activities. God may be transcendent, but his name is constantly invoked in prayers, when a hope or wish is expressed, or to take part in people's affairs. Also, in discussing the omnipresence of God, it was noted that Traditionalists believe that God manifests himself to them during times of worship and religious gatherings. The primary method through which God is worshipped is the offering of sacrifice. Traditionalists strongly assume the presence of God at all sacrifices.

However, in most Sierra Leone Traditionalists' rituals, God is approached indirectly through intermediaries, especially through a succession of ancestors (Harris and Sawyerr 1968, 15; Yambasu 2002, 64; Turay 1967, 51; Wyse 1989, 12; Parsons 1964, 166). This approach is to a greater extent influenced by the people's understanding of God as a chief who acts and is approached through his subordinates. So while everything is believed to be under God's control, intermediaries are postulated through whom access is possible. Nonetheless, in times of distress, the people may pray directly to God without any intermediaries. These prayers generally fall into either prayers of deliverance or prayers invoking blessings. Sacrifices and offerings are also made to God directly or indirectly, or concurrently with the ancestors (Conteh 2004, 90–107; Parsons 1964, 70–71, 88, 97).

Another name of God that the Limba use somewhat less frequently is 'God of Sacrifice' or 'God who accepts Sacrifice'. The Limba distinguish between what is offered to God or the ancestors and what is offered to the spirits. Sacrifice is offered to God and to the ancestors, whereas offering is made to nonancestral spirits. The Temne offer sacrifice in various rituals to God, to the ancestors, or to various nature spirits. Sacrifices to God are made for various purposes and at different levels—chiefdom, section, village/town, compound, household, and personal. Pouring libations, invocations, and prayer are all part of the ritual worship of God.

Lesser Gods/Deities

In the Temne and Kono supernatural orders, lesser gods/deities are next to the Supreme Being. The Temne speak of a shadowy figure called 'Chief of the earth' that controls and protects agriculture and perhaps controls the rain (NCDC 1993, 204; Gbla 1993, 23). He is said to own all the rice in the world. As such, at the start of each farming season, rice is planted for him in a special shed and left uncut. In the southern region of Temne country, it appears that his function as the protector of crops is now taken over by ancestral and nonancestral spirits. Among the Konike Temne, he is considered God Almighty's counterpart (Gbla 1993, 23).

There are four lesser gods the Kono generally acknowledge. The most important of these is the spirit of 'the Earth', who is prayed to alongside God and the ancestors for the fertility of the soil and for abundant crops (Parsons 1964, 166). She is thought to be 'the wife of God, and gives birth to all vegetation and sustains all animals' and people (Parsons 1964, 166). Similarly, the Mende postulate what is tantamount to an 'Earth deity', referred to as Grand 'Mother Earth'. Although it is not clear whether she is regarded and worshipped as a lesser god/deity, she is invoked in some of the most sacred oaths (Sawyerr 1968, 22). Also, in calling God to witness certain forms of swearing and cursing, the Mende are fond of using the expression, 'O you and your wife the Earth' (Harris and Sawyerr 1968, 8).

It is through the power of the spirit of 'the Earth', the Kono believe, that luxuriant vegetation is possible. The Earth is held in great respect because the life of the people is deeply rooted in it. As the conduct of the people is believed to affect the fertility of the earth, the Kono go to great lengths to maintain a good relationship with the spirit of the Earth in order to yield a good harvest.

Next to spirit of the Earth is the spirit who is responsible for the fertility of women (Parsons 1950, 270; 1964, 39). The spirit of fertility is represented by a sacred stone in the town of Gbamandu, where barren women, through the priest in charge, perform a special ritual to take away their barrenness. The last two gods are Kono river gods (Parsons 1950, 271; 1964, 155, 131). One of the river gods, is believed to be in all large rivers in snake or human form, and is the one to whom animals are offered by being thrown into the river by people seeking permission to fish (Parsons 1964, 155), and in a ceremony held close to the end of the secret society training of boys, when they demonstrate their skills before their parents (Parsons 1950, 271). The other river god helps the sons of chiefs to achieve the future success they may desire (Parsons 1950, 271; 1964, 131–132).

Angels
Among the ethnic groups under study, only the Limba speak of angels. In fact, very few other African ethnic groups speak directly of angels.[36] Until recently, the positions of angels and ancestors within the supernatural hierarchy were a matter of debate among the Limba. Although there are still a few who continue to debate this, at present, a majority of Traditionalists believe that angels, because they are natural spirits who act as direct agents of God's will and have an intimate relationship with him, are higher spiritual beings than the ancestors, who are human spirits and have attained their spiritual status by human design.

It seems that the Limba understanding of angels is greatly influenced by Islam and/or Christianity. The Limba word for angels, *maleken*, has its root from the Arabic word *mala'ikah* ('angel'). The Limba understand angels to be hylomorphic. They are natural spirits with wings, but are also capable of assuming human form when they appear to people, whether in dreams or in person. They communicate and have human needs. There are male and female angels. As children of God, they possess the moral attributes of love, kindness, and goodness towards people.

Angels are God's messengers and servants. In that regard, they carry God's messages and fulfil his plans. In their capacity as messengers and servants, angels play the role of mediator between God and humankind; they care for, protect, guide, guard, and help people. When an angel completes his/her service to the individual assigned to him/her, he/she takes his/her charge to the place of the dead (if the deceased is qualified to go there).

Ancestral Spirits

As in most African cultures,[37] the ancestors are of central importance in the lives of most Sierra Leone Traditionalists. To take the ancestors away from them is to 'destroy their roots in the past, their culture, their dignity and their understanding of *communion sanctorum*' (Hollenweger 1993, x; Setiloane 1978, 406). Ancestral veneration is evident all through Sierra Leone, even among converts to Christianity and in spite of Western sophistication. Avery noted, 'In Sierra Leone, sincere Christians, even ordained ministers, engage quite openly in...ancestral rites' (1971, 13).

Who Are the Ancestors?

In the Mende worldview, the spirits of the ancestors are next to God (Yambasu 2002, 64). The common words used in reference to the ancestors are 'grandfathers' and 'our forefathers' (Sawyerr 1968, 2, 16; Gittins 1987, 62–63; cf. Sawyerr 1996, 44–45). Some ethnic groups also demarcate between the dead who are ancestors and those who are not. Gittins differentiated between the ancestors and the dead in Mende belief (1987, 60–61). He used three terms, *ndoubla*, *halabla*, and *kambeihubla*, which are certainly used to refer to the deceased. *Ndoubla* in particular, he said, applies simply to the 'dead and buried' and does not carry any implications about ancestorship. They are the people who had not had the ceremony 'crossing the river' performed (Gittins 1987, 69). Additionally, most Limba, with the exception of the Warawara people, distinguished between the dead and buried, and those who have attained ancestorship.

Among the Temne, 'the word *kaerfi* literally means "a dead ancestor" '. Over time, *kaerfi* came to mean 'a dead person', and in contemporary times, it means a 'devil' (Turay 1967, 52). The spirits of the dead are represented by stones placed at each burial in a shrine called 'shrine of stones' located on the outskirts of most towns and villages (NCDC 1993, 204; Sawyerr 1970, 6). It seems that each family is expected to have a receptacle within the shrine that contains the stones that represent their dead heroes. In some areas, both men and women are included in the 'shrine of stones'; in others, there are separate shrines for men and women (NCDC 1993, 204).

As the stones in the shrine represent the spirits of dead relatives, a closest surviving family member later inherits each stone. For instance, the eldest daughter inherits her mother's stone; when the daughter dies, the second daughter takes her place as guardian of the stone. Similarly, the stone that represents the spirit of the father is inherited by the eldest son (NCDC 1993, 205). This tradition is meant to ensure that the spirit of the deceased is visited and that timely offerings are made to him/her. Also, it is to prevent the stones in any given receptacle from losing their significance on account of the inability of any living member to identify them.

The word most frequently used by Limba for the ancestors is the plural *Fureni be/Hureni* (lit., 'old people'). It has been suggested that *fureni be* is a lengthened form for the word *furu/huru* (breeze/wind/spirit). Alternate words for 'old people' are 'forefathers' and 'great grandfathers'.

Like many other ethnic groups in Sierra Leone, the Krio believe in the spirits of their dead relatives (Wyse 1989, 11–12). Although their worldview is strongly influenced by Christianity and Western culture, the Krio nevertheless continue to adhere to, and participate in, ancestral rites.[38]

'Great fathers' is the most commonly used word by the Kono in reference to the ancestral spirits. A less common word is 'the great ancestral forefathers'. The 'great fathers' are spoken of as 'new, fresh, young, and having white garments', roving 'back and forth' (Parsons 1964, 168).

The Abode of the Ancestors

The Mende conceive of their ancestors living in 'God's bosom' (Yambasu 2002, 64). Among the Temne, the ancestors live in 'the place of the dead' (Turay 1967, 52), which is sometimes said to be in the air

(NCDC 1993, 204). Evildoers cannot go right away to 'the place of the dead'; they first go to a place analogous of the Roman Catholic purgatory called *Yanama*, from which they may emerge and be forgiven after some time (NCDC 1993, 204).

Among the Limba, at the ceremony on the third day after burial, it is believed that the deceased joins the other dead at an undisclosed 'place of the dead'. The dead person is then considered 'an ancestor'.

The Krio refer to their ancestors as those who have died and gone into the 'world of truth' (Sawyerr 1967, 43). The phrase 'you who live in the world of truth' implies that the ancestors 'now know reality' (43) and 'do discern truth and therefore no longer subject to the effects of deception' (Sawyerr 1996, 45).

The Kono believe that their ancestors are in 'the place of the dead'. Each clan or family has its own 'place of the dead'. The residents of 'the place of the dead' are spoken of as 'fathers'. It is believed that the ancestors leave the 'place of the dead' and come to reside close to their burial place (Parsons 1964, 168).

Categories of Ancestors

Sawyerr has rightly stated that the ancestors seem to fall into several categories, some of which naturally overlap (1996, 43–44), which I have summarised as follows:

- Ancestors of a direct genealogy of a particular family or group of families.
- Ancestors who were community heroes whose memories have come down in history as the defenders of their community and of their ethnic group.
- Ancestors associated with professional expertise—smiths, hunters, and sacred specialists.

The Role of the Ancestors

The ancestors are closely involved in the life of the Traditionalists by manifesting interest in the welfare of the communities to which they belonged, and still belong. Not only do they belong to their respective communities, but they also order the lives that are led there. Even though spatially they are primarily associated with their graves, because of their spiritual characteristic, they are capable of following their children wherever they go, which makes it possible to call on them everywhere and from anywhere in the world. Not only are they ever-present, but they are also conversant with everything that goes on in the community.

Although the dead are physically removed from them, the Krio believe that they continue to watch over and influence them. People bring their problems to the ancestors and entreat them to intercede with God on their behalf, to bring good fortune and a better life to them, and so on (Wyse 1989, 12). These assumptions are clearly expressed at a graveside libation ceremony that continues to date (Sawyerr 1967, 41–49).

The ancestors play a more vital role in the life of the Kono than any aspect of their religiosity (Parsons 1964, 167). They are intermediaries between the living and God (166), with characteristics similar to those of humankind, but with a superior power and a supernatural ability to help the living. They speak to people in dreams and in strange events—for instance, 'if the first glass of wine was spilt' (168). Prayers are relayed through the stream of ancestors until they eventually reach God. People speak to the 'fathers' to keep their favour. They are addressed in idiomatic expressions of surprise, wonder, or inability to understand the happening—'O Great Fathers, I did not think of this'.

As in other African cultures,[39] it is on account of the ancestors' closeness to God, and the roles they play, that compel Sierra Leonean Traditionalists to uphold the ancestors in high regard (Yambasu 2002, 64). The question then is, 'Is the expression of this regard more proper worship or veneration?' Let us now look into this issue.

Ancestor Worship or Veneration?
The question of whether Africans worship or merely venerate their ancestors has been a matter of interest for several decades. The following are the arguments of two Sierra Leonean scholars who have contributed to the debate, albeit from opposite ends of the spectrum.

After a close look at ancestral rites, practices, and prayers, Sawyerr argued that ancestral cults constitute true worship (1966, 33–39). However, this worship, Sawyerr argued, 'falls short of Christian worship' (1968, 129). Much later, in another published work (1996, 55), after discussing his views and the views of several other scholars on the appropriateness of the term 'ancestor worship', Sawyerr concluded that 'Africans do worship their ancestors as they do their divinities', and this worship, he continued, 'consists of prayers, sacrifices, and divination on communal occasions or prayers and divinations on private occasions'. In Sawyerr's understanding, the rituals and practices offered to the ancestors both in public and in private constitute legitimate worship and are of the same nature as those offered to God.

Fashole-Luke posed the question, 'Do Africans worship their dead ancestors or do they venerate them?' (1974, 210). To him, the question is not just academic because it involves 'the problem of whether African ancestral cults are merely idolatrous practices', and 'the problem of whether the rituals and practices offered to the ancestors constitute true worship' (211). He challenged the reader to assess 'whether the quality of the so-called worship offered to the ancestors is of the same nature as that offered to the Supreme Being'. Fashole-Luke further argued that 'the phrase "ancestor worship" is emotionally charged, conjuring up primitive and heathen ideas of idolatry', while, in contrast, 'the phrase "ancestor veneration" is neutral' and does not present us with the negative images provoked by the phrase 'ancestor worship' (212). He thus strongly recommended we discard the phrase 'ancestor worship' and adopt the phrase 'ancestor veneration' in discussions pertaining to African ancestral cults.

Other ATR scholars have also challenged the word 'worship' as an inaccurate label to apply to ancestor veneration. As Mbiti put it, 'Africans themselves know very well that they are not "worshipping" the departed members of their family' (1989a, 9). King argued that ancestors are not objects of worship; rather, they are intermediaries and are considered 'a conveyor belt, a medium to reach an end, not the end itself' (King 1994, 24).

Having considered the preceding arguments, 'ancestor veneration' seems a more appropriate term for the regard a Sierra Leonean Traditionalist shows to ancestral spirits than does 'ancestor worship'. Sierra Leone Traditionalists venerate their ancestors on account of the mediatory role that they play between God and the living, and the service they render as elders of their families. The ancestors deserve veneration for what they are and do for the living.

Ancestral Veneration

The common, practical means through which the ancestors are venerated are sacrifices/offerings made for various purposes, which may be categorised as follows:

- Goodwill offerings to commemorate the death of an individual or to entreat the ancestor for some particular venture.
- Thank offerings to the ancestors for their assumed assistance towards a family member's success or recovery from severe illness.
- Propitiatory offerings to make amends for neglecting an ancestor, or at the time of a personal or national disaster.
- Mediatory offerings to request the ancestors to relay their petitions for safety to the appropriate spirits. (Sawyerr 1996, 47–48)

The items offered as sacrifices vary according to the purpose of the sacrifice, to the social and financial status of the bearer, and to the advice of the sacred specialist. If the ceremony requires the offering of an animal—it may be a cow, a sheep, a goat, or a chicken. An animal sacrifice may be either a blood sacrifice or a bloodless sacrifice. In the former, the animal is slaughtered. Some of the meat is cooked and eaten by the worshippers, while the remaining uncooked meat is distributed to various households. In the case of a bloodless sacrifice, the animal is set free after the ceremony and should be left for the remainder of its life to die a natural death because it belongs to God.

The offering of plants and fruits is also considered a bloodless sacrifice. Bananas, oranges, and kola nuts are the most common choices for fruit offerings. Rice can also be used as an offering.

In every case, three main items are present in a sacrificial ritual: water, kola nut, and moulded rice flour mixed with sugar. Often there is also wine/alcohol, charcoal, and a prepared meal. These items are all symbolic:

- Water in general stands for peace, harmony, and life. Among the Mende, Limba, and Krio, water cultivates harmony, cools and refreshes, and 'is also the simplest and most acceptable manifestation of hospitality' (Sawyerr 1996, 49).
- Rice flour, because of its whiteness, symbolises purity and cleanliness.
- Kola nut is a means of communicating with the supernatural.
- Alcohol represents happiness/merriment.
- Charcoal represents misfortune.
- A prepared meal is for joy and satisfaction.

I now investigate further how ancestral veneration is practised among the five groups.

Among the Temne, whenever there is a national crisis (Sawyerr 1970, 6), and at the start of the farming season (NCDC 1993, 204), sacrifices are made in the 'shrine of stones', which, as already mentioned, represent the spirits of the dead. In the former case, palm wine, rice, kola nuts, and a mat are offered (Sawyerr 1970, 6). In the latter, each family is expected to prepare food from which the leader takes and places a handful upon the stones for a successful farming season (NCDC 1993, 204–205). Also, an offering similar to that offered during a general crisis may be offered in commemoration of the dead (Sawyerr 1970, 6).

The Limba contact the ancestors for various purposes and at different levels.[40] Ancestral sacrifices may be offered in response to the advice of a sacred specialist whose advice was sought out for the appropriate response to some present or imminent misfortune. They are also offered for regular and recurring purposes, including the accession of a new chief, the dedication of a new house, and at important points in the rice-farming cycle. Heroes, sacred specialists, or 'the owners of swears make their own special sacrifices to dead predecessors (whether their actual ancestors or not)'.[41]

Awujoh is the joyous Krio celebration in veneration of the ancestors (Wyse 1989, 12).[42] Normally, it is held 'in honour of the dead to ask for their guidance, approval and goodwill, and it celebrates specific dates and anniversaries of the deceased, *three-day*, *seven-day* and *forty-day*'. For mainly economic reasons, the first two were dispensed of long ago. *Forty-day* and *wan year* (first anniversary of death) are maintained because of their importance. The Krio also set dishes of stew and rice on a table in the night for a newly deceased relative, and sometimes to assure relatives long dead that they are not forgotten. This practice is common to most of the ethnic groups.

The Kono venerate the ancestors with rites performed at the beginning of the farming season (Parsons 1964, 81), with the ceremonies for the protection of children by the ancestors known as *Tamba Tina* (47), in burial rituals (32–33), at graveside offerings to deceased brothers of maternal line (26), and in ceremonies at the village *Ko-tina* ('the giving place'), where gifts are given to ancestral spirits believed to abide there (75).

Nonancestral Spirits
Sierra Leonean Traditionalists, like most African peoples, believe that their world is full of a myriad of spirits (Harris and Sawyerr 1968, 1; Yambasu 2002, 60–61; Conteh 2004, 145). Various spirits play important roles among the people (Harris and Sawyerr 1968, 34–87; Gittins 1987, 73–98; Turay 1967, 52–55; Conteh 2004, 145–164; Parsons 1950, 271–274). We now look at the various categories of nonancestral spirits and their characteristics.

Nature Spirits
Nonancestral spirits are classified as either nature spirits or human spirits. Nature spirits (Harris and Sawyerr 1968, 3, 34–53; Gittins 1987, 73–85;

Conteh 2004, 145–148; Parsons 1964, 163) were created as such, and either they rove, disassociated, or they are associated with individuals, communities, and clans; or with natural features, such as mountains/ hilltops, lakes, forests, caves, trees, rivers, and springs—on account of their mysterious, fearsome, and somatic natures (Parrinder 1962, 44; Harris and Sawyerr 1968, 3; Turay 1967, 53; Finnegan 1965, 116; Conteh 2004, 45–46; Parsons 1964, 39, 131, 155). Although natural spirits may be good, bad, or ambivalent in their operations (Turay 1967, 52; Conteh 2004, 146–147; Parsons 1964, 168), most natural spirits are characterised by an unpredictable ambivalence and must therefore be treated cautiously.

Although people may be aware of the causes of a particular misfortune, suffering and accidental or inexplicable deaths are usually considered to be the acts of evil spirits. Natural disasters, such as floods and the consequent destruction, are attributed to the anger of nature spirits (Harris and Sawyerr 1968, 39–44; Conteh 2004, 147). Destruction caused by thunder and lightening, wind, and rain are similarly thought to be the work of spirits. Sierra Leone is 'a country in which natural forces often oppress at their most awesome, religious belief is accordingly inculcated by thunder-storms, great rains and winds' (1968, 3).

The acquisition of special skills or good fortune is often attributed to good spirits. It is believed that a person gifted with 'spiritual eyes' will take 'a good spirit' to become wealthy or renowned, or to attain certain skills. It is a common notion that people with outstanding abilities or talents have 'taken a spirit'.[43] Outstanding athletes, hunters, smiths, leaders in the secret societies, strikingly good drummers and singers, and, above all, diviners of various kinds are all believed to have obtained their outstanding abilities from spirits.[44] The patron spirits of secret societies[45] are highly revered.

Human Spirits

The next category of nonancestral spirits is human spirits.[46] These are the dead who have not been integrated into the ancestor cult, witches, wicked dead relatives, and ghosts. Witches, as well as wicked dead relatives who have not received respectable burial rites, are believed to become malevolent spirits who rove around in the night or day, inflicting mischief on the innocent, especially their enemies or infants.

Witchcraft

In many Sierra Leonean societies, the belief in witchcraft is very strong (Sawyerr 1996, 11–13; Turay 1967, 53; Shaw 1997, 856–76; Finnegan 1965, 116, 117; Conteh 2004, 151–157; Parsons 1964, 21, 53–54; Wyse 1989, 10).[47] Witches are believed to be everywhere acting invisibly. A person may practise witchcraft, potentially afflicting people by mystical means through the power and encouragement of evil spirits. This is usually done at night to avoid being discovered. In some societies, such as the Temne and Limba, a witch may be of either gender, so men and women might equally be suspected of witchcraft. However, this belief varies within Sierra Leone. By contrast, the Mende believe that witches are usually women. It is said that a witch leaves the body spiritually when 'asleep and goes out to attack another person, infant or adult' while their victim is also asleep (Sawyerr 1996, 11). Parrinder has strongly dismissed such a belief as a delusion, adding, 'People do not leave their bodies or destroy the souls of others. So in fact there are no witches, though many people believe in them' (1963, 92).

In most African societies, witchcraft is regarded as 'the greatest wrong or destruction on earth' (Magesa 1997, 68). It is considered the 'reverse of normal values and behaviour' of the community (Bourdillin 2000, 176), and for these reasons, practitioners of witchcraft in Sierra Leone 'are always considered to be evil and anti-social' (Finnegan 1965, 119).

Finnegan reported that most Limba Traditionalists, if asked why they believe in witchcraft, would 'often reply by saying that after all the witches confess' (1965, 119), and it is generally accepted that no one would confess to anything so terrible if they were not guilty; even today, this is still the most common explanation of this belief. Although witch-hunting is rare, there have been cases where accused witches have been made to confess under physical and psychological duress.

Witches are believed to acquire their power through their 'double eyes' (four eyes, two in front and two behind), which make them capable of seeing beyond the physical and ordinary. However, not all people with 'double eyes' practise witchcraft. For instance, people with exceptional abilities, such as sorcerers and traditional healers, are believed to have 'double sight'. It is also believed that twins and triplets possess 'double sight'. As Magesa noted, these individuals 'may possess the same powers as witches, but they are not necessarily malevolent' (1997, 180). Some use their double vision to secure wealth and fame through the spirits. Double-sighted individuals are good people who use their abilities to expose witches or others trying to harm people through mystical means.

Witches in Sierra Leone are believed to sometimes take on different forms to perpetuate mischief. Like other spirits, they are capable of taking the form of animals, reptiles, or birds (Harris and Sawyerr 1968, 74). Witches are associated with animals such as leopards, elephants, lions, snakes, owls, and vampire bats. Sierra Leoneans believe that even the bravest and strongest beasts are normally afraid of humans. In that regard, if the Limba hear that a wild animal has attacked a person, it is thought that the animal or reptile is not ordinary, and a witch must have entered it (Conteh 2004, 154).

The nightly cry of an owl is considered a supernatural manifestation of witchcraft. When an owl starts to hoot, people come out with sticks and metallic items and beat them together while using abusive and profane words against the witch who has sent the owl to come and carry out mischief.[48] When such words are uttered, the owl leaves and will not return for a long time. The same procedure is also followed when the hooting sound of a vampire bat is heard. The sound of a vampire bat indicates that witches are sucking blood from sleeping infants (Harris and Sawyerr 1968, 5).

Witches can also deprive people through spiritual means by stealing crops, plaguing or killing cattle, or causing harm and destruction on anyone who is seen as a threat to them politically or socially. Wicked, like-minded people may procure the services of witches to eradicate a political opponent or a rival in love affairs.

Self-preservation has required Sierra Leoneans to take certain preventive measures against both evil spirits and witchcraft by procuring protective charms, often through the aid of a sacred specialist.[49] Although a witch is considered to be powerful and is feared by most people, it is also believed that in the natural human existence, he/she 'is vulnerable to certain charms and spells and could be repelled by them' (Harris and Sawyerr 1968, 75). Charms may be sticks, stones, pieces of traditional cloth, or almost anything a person thinks is powerful.

In general, these charms are called 'medicines' (Harris 1950, 284–285; Conteh 2004, 156; Parsons 1964, 94). There is an almost endless variety of these medicines. Some are used for personal protection, such as amulets or talismans worn on the body called *Sehbeh*, or potions to be drunk or rubbed into the skin called *Manesi*. People also wear protective traditional clothes. These are often a combination of white, red, and black pieces of cloth sewn together into undervests and slips. Another is an outfit commonly called *Ronko*, which is a fearsome traditional brown or red gown with black vertical stripes, drenched in herbal medicines intended to make the user invulnerable.

A variety of medicines are also used for public protection. *Sehbeh*, either in leather bags with tiny chunks of kola nut spat on them or in a piece of traditional cloth, are often hung above the doorways of houses or on roofs. Charms are commonly buried or visibly hung around farms to protect them against evil spirits and to scare away thieves.

Medicines are believed to possess mystical power because they are visible symbols of invisible forces that come either directly from God or through the spirits. Mbiti noted that they are used to 'secure a feeling of safety, protection and assurance' (1989a, 196). A person's use of religious charms reflects invisible values and beliefs. These charms serve as 'visual aids' that give confidence and security to the user (Byaruhanga-Akiiki 1993, 192).

Other common means of protection against evil spirits or witchcraft include naming and exposing a witch, or invoking a 'swear' (Harris

1950, 284–285; Sawyerr 1996, 10; Parsons 1964, 167) as a kind of self-operating justice. Because Africans are afraid of the power of a 'swear', the accused will quickly confess if guilty. A 'swear' is considered an effective means of preventing or punishing the most profoundly antisocial of crimes.

On account of the belief that the spirit of a powerful person lives on after his/her death with the same passions he/she had when alive, the Traditionalists make sure that when a convicted witch dies, steps are taken to prevent him/her from surviving death to return and cause more mischief.[50] To this end, a sacred specialist is usually summoned and an offering is made to the ancestors to deactivate the power of witchcraft possessed by the deceased. In olden days, in an attempt to deactivate the spirit of a witch, the Temne and the Limba would dismember the corpse of a witch and bury its parts in different places (Sawyerr 1968, 107). That practice has long since been outlawed.

Ghosts

A ghost is 'an apparition or spectre of dead person' (Parrinder 1962, 137). Like many Africans,[51] Sierra Leone Traditionalists believe that a spirit becomes a ghost when a person has not received proper burial and is resultantly 'wandering about between this world and the next' (1962, 60). In Limba tradition, Ghosts are harmless, but are notorious for stalking and harassing their targets until something is done to appease them. Usually, this is accomplished by performing a second burial rite. It is on account of their habit of harassing the living that ghosts are considered to be evil spirits. Stories of ghosts haunting homes, offices, and people are still common among most peoples in Sierra Leone.

Offering/Sacrifice to Nature Spirits

Offerings are made periodically, or as required, to appease the spirits or as thanksgiving for a fortune received from the spirits. Offerings are made to benevolent or malevolent spirits by individuals, households, chiefdoms/villages/towns, or compounds. Offerings are usually made in the perceived 'home' of the spirit to which it is made; it is seldom made at the family/clan shrine where the clan spirit dwells, but may be made in caves[52] and forests, near lakes and springs, under huge/cotton trees,[53] on mountains, at shrines that have full-time priests, in secret society bushes, or at the home of a blacksmith. Items offered to these spirits are much the same as those used for sacrifices offered to God and to the ancestors. It should be noted, however, that Sierra Leone Traditionalists do not make offerings to witches or ghosts.

Human Beings
Sierra Leone Traditionalists believe and teach that there is a purpose for human existence; every individual has a role to play in the universe. In that regard, humankind is at the very centre of existence. Traditionalists 'see everything else in its relation' to humankind's central position (Mbiti 1989a, 90; cf. Okorocha 1994, 73). Humans, in the journey of life, must deal with the supernatural, along with animate beings and inanimate objects. This puts them in a position where they must strive to maintain a balance between personal identity as unique individuals, on one hand, and a communal identity, on the other. This advocates 'the integrative notion of "person" as a being-in-plenitude who can assert his/her being only in concert with other beings' (Yambasu 2002, 45). The Traditionalist's worldview as it relates to humankind may be considered from the viewpoint of humanity's origin and purpose in life.

In general, humankind is believed to have originated from God and is thus superior to and more intelligent than any of God's other creatures. A person, according to the traditional worldview, consists of a body and breath/spirit/soul (Parsons 1964, 161; Harris and Sawyerr 1968, 88; Sawyerr 1970, 82; 1996, 113; Conteh 2004, 170). The body contains the breath, which comes from God and makes humankind a living being. In addition to the body and spirit, humankind is endowed with a spiritual nature that enables him/her to relate with the supernatural. The relationship between God and humankind is based on the belief that humans are God's creation and that God provides and continues to provide for human existence.[54] As such, from the moment one wakes in the morning to the time one goes to bed in the evening, everything must be done according to God's wishes.

Human beings, as creatures of the earth (Parsons 1964, 166; Sawyerr 1996, 9; Conteh 2004, 170), are part of the natural order. As such, they share the universe with animate beings and inanimate objects, which are all part of God's creation. Since humans are a part of nature, they are expected to cooperate with it. It is 'the need to remain in harmony with nature' (Opoku 1993, 77) that has caused the African to incorporate the environment and its inhabitants into his/her 'religious perception of the universe' (Mbiti 1989a, 90). To be in harmony with nature is 'to be on good terms with one's entire social and spiritual world' (Zuesse 1991, 178).

It is on account of this understanding that Sierra Leone Traditionalists think that human beings, as the highest and most intelligent creatures, have a responsibility to take care of God's earth and all that is in it. It is the place where their ancestors are buried and it is the source of their livelihood. However, for economic reasons, and because of negligence and apathy, some are not putting into practice the teachings and beliefs they have inherited. Two issues call into question the Traditionalists' stewardship of God's earth:

- The indiscriminate cutting down of trees for firewood has led to forest depletion and has left some villages looking like deserts. They have been stripped of their trees, making these communities vulnerable to even the mildest storm that blows. Wood is the most common fuel used for cooking by people without electricity or kerosene stoves.
- The pollution of many rivers and streams through the improper disposal of garbage and other waste. Most people think that because rivers and streams empty into the ocean, anything dumped into them will be carried there and eventually rot away.

Although most of the published series on ecology have not addressed ecology in ATR,[55] the contribution of ATR to the 'ongoing world-wide concern about the environment cannot be overemphasised' (Opoku 1993, 78).

Lifecycle/Rites of Passage

Because of the belief that humankind is a spiritual being (Harris and Sawyerr 1968, 1; Sawyerr 1996, 9; Conteh 2004, 176), religion pervades every aspect of the Traditionalist life, from conception to the afterlife. Life is a 'holistic' journey, which begins and ends with God, who is consulted every step of the way. Awareness of the divine presence and intervention in the journey of life is reflected in the rites of passage that mark important stages and events in the life of the Sierra Leone Traditionalist (Wyse 1989, 11–12; Conteh 2004, 176–228). The religious tenets of Sierra Leone Traditionalists, like those of most Africans, have formed the matrix of every aspect of Sierra Leone traditional culture. As Mbiti rightly observes,

> Wherever the African is, there is his religion, he carries it to the fields where he is sowing seeds or harvesting a new crop; he takes it with him to the beer party or to attend a funeral ceremony; and if he is educated, he takes religion with him to the examination room at school or in the university; if he is a politician he takes it to the house of parliament. (1989a, 2)

In ATR, 'all acts from birth to death and thereafter bind the person as a communal being to everyone around themselves, especially those who have passed on to the metaphysical world and those still to be born' (Oosthuizen 1991, 41).

Pregnancy and Childbirth

As soon as a woman knows that she has conceived, religious observances begin, because it is believed, in the first place, that life is from God and pregnancy is a result of his blessings. It is on account of this belief that Traditionalists condemn abortion. The Limba argue that the foetus is God's and has the right to life from the time of conception (Conteh 2004, 180). The Mende believe that the life/spirit is from God and enters the mother's body, 'thus inspiring and giving life to her blood, that is to the foetus' (Sawyerr 1996, 68). Sawyerr (1968, 26) has noted that the unborn is one level of the three-tiered hierarchy of relations embraced within African traditional communities. Thus, abortion is frowned upon and strongly discouraged. The unborn child is vulnerable, defenceless, and voiceless. Its only defence, protection, and voice is the society. Traditionalists see themselves as being the voice of the voiceless and as protecting the community from disaster when they stand against abortion. Rape and poverty are not considered appropriate reasons for abortion; however, abortions that are deemed medically necessary seem to be mildly tolerated.

Religious observances are also required during pregnancy to thwart the clandestine actives of evil spirits (Conteh 2004, 178–179; Parsons 1964, 36–37). Further, certain precautions are taken by the pregnant mother for her own protection and that of her baby (Sawyerr 1968, 19; Conteh 2004, 179).

When the child is eventually born, it is named at a naming and out-dooring ceremony (Harris and Sawyerr 1968, 92; Conteh 2004), which is followed by a thanksgiving sacrifice generally consisting of kola nuts and rice flour mixed with sugar and salt, presented to God through the ancestors. For the Krio, this ceremony is a mixture of traditional and Christian rites (Wyse 1989).

The ceremonies that 'accompany pregnancy, birth and childhood' signify 'that another religious being has been born into a profoundly religious community and religious world' (Mbiti 1989a, 117). In many African cultures, much goes on in the life of the child between birth and puberty: '[m]any rites are performed and many prayers are said to enhance' the child's vital powers. The child also 'learns the traditions and patterns of the life of the family, the village and the clan, through pure curiosity…but also through various forms of instruction from parents, the neighbours, the grandparents, and peers' (Magesa 1997, 94).

Initiation—Secret Societies

For the Mende, Temne, Limba, and Kono, the next important phase of a child's journey in life is his/her initiation into a secret society

(Parsons 1964, 149–154; Harris and Sawyerr 1968, 1; Dorjahn 1982, 35–62; Gittins 1987, 147–154; Conteh 188–194). This initiation plays a crucial role in the child's road to adulthood.

Among the men, the *Poro* society is found in many Sierra Leonean ethnic groups (Little 1949, 199; Parrinder 1962, 95–96; Dorjahn 1982, 35–62; Conteh 2004, 188, 190–191; Parsons 1964, 149–156). The *Poro* society 'can be traced back for several hundred years and is related to other West African societies' (Parrinder 1967, 96).[56] Among the Mende and Kono women, the *Sande* society (Little 1949, 200; Parsons 1964, 143), and among the Limba and Temne women, the *Bondo* society (Turay 1967, 53; NCDC 1993, 204; Conteh 2004, 188, 192–194), are prominent. The Krio have secret societies such as *Gunugu*, *Ojeh*, *Hunting*, and *Geledeh*; many belong to the Western mystical institution of Freemasonry; and some in the interior have participated the *Bundo* and *Poro* societies (Wyse 1989, 12). The men's societies are not operated in Freetown, where only the women's *Bondo* society is seen.

Some Limba have argued that their secret societies have no human origin. They simply say, 'We met it' (Ottenberg 1994, 364)—this has led to the belief that secret societies were established by God and are maintained by him.[57] In that regard, some educated Limba are strongly convinced that these institutions should be rightly called 'secret sacred societies'. These societies are 'secret' in the sense that no member of the opposite sex, or child who has not yet been initiated, may know about the rituals or take part in the dances. They are not 'secret societies' in the sense of having a concealed or limited membership, but this does not mean that all persons of an appropriate age and gender are included in the society's rituals (Finnegan 1965, 77).

Initiation into these societies is meant to equip an individual for adult life—through learning certain medicinal, magical, and technical skills patterned by these societies—and to honour the initiates.

Because secret societies are considered sacred, the process of initiation is preceded by certain religious activities. The bush is cleansed from evil forces and consecrated to prevent unwelcome spiritual forces from entering it and causing havoc. This is usually followed by a sacrifice made to God through the ancestors for the well-being of the participants, both the officials and the initiates. Completing the necessary religious ceremonies before the candidates are initiated is an attempt to present the officials, the candidates, and the bush to God's care and control. The 'idea of rebirth is characteristic of many of these initiation rites' (Parrinder 1962, 96). In general, after the emergence from the bush, initiates are now considered to be adults.

Marriage
In most African cultures, marriages are believed to come from God.[58] In the Traditionalist worldview, it is believed that God makes marriages, whether prearranged or otherwise, happen.[59] Because God created marriage and directs people to their rightful partners, it is believed that he is also the one who sustains marriages. Thus, at all weddings, God is entreated for his blessing and for the creation of a peaceful and stable home.

Death and the Afterlife/Next World
There are several myths/stories about the origin of death in SLIR (Parrinder 1962, 41–42; 1969, 54; Harris and Sawyerr 1968, 9; Finnegan 1967, 233–235). In these stories, God did not intend for humankind to die; he gave to different animals preventives of death to take to humans, but in each story, the appointed animal did not get to humankind in time and, as a result, death came into the world. Traditionalists consider death as inevitable. It is the ultimate end of every created being. Therefore, life must be spent wisely and respectfully. Death is feared because it physically snatches a person from his/her community. The deceased is deprived from a physical communal life and activity.

It seems as if Sierra Leone Traditionalists only make provision for life beyond the grave if one is accepted as an ancestor. However, at death, it is generally believed that the spirit leaves the body and assumes a spirit existence, and the buried body decays in the grave. The 'good dead' spirit continues to be good. Under this category fall the ancestors and those who did not perform heroic acts to attain ancestorship but did lead a decent and praiseworthy life. The 'bad dead' spirit is believed to become evil and may become a ghost and taunt the living. For most Traditionalists, the grave appears to be 'the seal of everything, even if a person survives and continues to exist in the next world' (Mbiti 1989a, 160).

Sin and Salvation
Sin

The Sierra Leonean traditional community, like any African community, is governed by rules, most of which were established by the ancestors or the elders of the community for the guidance of its social and religious life (Conteh 2004, 229; Harris and Sawyerr 1968, 102–103). From an African ethical standpoint, violation of any of these rules constitutes sin or wrongdoing (Mbon 1991, 102; Magesa 1997, 166–172), and sin consequently 'creates disharmony and brings about the disintegration of the society' (Asante 2001, 361). Sin injures the African 'philosophical principle of, I am because we are, and since we are, therefore I am' (Mbiti 1970b, 65). In view of that, sin is regarded as an agent destructive to spiritual, personal, and social harmony. It is therefore condemned. Sin and offences in SLIR may be classified as follows:

- Sin against God or the ancestors.
- Sin against humans.
- Sin against nature, the spirits, or secret societies.
- The infraction of taboos or clan norms.
- The intentional destruction of animals, reptiles, or birds.
- Sexual sins, adultery, incest, homosexuality, and rape.

Homosexuality in Sierra Leone

As in most African cultures, Sierra Leoneans are quite traditional on sexual morality, and there is a basic cultural value in African heritage in which sexuality is sacred and respected. As such, homosexuality is seen as not only a sin, but also a perversion. All of the country's religious traditions regard it as hideous, and anyone of such sexual orientation is considered an outcast. Even the question upset some of the Traditionalists, Muslims, and Christians I interviewed.

The legal status of homosexuality in Sierra Leone is unclear.[60] It appears that the government does not want to discuss the issue for fear of offending religious leaders and institutions that have contributed greatly in bringing the decade-long civil war to an end, restoring peace to the country. As such, homosexuality in Sierra Leone is still not a matter of public discussion.

Some of my interviewees believe that the lifestyle does exist discreetly. In Sierra Leone, many girls are very jealous when their friends befriend other girls, and this sometimes leads to fierce fights. One of my interviewees told me that a wealthy lady once proposed to marry and take care of her. This suggests that there are some Sierra Leoneans, especially women, who are interested in same-sex relationships. It is rumoured that homosexual men may recognise each other by wearing earrings, and lesbians by wearing ankle bracelets. Although I did not find any evidence to support these rumours, I also did not find anyone who openly professed to be a homosexual.

It is probably because homosexuality is a taboo subject, and very little has been written on homosexuality in ATR. Mbiti (1989a, 144) only listed homosexual relations as one of the sexual sins in ATR. Magesa stated that 'active homosexuality is morally intolerable' in Africa, 'because it frustrates the whole purpose of sexual pleasure and that of human person's existence in the sight of the ancestors and God'; in that regard, gay 'or lesbian orientations cannot be allowed to surface, let alone be expressed actively' (1997, 146).

In the present religious climate, Sierra Leone Traditionalists are not ready to entertain in-depth discussion on homosexuality. In fact, they cannot fathom why a sane person should even think about having a romantic and sexual relationship with someone of the same sex. As one interviewee put it, 'Acceptance of such a practice in our community will invoke inexplicable calamities on us'.[61]

Salvation

As African societies are *sensu communis*, provisions are made by which an offender may be made whole and restored to the community.[62]

Depending on the nature of the crime, this wholeness and restoration is accomplished either through personal or communal rituals of cleansing or through the offering of sacrifice. In the Sierra Leone traditional worldview, these rituals are the 'natural means of restoring the vitality' of the individual community (Sawyerr 1996, 123).

Salvation is freedom from wrong doing, deliverance from evil forces, and a state of well-being with oneself, the supernatural, and the community. As Okorocha (1994, 86) put it, it is a 'state of being at peace with the spirit world by living one's life in line with the traditional decorum'. It is also a deliverance from the 'physical and immediate dangers that threaten individual or community survival, good health and general prosperity or safety' (Mbiti 1989b, 67). In this regard, 'salvation meant wealth, health, and prosperity with no reference to moral scruples' (Okorocha 1994, 63).

The African concept of salvation is highly based on 'contemporary realities' (Okorocha 1994, 63). It is not something to be experienced at 'the end of time' (Mbiti 1989b, 67; cf. Mugabe 1999, 246). There is 'no anticipation of a final day when the present cosmic order will be 'judged, or dissolved' and replaced by 'a new heaven and a new earth', and 'there is no clear hope of a hereafter free from suffering' (Okorocha 1994, 85). Rather, salvation 'has been experienced in the past, and it is being experienced in the present' (Mbiti 1989b, 67). In a nutshell, salvation is conceived 'in terms of concern for the ills and successes of community life' (Asante 2001, 359). To be saved is to be 'delivered from sin into fullness of life' and be 'empowered to live a community-centred life' (360).

Sacred Specialists
Sacred specialists are people who are believed to have received spiritual abilities either from God or from the spirits. Because of their spiritual giftedness, sacred specialists play a vital role in the life of the individual and of the community. They are human mediators between the supernatural and the people. In some cases, they play a part in one's life from conception to death. They also help and guide people to maintain personal and communal religious values. Priests, diviners, and herbalists

are the three main categories of sacred specialists in Sierra Leone ATR (Gittins 1987, 179–201; Shaw 1985, 286–303; 1996, 30–55; Wyse 1989, 10; Parsons 1964, 12, 69, 71). Sacred specialists are believed to have 'double eyes'—two additional, invisible eyes that enable them to see and know what transpires in the worlds of the spirits, of the dead, and of witches (Conteh 2004, 242; Shaw 1985, 287; Gbla 1993, 93).

In the priesthood, there are different categories of priests. In Limba culture, priests (*banaben*) are either lay or professionals. Lay priests are usually the heads of families or compounds without community status for their priesthood. Professional priests have community status and are believed to have received their call either from God or from the spirits. There are two categories of professional priests: the chief priest, called *Bagbendekolo*, and his assistant, who is known as *Bagbayha*. Among the Kono, the priest that performs ceremonies for protection is called *Nyamoe* (Parsons 1964, 69), and the one that performs purification rites is known as *Bengene* (71).

Priests may receive training from an experienced priest or elder (Conteh 2004, 244; Parsons 1964, 155–156). All categories of priests connect people to the supernatural through sacrifice, prayers, offerings, and libations.

Diviners (Gittins 1987, 180–183; Shaw 1985, 287; Gbla 1993, 93–95; Conteh 2004, 245–248; Parsons 1964, 81) are believed to discover the solution to problems through inspiration or the manipulation of objects using various techniques. In addition to their role as fortune-tellers and seers, they also offer counsel and comfort, and give assurance and confidence to people; they expose thieves and interpret messages from the spirits and from the dead. There are different kinds of diviners, all of which use objects as mediums to achieve their results. But each uses different methods of divination.

Herbalists (Gittins 1987, 180; Gbla 1993, 96–97; Shaw 1996, 32; Conteh 2004, 248–249), as the name implies, are sacred specialists who use medicines/herbs and wild plants from the bush to make medicines for protective and curative purposes. They are believed to have an outstanding knowledge of the curative properties of herbs, plants, bark, and roots. They are gifted in curing minor, life-threatening, mental, and witchcraft-related illnesses.

CONCLUSION

This section has attempted to produce a systematic study of the fundamental tenets of the indigenous religion of the Mende, Temne, Limba, Krio, and Kono—five major ethnic groups of Sierra Leone—and to provide an overview of SLIR that should equip all the parties involved for a better understanding of ATR.

Foremost in SLIR is the belief in a Supreme Being believed to be a transcendent being living above in the sky, out of the physical reach of people, but whose presence is assumed in worship and in the establishment of and participation in human activities. As such, God is both transcendent and immanent—two of his intrinsic attributes. These two attributes, along with the other four identified—omnipotence, omnipresence, omniscience, and all-seeingness—portray God's character and abilities, as well as the qualities of his nature. God's activities as creator and ruler show that he is the ultimate causation of all existence who continues to influence the lives and activities of humankind. Although the Supreme Being is believed to be immanent, the Traditionalists usually approach him indirectly through intermediaries, especially the ancestors, on account of the understanding of God as a chief who acts and is approached through his subordinates. However, in times of distress, the people may pray directly to him without intermediaries. These prayers generally fall into either prayers of deliverance, or prayers that invoke blessings. Sacrifices and offerings are also made to God directly, indirectly, or concurrently with the ancestors.

In the religious hierarchy of the Temne and the Kono, lesser deities are next to the Supreme Being. The Limba speak of angels with striking affinities to those of Islam and Christianity. For the Mende and Krio, next to the Supreme Being are the ancestral spirits, which are third in the spiritual hierarchy of the Temne, Limba, and Kono. ATR scholars have debated the question of whether or not the ancestors are worshipped.

Two Sierra Leonean scholars, Sawyerr (1966, 3, 33–39; 1996, 43–55) and Fashole-Luke (1974, 210–212), have given strong voices to this debate.

Last in the hierarchy of the supernatural are the nonancestral spirits, which are believed to be numerous and have been classified into nature spirits, which were created as such, and human spirits, which are the spirits of dead humans and include ghosts and witches. All of these inhabit the universe and may be good, evil, or ambivalent.

In order to preserve themselves and their interests, Traditionalists take certain measures to protect against or eradicate both evil spirits and witchcraft. This is often accomplished though procuring a variety charms to drink, wear, hang (on oneself, house, or farm) or rub. The invocation of a 'swear' is considered effective in preventing or punishing the most profoundly antisocial of crimes. Offerings are made to benevolent and malevolent spirits by individuals, households, and communities.

Outside the supernatural realm is humankind, created from the earth with a body and breath, which is the source of life for the body. The spiritual nature of a human being gives him/her a yearning to be in constant harmony with God. Humankind shares the universe with God's other creatures and, although superior to and more intelligent than all of God's other creatures, is expected to embrace and live in harmony with the rest of creation, both animate beings and inanimate things. Because the Traditionalists have a spiritual and physical connection to the earth—which is not only their origin, but also the place where their ancestors were laid to rest—they exhibit an ecological consciousness.

Life is full of puzzles, none of which can be solved without the help of God. Therefore, the Traditionalist dependence on God as the ultimate source and sustainer of everything is evident throughout the entire lifecycle—from conception to death, and, in some instances, even after death. Throughout all of life's stages, God is a focal point.

At the end of this life, the breath departs from the body, which is buried and decays in the grave. It seems that the Traditionalist has no common belief about the destiny of humankind after death, except for those who go on to become ancestors.

As humankind tries to maintain a cordial relationship with the supernatural and the rest of creation, there are rules for the guidance of the socioreligious life of the individual and of the community. These rules were established by the ancestors and the elders, and any failure to follow them is considered an act of sin. Traditionalists despise sin because it is destructive to the social and spiritual well-being of the offender and his/her community. Prescribed procedures must be followed by the offender in order to obtain forgiveness and be reconciled with his/her victim, with the community, and with God. Only then would the offender be considered saved.

Salvation, then, is a state of being in harmony with the supernatural, the community, and oneself. It is deliverance from the physical and contemporary dangers that militate against the individual or community existence. It is a state of spiritual and physical prosperity. Salvation in the African context is primarily based on contemporary realities. It is experienced in the here and now.

This chapter concluded with a discussion of sacred specialists. Most Sierra Leonean communities have sacred specialists who act as intermediaries between the supernatural and the people, believed to be gifted with 'double vision', which gives them the ability to see and reveal things in the worlds of the spirits, the dead, and witches that are concealed from ordinary human eyes. They are also gifted with the ability to prevent the evil activities of malevolent spirits and witches, to communicate with the dead, and to provide help for the physical, spiritual, and the social well-being of the living. Three main categories of sacred specialists are identifiable: priests, diviners, and herbalists.

ENDNOTES

1. ATR and SLIR are used interchangeably in this study.
2. Steady (1976, 216) excepted the Krio from this generalisation by stating that, for the Krio, 'Sierra Leone Christianity is the traditional religion, and Western ethics and culture form part of their multi-faceted life-style and ideology'. Steady based her argument on the observation that Christianity, in its Western forms, has constituted a vital part of Krio socioculture for well over a century and a half—ever since the Krio have been identifiable as a people group. While her point is valid insofar as the Krio have adopted a Eurocentric cultural lifestyle due to the influence of Christianity, we should not forget the fact that the Krio are an invented people group identified by a common sociohistory, while the various groups of repatriated ex-slaves that were settled in Sierra Leone in the eighteenth and nineteenth centuries—and eventually constituted the Krio people—were ethnically Africans whose indigenous religion would have otherwise been ATR. The African features of ancestral piety, rites of passage, music, traditional dish, and mode of dress in Krio culture that Steady identified as African influences (1976, 219) are not in fact outside influences but Krio culture (see Wyse 1989, 1–18; Sanneh 1983, 83–89). Notwithstanding 'their Western veneer, the Krio' are 'very much Africans, and shared the same fears, customs, superstitions and worldview of other less Westernised Africans' (Wyse 1989, vii). Wyse made it clear that the Krio adopted Christianity when he argued that the Krio, like most Sierra Leoneans, 'believe in a supreme being and an after-life, although this belief has perhaps been modified by their adoption of Christianity and other facets of Western civilization' (10). Edward Blyden strongly opposed the indiscriminate emulation of European culture in the Krio community, stirring controversy and debate by arguing that the Krio had thereby become 'de-Africanised' (Wyse 1989, 10). Under his influence, many Krio embraced more of the African culture, adopting African names and traditional dress. The Recaptives, one of the groups of the repatriated former slaves, are noted to have 'preserved a great deal of their religious customs and traditional practises although they were living in villages which were self-consciously Christian' (Sanneh 1983, 83). In view of the aforementioned argument, we can reasonably conclude that although the Krio are greatly influenced by Christianity, their indigenous religion, like that of other ethnic groups in Sierra Leone is, ATR.

3. The external and internal influences and impact on Sierra Leone religion and culture are noted in Harris (1950, 297), Yambasu (2002), Turay (1967, 50–55), NCDC (1990, 205–206), Ottenberg (1984, 437–454; 1988a, 437–465), Conteh (2004, 49–52), and Parsons (1964, 226–240).

4. See Mosley (1995) and Ivan Karp and D. A. Masolo (2000) for extensive discussions on African philosophies.

5. A 'swear' is a curse that acts spiritually through a material object. It is believed to be capable of consciously pursuing and discriminating culprits. It can spiritually pursue the guilty and possibly his/her relatives also by its own divine means, and it is believed it can make no mistake.

6. The most important religious cloth is the *Ronko*.

7. Most of the stone sculptures in Africa are still found in Sierra Leone, Nigeria, Congo, and some in Zimbabwe (Parrinder 1969, 14).

8. See Harris (1950, 277–296), Harris and Sawyerr (1968), Gittins (1987), and Yambasu (2002, 60–73) for Mende religion. For Temne religion, see (NCDC 1993, 204–205). For Limba religion, see Finnegan (1965, 106–122) and Conteh (2004, 66–168). For Krio religion, see (Wyse 1989, 1–18). And for Kono religion, see Parsons (1950, 269–276; 1964, 166–169).

9. Parrinder (1962, 25) represented the relationship between spiritual powers with a triangular formula. At the apex is the Supreme God, on one side of the triangle is the ancestors, and on the other side of the triangle are the gods or nature God; at the base is the earth where the dead are buried and where humankind and its intermediaries. Idowu (1977, 139) stated that the beliefs in God, the divinities, spirits, ancestors, and practise of magic and medicine are the five components that make up ATR. In Mbiti's opinion (1989a, 7), the beliefs in God, spirits, and divinities are some of the elements of African religious beliefs. According to Magesa (1997, 35–36), 'God, the ancestors, and the spirits are all powers or forces that impinge on human life in one way or another'.

10. Smith (1950, v) provided us with references of scholars that have collected evidence that most Africans have a belief in a Supreme Being. While working as a missionary in Africa, Smith was asked by Emil Ludwig, 'How can the untutored African conceive God?' Ludwig was surprised when Smith responded that it was irrelevant to persuade 'Africans of the existence of God, they are sure of it'. In disbelief, Ludwig asked, 'How can that be?' Smith went on to say, 'Deity is a philosophical concept which savages are incapable of framing' (1). While it is likely that Ludwig's statements simply express a gross misunderstanding of the African nature, if they were ever applicable, it is clear that they are now outdated.

11. See NCDC (1993), Parsons (1950, 260–270; 1964, 163–169), Harris (1950, 278–290), Yambasu (2002, 61–64), and Conteh (2004, 66–109) for the respective theistic accounts about God of the ethnic groups under study.

12. In African traditional life, 'even to a child the Supreme Being needs no pointing out', says an Ashanti proverb (Ikenga-Metuh 1981, viii).

13. Cf. Parsons (1950, 260–263), Harris (1950, 278–280), Harris and Sawyerr (1968, 1–9), and Conteh (2004, 67–79).

14. See also Gittins (1987, 49).

15. The 'withdrawal theory of God' is common among the Africans. Some ethnic groups in 'Ivory coast, Ghana, Togo, Dahomey and Nigeria, at least, say that God was formerly so near to men that they grew over-familiar with him' (Parrinder 1969, 31).

16. Mandigo is one of the ethnic groups mainly living in the north with the Temne.

17. Smith (1950, 3) has cautioned, 'Etymological methods are not invariably helpful and indeed may lead astray'. As truthful as this statement may be, the etymological explanation is of theological importance to the Limba and throws light on some of the attributes of God.

18. Finnegan (1965, 107) argued that the Limba do not 'have any explicit theology about Kanu'. The theological ideas expressed in this etymological explanation prove otherwise.

19. Similarly, Parrinder (1962, 34) stated, 'An apparent identification of God with the sun has been thought to exist among peoples in the northern parts of Ghana and Nigeria. However, although they use a word for the Supreme Being, which means "the sun", they are not sun-worshippers'. The same can be said in many African cultures. Among some East and West African peoples, the sun 'is such a potent representation of God that' he is 'simply named after it or in reference to it' (Magesa 1997, 59).

20. The Nuba people of Sudan also refer to God as *Masala* ('the great Mother') (Smith 1950, 215; Mbiti 1970a, 334).

21. The Kuranko are another ethnic group of Sierra Leone. As the closest neighbours in their homeland, they are also one of the ethnic groups with which the Limba have intermingled.

22. The Islamic, Kuranko, and Temne sources show how foreign influences have impacted Limba culture. The Temne full name of God is *Kuru Masaba* ('God Supreme').

23. Cf. Wyse (1989, 10). We should note here that the majority of Krio words have an English origin (Alie 1990, 78). The English word 'God' is similar in pronunciation in Krio.

24. See the works of Smith (1950) and Mbiti (1970).
25. In some other African cultures, the name for God is sometimes the same as the word for sky. The Supreme Being among the Tiv people is *Aoundo*, which is the name for the 'above and firmament' (Downes 1971, 17). The Nupe refer to God as the *Etsu na da sama* ('the God who is in the sky'). In Nuer religion, the Supreme Being *Kwoth* is the spirit who lives in the sky (Evans-Pritchard 1956, 5). In Yoruba, Olorun means 'Lord of the sky or of the heavens' (Lucas 1948, 35–36).
26. See Harris (1950, 278–279) and Harris & Sawyerr (1968, 6–7) for a detailed version for the Mende story, and Finnegan (1967, 231–233) for the Limba story.
27. In ATR, the transcendence of God is considered in several ways: in terms of time, space, distance and outreach, worship and exaltation, God's limitlessness, humankind's understanding of God, and God's supreme status in relation to other beings, divinities, objects, and human institutions (Mbiti 1970a, 12–16). God's immanence is generally conceived of as God's involvement in the affairs of the African (16–18).
28. Cf. Finnegan (1967, 274–275). Finnegan states, 'Limba do not generally speak of *Kanu below*, but occasionally this term is used (especially in Kamabai, I think) to cover all the spiritual agencies other than Kanu (above)—i.e. spirits, the dead and, especially, witches. This terminology may possibly be an effect of mission teaching' (1967, 274–275; cf. 236). The statement that 'Limba do not generally speak of *Kanu below*, but occasionally' may be true in the 1960s and perhaps in the early 1970s. This is no longer the case in the past three decades. As a Limba growing up in Sierra Leone, I was familiar with the phrase *Kanu below* before even starting my secondary schooling. The concept played a vital role during my fieldwork, as is shown in the discussion of nonancestral spirits.
29. A similar ideology is found among the Yoruba: things that receive *Olodumare's* approval are easy to do and the things that do not receive *Olodumare's* sanction are difficult to do (Awolalu 1979, 14).
30. Sierra Leoneans are generally afraid of 'curses'/'swears' relating to thunder and lightening.
31. In most African societies, 'creation is the most widely acknowledged work of God' (Mbiti 1989a, 39).
32. The idea of God owning humankind is a popular concept in African traditional theism (Mbiti 1970, 72).
33. In Africa, myths and accounts about the order of creation vary widely (Mbiti 1970a, 48–52).

34. The concept of creation *ex nihilo* is also reported among several African groups (Mbiti 1989a, 39–40).
35. For information on the governing work of God as chief/king and judge in Africa, see Mbiti (1970, 71–78).
36. The Nuer people talk about the 'little gods' who are the *malaika* ('angels'), from the Arabic word *mal'ak* (Nadel 1954, 247). Lockyer, a British missionary to Kenya, recounted a story of angelic encounter told to him by a native Mau-Mau who converted to Christianity:

> One dark night the men of the Mau-Mau tribe were climbing the hill up to the school to capture and kill the missionary children, and fulfill one of their vows by eating a white man's brain. Suddenly men in white robes appeared all around the school, with flaming swords, and the natives ran back down the hill. Then the new Christian asked, 'Who were these men; were they angels?' A missionary replied, 'We do not have enough men on the staff to surround the school, and we have no flaming swords.' With wide eyes the native shouted, 'They were angels!' (Lockyer 1995, ix)

This story suggests that although the belief in angels appears to be less prominent in AR, some ethnic groups, such as the Mau-Mau people, hold some belief in angels. The Mau-Mau man's question and the missionary's response suggest that the Mau-Mau man's knowledge about angels may have predated his conversion to Christianity. A solid effort by scholars to examine Africa angelology might reveal even more groups with such a belief.

37. Every work on ATR has something to say about ancestral spirits.
38. See Sawyerr (1967, 41–49) for a synopsis of a Krio Sunday graveside libation ceremony in Freetown after a bereavement. This practise still continues especially in the first day of the New Year.
39. See Setiloane (1978, 407) and Mbiti (1989a, 82).
40. Cf. Finnegan (1967, 20).
41. Finnegan (1965, 110).
42. Cf. Sawyerr (1996, 45).
43. See Gittings (1987, 74–82), Turay (1967, 53), and Conteh (2004, 146–147).
44. Harris and Sawyerr (1968, 44–46) classified these spirits as 'land spirits' because they cater for the land activities of the people.
45. See the subheading Initiation—Secret Societies for a discussion on secret societies.

46. See Gittins (1987, 92–97), Mbiti (1989a, 74–89), and Magesa (1997, 53–57).
47. See Magesa (1997, 179–189) for a discussion on the English and African usage of the word.
48. It is said that witches do not like curses or profanity to be used against their mothers.
49. This African method of protecting oneself and one's interests against malevolent spirit(s) has also been referred to by scholars as magic. Parrinder (1962, 114) referred to this act of mystical protection as 'Personal Magic', and Mbiti (1989a, 193–194) saw it as 'good magic'.
50. Cf. Sawyerr (1968, 107).
51. Cf. Ferdinando (1996, 113).
52. Most of the people who go to perform religious rites in caves are those who have personal spirits. Because of their fearsome nature and homelike structure, caves are considered to be the home of many spirits. Offerings to personal spirits for forgiveness, thanksgiving, and prosperity are made in caves.
53. Cotton trees are believed to be the meeting places of witches. They are considered powerful spiritual centres for evil spirits.
54. In the story 'The dog and the rice' (Finnegan 1967, 238–239), *Kanu* created the Limba people, provided them with food, and taught them the techniques of farming. In several African stories, God created and put humankind in a state of paradise with all the necessities of life (Mbiti 1989, 93–94).
55. Harvard Divinity School's 'Religions of the World and Ecology' series and the World Wide Fund for Nature's 'World Religions and Ecology' series have nothing presently on ATR and ecology.
56. Cf. Parson (1964, 149). For various stories and myths about the origin of Poro, see (Parrinder 1967, 96–103).
57. Cf. Finnegan (1965, 107–108).
58. See Magesa (1997, 121).
59. Prearranged marriages are common in Africa (Mbiti 1989a, 133–134).
60. Homosexuality is illegal in most countries in Africa, which portrays the widespread homophobia on the continent. Several heads of state have openly condemned homosexuality, claiming that it is not an African phenomenon but rather a Western decadency. Countries in the forefront of condemning homosexuality are Zimbabwe, Namibia, Uganda, Somalia, and Egypt. In spite of that, the matter of homosexuality is rapidly coming out of the closet in Africa. Among the countries in Africa that have legalised homosexuality, South Africa is the only country that stands at par

with Western countries in the discussion and promotion of the rights of homosexuals. Gay and lesbian activities are visible in South Africa, and it is an offence to discriminate against anyone on the basis of sexual orientation. In South Africa, as in the West, homosexuals hold positions of trust in government and public sectors. They also organise and participate in annual gay pride parades. In spite of the protection homosexuals enjoy from the government, the Traditionalists, and most religious groups, consider their lifestyle unacceptable and sinful.

61. Gbagbo Mansaray, interviewed 25 June 2006, in Makeni Town, Sierra Leone).

62. This tradition abounds in ATR (Sawyerr 1996, 121; Mbiti 1989a, 205–206).

CHAPTER 3

ISLAM IN SIERRA LEONE

Islam is a major religion not only in Arabia, where it began, but also in almost every part of the world to which it has spread, especially in Africa, where it has attracted millions of converts and has maintained a unique relationship with indigenous religioculture. Much has been written about Islam. However, Islam in Sierra Leone, as in any African country, must be studied and understood in its context for fruitful inter-faith dialogue.

This chapter provides a chronological overview of the advents of Islam into Sierra Leone and describes its basic tenets, as well as its encounters with indigenous religion and practices.

THE ADVENT AND EXPANSION OF ISLAM

By the end of the eleventh century, Islam had become firmly established in the Sudan north of Sierra Leone near the Sahara (Olson 1969, 47). It has since spread into Sierra Leone as far as the Gulf of Guinea and the

Atlantic coast. Very little has been written about Islam's early expansion in Sierra Leone, or of its influence on Sierra Leonean culture and religion.

From the sixteenth to the eighteenth centuries, Mande Muslim traders migrated to the Guinea–Sierra Leone hinterland seeking land and trade relations (Skinner 1978, 34–35; cf. Triminghan and Fyfe 1960, 36). They settled in villages along the trade routes of Sierra Leone, forming villages of their own where they combined cultivation with their trade. The Mande were accepted by the indigenes among whom they settled and with whom they intermarried (Triminghan and Fyfe 1960, 36). The Mande were instrumental in the development of Islamic institutions and concepts in Sierra Leone.

Another account of the infiltration of Islam into Sierra Leone recounts its expansion south from the Sudan through small groups of Fula and Mandingo traders in the eighteenth century (Fyle 1981, 27; cf. Bah 1991, 464). Upon arrival in any place, and during their temporary or permanent stay, the Fula and Mandingo opened schools to teach Arabic and the tenets of Islam (Alharazim 1939, 14; cf. Parsons 1964, 226; Bah 1991, 464). Many of the people and their leaders rallied around these teachers, embraced the Muslim faith, and became the patrons of their teachers (Alharazim 1939, 14). The Mandingo intermarried with the indigenes and formed new clans. For instance, among the Tonko, Warawara, and Biriwa Limba peoples, Mandingo Muslims took wives and had children, which resulted in the Samura, Kamara, and Kargbo clans of Tonko; the Mansaray clan of Warawara; and the Conteh clan of the Biriwa (Fyle 1981, 28). The Mandingo became involved in local politics and were made rulers among the Limba, and fought on the side of the Limba in battles against other ethnic groups.

In spite of this seemingly fruitful interaction between the Mandingo and the indigenes, these early Fula and Mandingo immigrants did not succeed in establishing Islam in Sierra Leone to any strong degree (Fyle 1981, 29).

A major Islamic breakthrough came about through the 1727 political and economic war between the Fula and the Yalunka (Alie 1990, 43; Bah 1991, 465). This war, known as the Futa Jallon Jihad, resulted in a significant wave of Muslim migration into Sierra Leone. The jihad dispersed many peoples over a wide area, and through the attacks on the hinterland, the development of trade, and the significant role played by Qur'anic teachers, proselytisers, scribes, mediators, counsellors, and makers of protective amulets contributed to the large-scale Islaminisation of Sierra Leone's Northern Province (Bah 1991, 465; Fyle 1981, 31; Alie 1990, 43). New Muslim rulers and converts helped spread Islam into many parts of Sierra Leone.

When the colony (later called Freetown) was founded in 1787 for the settlement of freed slaves (Fyle 1981, 34; Alie 1990, 51), Muslim traders and missionaries in the hinterland traveled to the colony to foster business and social relationships with the Europeans. Some of the administrators and managers of the colony paid return visits to the northern hinterland. Two of the Muslim traders who visited the colony in 1794 and established trade contacts were Fendu Modu and his son Dala Modu (Fyle 1981, 43; Jalloh and Skinner 1997, 11–13). Dala Modu eventually moved and settled in one of the outskirts of Freetown. They used their wealth to sponsor Muslim clerics and provided infrastructures for the promotion of Islamic institutions and teachings. The growing business opportunities in the colony brought many more Muslims from the north, and before long, there were small communities of Muslims in and around Freetown, especially in the east end.

After the abolition of the slave trade in 1807, Sierra Leone was found suitable to set up a British court that would try owners and crews of captured slave vessels (Fyle 1981, 38; Sanneh 1983, 72). Thus, slaves captured on board slave ships were emancipated in the colony (Hildebrant 1990, 81–82). These slaves were called Recaptives on account of 'being captured the first time and enslaved, they had been recaptured and freed by the British Navy' (Fyle 1981, 38). They began to arrive in the colony in 1810.

Most of the Recaptives put ashore from these ships time after time were Christians, but some, particularly the Aku from Yorubaland, were Muslims who had been converted during the Fulani jihad and afterwards (Wyse 1989, 9). The Aku were sent to Fourah Bay in the east and to

Fula Town in the northeast of Freetown (Alharazim 1939, 13; cf. Wyse 1989, 9; Alie 1990, 74). The Aku secured the services of some of the Fula and Mandingo Muslim teachers to teach their children and to make converts to the faith of Islam (Alharazim 1939, 13–14). Mosques were built in Fourah Bay and Fula Town, and converts from adjacent villages rapidly poured in. Converts 'travelled on foot from Waterloo' village to join other believers at Rokel, Hastings, Wellington, and Kissy villages for the congregational prayers on Fridays, as well as on special festival days—these comradely meetings were known as *Arootas* (Alharazim 1939, 14). Muslim influence continued to spread throughout the colony and beyond. Prayer places and Qur'anic schools were found in many parts of Freetown. In 1891 the colony comprised 10 percent Muslims; in 1901, 12 percent; 1911, 14 percent; in 1921, 19.5 percent; in 1931, 26.2 percent.

Mass conversion to Islam in the late nineteenth century was largely on account of the conquests of Samori Turay the Mandinka warrior (Fyle 1981, 33). By the start of the twentieth century, a considerably large number of certain ethnic groups were solidly Muslim (Olson 1969, 48). It was during the twentieth century that Islam spread more deeply (Triminghan and Fyfe 1960, 36).

In 1890 the British Colonial Office directed the Sierra Leone government to urge Muslims to apply for government financial aid to education. On account of the realisation that Qur'anic education would not provide them with European forms of employment, as well as the desire to transform their traditional educational system to a modern form like those of the existing Christian and government schools, the Muslims took advantage of the offer. A building was provided and a grant for the salaries of teachers (Anderson 1970, 177). All the schools opened in Freetown and the hinterland received grants from the colonial government.

Blyden, a Christian and an astute student of Islam, who taught himself to speak Arabic, maintained close relations with the Muslim community in Freetown. He urged the British authorities to involve Muslim Africans in their colonial enterprise. On account of his interest in Islam and concern for the welfare of the Muslims, the British appointed Blyden as director of Islamic education in 1901. During his tenure, Blyden trained many Muslim youths, most of whom became the founders and leaders of the Progressive Islamic Organisation after World War I (WWI). At the end of WWI, Muslims in Sierra Leone were exposed to the wider Islamic world. Many had made the annual *Hajj* ('pilgrimage') to the Holy land of Mecca and had travelled to other major Islamic centres such as Morocco and Egypt. Some had gone to study abroad. Bilateral arrangements were made to have Arab teachers in Islamic Schools in Freetown. About 1928, the Sierra Leone Muslim Congress was established in Freetown with the objectives of education, the promotion of Islam, and the unification of Muslims in Sierra Leone. Within a few years of their establishment in Sierra Leone, around 1937, the Ahmadiyya Missionary Organisation opened schools in many parts of the country. Some of the best secondary school final results have been produced by the Ahmadiyya secondary school in Freetown.

Many prominent Sierra Leonean Muslim leaders such as the late Sheik Jibril Sesay, founder of the Alimania Youth Organisation in 1942, and the late Sheik Basariah, who founded the Basariah wing of Islam, contributed immensely to the development of Islamic education and religion in Sierra Leone (Khanu 2001, 38).

Through several Islamic Organisations—such as the Sierra Leone Muslim Reform Society, the Pilgrims' Association, the Supreme Islamic Council, and the Islamic Call Society of Libya—many Islamic colleges have been opened in Freetown and the hinterland (Khanu 2001, 38). The Ansarul Islamic Mission, founded in 1974, has fourteen secondary and sixty primary schools in the country.

Since the mid-1970s, huge profits generated by petroleum products controlled by Muslim or pro-Islamic countries outside the sub-Saharan region, such as Saudi Arabia, Kuwait, Iran, and Libya, led to a considerable increase in grants for Muslim missionary enterprises. Food was also shipped by Islamic countries to feed the needy. All this contributed to the increase of Muslim organisations in Sierra Leone.

During the All People's Congress (APC) political regime, Sierra Leone became a member of the Islamic Conference Organisation (ICO) to support the cause of the Palestinians and to deny Israel recognition (Jalloh and Skinner 1997, 153; cf. Bah 1991, 473). Because of grants, the government has pledged itself to follow a course that many Sierra Leoneans do not understand.

In a nutshell, Islam came into Sierra Leone sometimes through the effects of war, but more often by peaceful means. Many foreign Muslim traders, missionaries, military leaders, and Sierra Leonean Muslim and non-Muslim leaders played roles in the development of Islamic influence in the colony and hinterland of Sierra Leone.

The main Muslim groups in Sierra Leone are the Sunni, Shi'a, and the Ahmadiyyas. The Sunni and Shi'a are the largest.

BASIC TENETS AND PRACTICES OF ISLAM

Sources of Islamic Teachings and Practices

Like most Muslims the world over, Muslims in Sierra Leone look to the Holy Qur'an as the fundamental source of religious doctrine. It forms the basis of all Muslim teachings, laws, and discussions relating to religion. The Holy Qur'an is also referred to as *Al-Kitab Allah*, 'the book of Allah' (Pratt 2005, 31; cf. Ali 1992, 1).[1] The word *Qur'an* is derived from the root word *qara'a*, which means 'he collected together things', and also, 'he read or recited' (Ali 1992, 1; 2002, I-25). The Qur'an is 'a revelation from the Lord of the worlds' (26:192), or the revelation from God, 'the Mighty, the Wise' (39:1) to the Prophet Muhammad (47:2) through the angel Gabriel in the Arabic language (Aziz 1993, 43) in the lunar month of Ramadan at *Laylatul Qadr*, 'Night of Power' (Nelson 2005, 104, 109), at various times during a period of twenty-three years (Ali 1992, 3; 2002, I-26; Aziz 1993, 43). Ninety-three chapters were revealed at Mecca during a span of thirteen years, and the remaining twenty-one chapters were revealed at Medina over a period of ten years (Ali 1992, 4; 2002, I-27; Aziz 1993, 46).

The Meccan revelations were concerned with ethical and spiritual teachings, and are eschatological in nature, with emphasis on the Day of

Judgment (Khanu 2001, 22–23). They were meant to ground Muslims in their faith in God (Ali 2002, I-28).

The Medinan revelations were about social laws, and political and moral issues (Khanu 2001, 23). They were meant to translate faith into action (Ali 2002, I-28). Muslims consider the Qur'an to be a 'flawless and timeless book, intended as the perfect guidance for all humanity— not just group of people in a specific age and time' (Nelson 2005, 100).

Although it is believed that the Qur'an is the final revelation of God, and the primary scriptural and authoritative source of Muslim faith and life, it does require interpretation. Believers cannot proceed in their faith journey without the guidance of the Qur'an as interpreted and lived out by the Prophet Muhammad, the one who went on further to explain the deeper meanings contained in the Qur'an and filled out its general exhortations with essential detail (Nelson 2005, 101). For instance, the Qur'an tells Muslims to pray five times a day, but it does not say how. During Prophet Muhammad's time, believers had the opportunity to consult him regarding how to do things or to find answers to issues. Since the Prophet is longer accessible, Muslims now depend on another source—the *Sunna* ('trodden path' or 'tradition', especially that of the Holy Prophet's life)—which comprises sections of narrative material called the *Hadith* (Pratt 2005, 41; Ali 1993, 22; Aziz 1993, 50; Khanu 2001, 23; Peters 2003, 161). The *Sunna* is used in Islam to indicate the customary behaviour and sayings of the Holy Prophet (Ali 1992, 22; Peters 2003, 52, 161–165).

A third source of Muslim guidance is the *Shari'a*, which means 'that which is prescribed' or 'the path to be followed', believed to be given by Allah for the guidance of all his people (Pratt 2005, 88). The life of the Muslim is structured according to the *Shari'a*, which is based on legalistic chapters in the Qur'an that are believed to represent God's revelation of the law in its fullness. The Qur'an commands the doing of justice, and it is by the way of *Shari'a* that this doing of justice is interpreted. It is the temporal application of divine justice (Pratt 2005, 89). The entire Muslim *ummah* ('community') is expected to live according to the *Shari'a*, but because Sierra Leone is not a Muslim country and Muslims in the country are very tolerant, *Shari'a* law is not strictly enforced, and the sometimes severe punishments it requires are rarely implemented.

There are two primary sources and three secondary sources of *Shari'a* (Pratt 2005, 90). The Qur'an and the *Sunna* constitute the primary sources, which have already been dealt with, and the three secondary sources are *Ijma*, *Qiyas*, and *Ijtihad*, which I now proceed to discuss briefly.

Ijma—the legal consensus of the community—is a vital operative machinery meant to regulate legal supposition and custom (Khanu 2001, 23; Pratt 2005, 91). It is the consensus of opinion among the companions of the Prophet Muhammad and the agreement reached on the decisions taken by Muslim scholars/jurists in respect to various matters (Pratt 2005, 91). It is a means for total unanimity—the rule of the majority.

Quiyas ('analogy') refers to the process of reasoning adopted where there is no clear directive from the Qur'an or *Sunna*, but where there are parallels or analogical instances (Pratt 2005, 91).

Ijtihad ('to endeavour', 'individual thought', or 'to exert oneself') is vital in finding the legal elucidation to new problems (Khanu 2001, 23; Peters 2003, 175; Nelson 2005, 102). It is the process of consultation and the use of rational argument in order to arrive at a binding decision (Pratt 2005, 91).

The result, when these secondary sources are applied, 'leads to an extension of law beyond that which is found directly in the Qur'an and the Sunnah' (Pratt 2005, 92). It is from the Qur'an, the *Sunna*, and *Shari'a*—and its components—that Muslims in Sierra Leone derive most of their beliefs, teachings, and practices.

Islamic Tenets and Teachings

The basic beliefs/teachings, and some of the practices, of Islam are summarised in the Qur'an as follows:

> It is not righteousness that you turn your faces toward the East and the West, but righteous in the one who believes in Allah, and the Last Day, and the angels and the Book and the prophets, and gives

away wealth out of love for Him to the near of kin and the orphans and the needy and wayfarer and to those who ask and to set slaves free, and keeps up prayer and pays the Zakaat; and the performers of their promises when they make a promise, and the patient in distress and affliction and in time of conflict. These are they who are truthful, and these are they who keep their duty. (2:177)

The *Kalima*, known as the 'brief expression of faith', summarises the five basic beliefs of Islam, which are God, angels, prophets and messengers of God, books of God, and life after death (Aziz 1993, 4). I now briefly look at these basic beliefs of Islam.

The Supreme Being

The Supreme Being in Islam is God, whose proper name is Allah. Muslims believe and teach that there is one, and only one, God, who is unique in every respect, and there is nothing that bears any likeness to him (20:8, 112). Allah is 'the Lord of the worlds' (1:1, 26:192); as such, he is not just the God of the Muslims—or the God of a chosen race, religion, or nation—but the one and only God for all peoples (Aziz 1993, 10).

The Qur'an tells us a great deal about Allah. Sura 59:22–24 mentions several of his attributes and activities. On the basis of references in the Qur'an, Muslims list ninety-nine names of God, also referred to as the Most Beautiful Names, which portray the attributes, qualities, and activities of Allah (Baldock 2004, 50, 213–221).

Ali has suggested that most of the attributes of the Divine Being that are mentioned in the Qur'an 'are, as it were, offshoots of any one of the four essential attributes mentioned in the opening chapter' (Alie 1992, 56). He went on to mention that God is *al-Wahid/Ahad* ('the One'), *al-Hayy* ('Ever-Living'), *al-Quayyum* ('Self-Subsisting'), *al-Ghani* ('Self-Sufficient'), *al-Awwal* ('the First'), *al-Akhir* ('the Last'), *al-Quaddus* ('Holy'), *al-Samad* ('on Whom all depend and He depends not on any'), and *al-Haqq* ('True'). Ali further categorised God's attributes and activities as relating to his love and mercy,[2] his glory, power, and greatness,[3] his knowledge,[4] and his activities.[5]

It appears the most significant attributes are 'beneficent' and 'merciful', since every sura in the Qur'an, save sura 9, is prefaced with the phrase, *Bismillah-ir rahman-ir rahim* ('In the name of Allah, the Beneficent, the Merciful'). *Rahman* and *Rahim* apply to two different states of the exercise of God's mercy. *Rahman* is when humankind has not done anything to deserve God's mercy and God exercises his unbounded mercy in bestowing his gifts on him/her. *Rahim* is when humankind does something to deserve God's mercy, and God's mercy is, therefore, repeatedly exercised for him/her (Ali 1992, 53; Aziz 1993, 11). In other words, it is *Rahman* that creates for humankind all the necessities that make life possible on earth, and it is *Rahim* that gives humans the fruits of their labours; or, again, it is *Rahman* that, by God's revelation, shows humans the right path to develop their faculties, and it is *Rahim* that rewards the faithful for the good they do (Ali 1992, 53).

Angels

An angel (*mala'ikah*) is a spiritual and nonmaterial being created from light. Angels vary in rank and status (Aziz 1993, 13; Nelson 2005, 104) and have many tasks. They carry out God's will and act as intermediaries and messengers between God and the world; they record the deeds of humans; and they listen to the prayers of believers and deliver salutations to God and God's prophets (Nelson 2005, 104). Nelson has noted that 'when Allah refers to Himself as "We" in the Qur'an, He is indicating that while He is the ultimate actor, for example in the process of creation; He also delegates certain actions and duties to angels' (101).

Prophets and Messengers of Allah

As well as the previously quoted sura 2:177, several other suras (2:185, 3:179, 4:171, 59:19) speak to the importance of the believing in the prophets and messengers who were endowed with divine revelations and sent by God as teachers, 'bearers of good news and as warners' (2:213). The Qur'an teaches that God sent prophets to all nations on the earth, at various times (10:47, 16:36, 16:84, 16:89, 35:24). All Muslims are required to believe in all these messengers of God without distinction (2:136, 2:285, 3:84, 4:150–152), because all were sent as part of one system (5:19, 23:44, 57:26–27). Their message is the same and came from one and the same source—God—so that people would submit to his will and his law.

The Qur'an mentions twenty-five messengers and prophets, and states that there are more unmentioned ones. Some of the prophets mentioned in the Qur'an are Adam, Noah, Abraham, Moses, David, and Jesus Christ, from the Bible (Ali 1992, 83–92, 95–112; Aziz 1993, 16);[6] Luqman, Hud, and Dhul-Kifl (Ali 1993, 16; 1992, 93–94); and Muhammad (*Muhammad al rasul ullah*), who is the last of the prophets and was chosen by God to be the seal of the prophets even before the time of Adam (Nelson 2005, 99; Pratt 2005, 80).

After Muhammad, no other prophet or messenger will come from God because Muhammad came with the teachings from God meant for all peoples and for all times. Muhammad is believed to be the perfect example of how all human beings should behave in relation to God and the 'rest of creation—at all times' (Nelson 2005, 99). He came to unite all peoples with a single religion in order that humankind may live peacefully as one people (Aziz 1993, 18).

Books of God—Holy Scriptures
Muslims refer to the original revelations of the prophets as 'books of God' because they were intended to be conserved together (Aziz 1993, 20). God has revealed his teachings for guidance through selected people—the prophets and messengers—to convey them to the peoples of their times. These prophets and messengers brought special books, as in the case of Moses (Torah), Jesus (Gospel), and Muhammad (Qur'an) (sura 3:3). Muslims are required to believe not only the teachings of the Prophet Muhammad, but also the teachings of all the prophets before him that were revealed by God (Aziz 1993, 21; Nelson 2005, 99).

However, as the seal of the divine scriptures, the Qur'an claims to be a verifier of previous scriptures (2:89), a guardian over other scriptures (5:48), a judge in deciding their differences (16:64), and that which makes manifest and perfects their teachings (26:1, 5:3). The Qur'an is unequalled in its recording and preservation (Ali 1992, 26–29). The astonishing fact is that the word of God that came to the Prophet Muhammad over fourteen hundred years ago remains fully intact and completely preserved (Aziz 1993, 20–21). Believers continue to claim that the Qur'an is the only authentic and complete book of God, which is being protected from being lost, corrupted, or concealed.

Afterlife

The human being has not only a body, but also a *rub* ('spirit'), or a *nafs* ('soul'), which leaves the body at death (Peters 2003, 257) and enters into a spiritual interspace that resembles purgatory (Nelson 2005, 105). The state of the soul during this period depends on the quality of one's life before death: 'Just as our physical actions and habits affect the body and leave their impressions upon it, so does the good or evil of our deeds affect the spirit and leave an impression upon it' (Aziz 1993, 23). The souls are called from their place to the Day of Judgment when everyone is judged according to their deeds in this world, which determines the final resting place in either the garden or the fire. Our journey on earth is the shortest but most crucial part of the process (23:112). It sets the stage for eternity; therefore, humanity is called to make provision for the hereafter (*Akhirah*) by acting according to God's divine guidance (Nelson 2005, 105).

Practices

Islam is not just about belief; 'it is also very much about a religion in action', and as such, the Muslim's 'life is given visible and daily concrete expression by way of the obligations to fulfill the requirements of piety' (Pratt 2005, 83).

Islam is built on five pillars of religious duty (*arkan*), namely, *Shahadah* ('witnessing/testifying'), *Salat* ('prayer'), *Sawm* ('fasting'), *Zakat* ('charity/almsgiving/poor tax'), and *Hajj* (pilgrimage'). *Shahadah* is a state of faith; the other four are practices of faith meant to cater for the believer's spirituality and satisfy his/her physical needs 'through the ongoing process of interacting with God, with the self, and with Creation' (Nelson 2005, 106).

Shahadah

Shahadah is the creed or testimony of faith acknowledging that there is none worthy of worship except Allah and that Prophet Mohammad is his messenger (Baldock 2004, 50). This two-part creedal statement affirms the oneness of God (*twahid*) and the speaker as a believer, who, as such, is a person who submits to the will of Allah (Pratt 2005, 84). Muslims are obligated to recite it frequently, everyday, as a reminder of their devotion to God and to the path of Muhammad (Nelson 2005, 95).

Salat

Salat is the observance of the five daily prayers—*al-Fajr*, which takes place in the morning right before sunrise; *al-Zuhr*, around mid-day between noon and early afternoon; *al-'Asr*, afternoon, midway between midday and sunset; *al-Maghrib*, between after sunset and the end of evening twilight; and *al-isha*, one or two hours after sunset (Pratt 2005, 84)—and is obligatory for every mature and sane Muslim, and, in the case of women, those free from menstruation or confinement due to childbirth.

In *salat*, a Muslim prays directly to God and recites verses from the Qur'an. The *al-Fatiha* ('the Opening') chapter of the Qur'an is recited often, at least twice in each of the five daily prayers. Other obligatory prayers are the Friday noon congregational prayer (*al-Jumma*), which replaces the usual noon prayer (*al-Zuhr*), and the funeral prayer (Pratt 2005, 85). There are also other highly recommended prayers, including those accompanying the obligatory and the great festival prayers *Idul-Fitr*, *Idul-Adha*, and *Maulidu 'l-Nabi*. In addition to all these prayers, Muslims express gratitude to God and seek his favour every step of the way from birth to the grave.

Salat is preceded by the performance of *Wudu* ('ablution'), the purification three times of the hands, mouth, face, and feet, and facing the *Qiblah*—the direction of the *Ka'ba* in Mecca, the symbolic house of God originally built by Abraham (Baldock 2004, 51–52; Pratt 2005, 84–85).

Sawm

Every healthy and mature Muslim is required to fast from dawn to dusk, once a year, during the entire month of Ramadan. During this period, a Muslim is to abstain from food, drink, and sex (Aziz 1993, 31; Nelson 2005, 108; Pratt 2005, 86). The month of Ramadan is considered a time for spiritual curing. It is the time when Muslims 'purge all of the bad habits built up' during the year, and 'it is a time that has been designated by Allah for cleansing the heart by way of fasting, prayer, and reflection' (Nelson 2005, 108; cf. Aziz 1993, 32). It provides an opportunity for Muslims to see who they are, correct their weaknesses, and broaden their spiritual horizons. As already mentioned, it was during Ramadan that Allah revealed the Qur'an to the Prophet Muhammad.

Zakat

The root meaning of *Zakat* is 'to purify', that is, a Muslim purifies his/her wealth by giving it away (Nelson 2005, 109; Baldock 2004, 52). *Zakat* not only purifies the wealth of the giver but also purifies his/her heart from selfishness and greed. In turn, it purifies the heart of the recipient from envy and jealousy, from hatred and uneasiness, and it replaces it with sincere appreciation, goodwill, and blessings for the giver. *Zakat* is generally 2.5 percent of the yearly savings for a rich businessman or woman (cf. Pratt 2005, 85), 10 or 20 percent of the produce for farmers, and 25 percent of found treasure, such as (nongambling) lottery or a found precious item. This money, produce, or found treasure is distributed among the poor and needy, wayfarers in need, new Muslim converts, Muslims in debt, employees appointed to collect *Zakat*, and Muslims in service through the research, study, or propagation of Islam. It is also used to fund the liberation of Muslim prisoners of war. Muslims who can afford it may also go above and beyond what they pay as *Zakat*, in which case the offering is a strictly voluntary charity (*sadaqa*), which, in Sierra Leone, is better known as sacrifice. Parallel to *Zakat* in Sierra Leone is the *Zaqatul Fitri*, a gift of rice given to the poor at the end of Ramadan.

Hajj

Hajj is the pilgrimage to Mecca during the month of *Zul Hijja/Dhu 'l-Hijja* (Aziz 1993, 33; Baldock 2004, 54; Pratt 2005, 86). This pilgrimage to Saudi Arabia is compulsory at least once in a lifetime for those who have the ability and financial resources to make it. Muslims from all walks of life and every part of the world gather in Mecca in response to the call of Allah. It has been noted that *Hajj* is the cure for a lifetime, in the same way that *Salat* is the cure for the day and *Sawm* is the cure for the year (Nelson 2005, 109–110). *Hajj* commemorates the rituals observed by Prophet Abraham and his son Ishmael, who were the first pilgrims to the *Ka'ba*. *Hajj* is likened to the Judgment Day, when all soul will be gathered and judged according to their deeds (110). It is also the time when members of the global *ummah* congregate 'to pledge that there is only one God for the whole of humanity and that all persons are equal, regardless of race, nation, wealth or status' (Aziz 1993, 33; see also Nelson 2005, 110). The chief features of the *Hajj* are the *tawaaf*, the circumambulation seven times of the *Ka'ba*; the gathering of the pilgrims on the plain of *'Arafa* to glorify God (Aziz 1993, 33–34; Baldock 2004, 55; Pratt 2005, 87); the stoning of 'devil-posts', or pillars symbolising the rejection of all that comes between humankind and the Divine; and the concluding 'Feast of Sacrifice', the *Eidul-adha*, commemorating the animal sacrifice Abraham made in place of his son, symbolising the surrender to the divine will which is associated with the sacrifice of the lower (or animal) self (Baldock 2004, 55–56; Pratt 2005, 87). Although it is not essential to complete the *Hajj* and make it valid, many believers also take this opportunity to visit to the tomb of Prophet Muhammad at Medina.

ISLAM'S ENCOUNTER WITH TRADITIONAL BELIEFS AND PRACTICES

Islam did not, by any means, encounter godless Sierra Leonean indigenes. The people whom Muslim traders and clerics encountered already knew God. The first modern religious changes in the Kono homeland were brought about by the introduction of Islam (Parsons 1964, 226). It is reasonable to say the brand of Islam, which evolved in Sierra Leone, was an accommodating one. Islam gained influence among the indigenes of Sierra Leone because it was brought by other Africans who retained many traits and accoutrements of traditional ethnic culture (Anderson 1970, 177). As such, Islam was able to adapt itself to the culture of the people. Muslim leaders approved of, or at least tolerated, traditional practices such as sacrifice and polygamy. This attracted many people to Islam. Even less of a demand for change was made with regard to charms and medicines. Islam accepted traditional religion with an over-lay of Muslim belief and practice. Much of the Islamic worldview was superimposed on the indigenous religion of the people, bringing the two faith traditions together.

As already discussed, Sierra Leone Traditionalists believe in the existence of a myriad of both good and evil spirits. On account of their belief in the existence of evil spirits and the practice of witchcraft, self-preservation has demanded that Sierra Leone Traditionalists take certain preventative measures by procuring protective charms.

Muslim men called *alfa* or *morimen* (because they were powerful in the use of 'medicine') adopted the making of charms from the indigenes (Skinner 1978, 57–58) and took advantage of the opportunity to make a living by producing and selling these charms. They made charms out of various objects with verses from the Qur'an written on paper and enclosed in pouches (1978, 58; 1964, 227), which were used by warriors, farmers, and traders. These charms are believed to bring prosperity or victory and to ward off evil spirits. Many Muslims also use these charms. Qur'anic verses were also written over doors as a form of protection, or written on boards and placed on farms or in trees to prevent robbery and vandalism (1978, 58). A potion called *lasmamie* was made by writing Qur'anic verses on a board and then washing the writing into a receptacle and adding a drop of perfume and pouring it into a bottle to be rubbed for protection, imperviousness, and good luck (Khanu 2001, 46; Parson 1964, 227).

One of the strongest Muslim influences on the Kono was on the use of magic and 'medicines' (Parsons 1964, 227), and I add that this is true of most ethnic groups in Sierra Leone. In addition to making charms, Muslim men used prayer, divination, potions, and magic tablets to identify culprits and to protect and cure people (Skinner 1978, 58). Most of the sacred specialists in Sierra Leone since the advent of Islam have been Muslims.

Muslim clerics are known to have joined the *Poro* secret society and were provided with roles that suited their familiarity with the sacred Arabic script. They were asked to use their knowledge of magic squares, the basis of Islamic talismans, to provide powerful medicines for the society for the use against their detractors (Sanneh 1983, 235). In many communities in Sierra Leone, Muslim clerics were and are still key figures in conducting traditional rituals and sacrifices (Khanu 2001, 46). The fact that Islam in Sierra Leone incorporated aspects of traditional religious practices made it more acceptable and appealing to the indigenes.

However, not all Muslim missionaries were prepared to tolerate the accommodating brand of Islam practised in Sierra Leone. The Ahmadiyya movement, which was established in Sierra Leone in 1937 by missionaries from Pakistan, aimed at purifying West African Islam (Bah 1991, 469). Ahmadiyya missionaries were interested in three major goals (469–470):

- To reform and purge Islam of all its corrupted forms.
- To modernise Islam or to keep up with modern trends and developments.
- To challenge Christianity.

Although some Muslims refer to the Ahmadiyya movement as a cult, it is perhaps on account of the first of these goals that there are not many Ahmadiyya followers in Sierra Leone.

The greatest impact on ATR by Islam came in the 1970s with the rise of Islamic economic might. This affected the whole of sub-Saharan Africa economically and culturally. President Moammar Quadafi of Libya was prominent in promoting Islam through financial might. In 1975 he started building beautiful and expensive mosques, cultural centres, schools, and universities. All this came with a price. Muslims and institutions that received these favours were expected to promote the North African brand of Islam. Thus, the syncretistic type of Islam long practised in Sierra Leone required a total overhaul if it expected such grants.

This development called for a complete exclusion of African practices such as divination and the use of protective charms from Islam. Today there are Muslims in Sierra Leone who consider most traditional religious practices to be satanic. In recent years, they have been working hard to minimise what they consider to be heathen practices in Islam. ATR and culture are openly preached against today. This continues to baffle the Traditionalists and, as Khanu put it, one can almost hear the indigenes say, '[A] new teaching has come into Islam' (2001, 46).

The influence of Islam on Sierra Leonean culture and religion is evident in indigenous rites of passage (e.g., the naming ceremony of a newborn as noted in the previous chapter). The Mande settlers not only played an important role in the development of Islamic institutions and concepts in Sierra Leone, as already stated, but they also made an impact on the indigenous culture. Several ethnic political titles for male Temne, Limba, and other northern chiefs derived from Arabic words were introduced through their influence (Skinner 1978, 61). By the late eighteenth century, the following were in use: *Almami* ('king', 'chief', 'subchief'), *kande* ('chief'), *mansa* ('king', 'chief'), *farima* ('chief', originally a warlord), *alkali* ('chief', 'subchief', 'judge'), and *santigi* ('village chief', 'section chief'). During the same period, northern clan names such as Sankoh, Turay, Sesay, Koroma, and Kamara were derived from Mande settlers.

Other indications of Muslim influence on indigenous culture are the introduction of Arabic loan words such as *sathka* ('sacrifice'), the modification of the original name (*Kuru*) of the Supreme Being by Temne Muslims to *Kuru Masaba*, and the introduction of Arabic names for people such as Momodu (Muhammad), Lansana (al-Hasan), Brimah (Ibrahim), and Suliman (Sulaiman) (Skinner 1978, 58–60).

Conclusion

This chapter sought to provide an informed knowledge of Islam as practiced in Sierra Leone as a means to interreligious cooperation and dialogue. When Islam immigrated into Sierra Leone, the indigenes they encountered already knew God and had their own religious system. In general, wherever Muslims settled, they disseminated their beliefs and established institutions for worship and learning. Muslim traders and clerics/missionaries opened Qur'anic schools to teach Arabic and Islamic tenets.

Practitioners of Islam are considered 'People of the Book' because they have scriptures, which claim to come from or be inspired by God, as the primary sources of their beliefs and teachings. Islam is a way of life, expressed and practised by believers through worship, prescribed duties, and actions.

Islam was favoured by the masses because it was brought by other Africans and was presented by its forebears as an African religion, which resulted in an accommodating brand of Islam that still exists in Sierra Leone. Muslims accepted and adapted Sierra Leonean indigenous religiosity and culture, with an overlay of Islamic belief and practice. This syncretistic approach and lesser demand on the indigenes attracted many people to Islam.

Statistically, the number of Muslims in Sierra Leone has always been greater than the number of Christians. Although, in recent years, Christianity has been making strides and growing, Muslims still significantly outnumber Christians.

The effects of Islam on ATR and vice versa in Sierra Leone are evidently clear. Although ATR continues to be marginalised in Sierra Leone, one would be naïve to think that it has not influenced the worldviews of Islam.

ENDNOTES

1. See Ali (1992, 1–2) for additional names of the Qur'an.
2. God is *al-Rauf* ('Affectionate'), *al-Wadud* ('Loving-Kind'), *al-Latif* ('Benignant'), *al-Afuww* ('Pardoner'), *al-Shakur* ('Multiplier of rewards'), *al-Salam* ('Author of Peace'), *al-MUmin* ('Granter of security'), *al-Muhaimin* ('Guardian over all'), *al-Jabbar* ('Restorer of every loss'), *al-Barr* ('Benign'), *Rafi al-darajat* ('Exalter of ranks'), *al-Wasi* ('Ample-Giving'), *al-Wahhab* ('great Giver'), and *al-Razzaq* ('Bestower of sustenance').
3. God is *dhul-Jalal wal* Ikram ('Lord of glory and honour'), *al-Karim* ('Honoured'), *al-Majid* ('Glorious'), *al-Hamid* ('Praiseworthy'), *al-Zahir* ('Ascendant over all'), *al-Qahhar* ('Supreme'), *al-Aliyy/Mutaal* ('High'), *al-Quadir/Muqtadir* ('Powerful'), *al-Aziz* ('Mighty'), *al-Qawiyy/Matin* ('Strong') *al-Mutakabbir* ('Possessor of every greatness'), and *al-Azim/ Kabir* ('Great').
4. God is *al-Alim* ('Knowing'), *al-Hakim* ('Wise'), *al-Sami* ('Hearing'), *al-Khabir* ('Aware'), *al-Basir* ('Seeing'), *al-Shahid* ('Witness'), *al-Raquib* (Watcher'), and *al-Batin* ('Knower of hidden things').
5. God is *al-Khaliq* ('Creator'), *al-Bari* ('Maker/Creator of soul'), *al-Musawwir* ('Fashioner of shapes'), *al-Badi* ('Wonderful Originator'), *al-Wakil* ('Having all things in his charge'), *al-Waliyy* ('Guardian'), *al-Hafiz* ('Greatest Judge'), *al-Hasib* ('One who takes account'), *al-Muntaquim/dhu-Intiqam* ('Inflictor or retribution'), and *al-Muqit* ('Controller of all things').
6. See Ali (1992) for a detailed reading of the history of these biblical prophets.

CHAPTER 4

CHRISTIANITY IN SIERRA LEONE

Christianity is another of the world's major religions that has impacted
Africa both for better and for worse. Like Islam, Christianity in Sierra
Leone must be studied and understood in its context to establish productive interreligious cooperation and dialogue. This chapter follows
the same pattern as the previous segment. It outlines chronologically
the advent and expansion of Christianity into Sierra Leone, describes its
basics tenets and practices, and concludes with its encounters with ATR.

ADVENT AND EXPANSION OF CHRISTIANITY

The expansion of Western missionary Christianity[1] in Africa has been
attributed to the arrival of freed Christian slaves in Sierra Leone, West
Africa, at the end of the eighteenth century. Earlier, beginning in 1605,
Jesuit priests from Portugal had tried unsuccessfully to establish a Christian post in Sierra Leone (Olson 1969, 201; Fyle 1981, 19; Hildebrant
1990, 81). Although these efforts of the Roman Catholic Church (RCC)
failed (Alie 1990, 101–102; Fyle 1981, 19; Sanneh 1983, 66; Olson 1969,

201–203), they laid the groundwork for many later missionary endeavours (Olson 1969, 67–212; Parrinder 1969, 124–126; Fyle 1981, 19; Sanneh 1983, 60–83; Alie 1990, 101–110), including contemporary ones.

Sierra Leone 'was the first Protestant mission field in tropical Africa' (Olson 1969, 15) and hence 'a Protestant stronghold' (Hastings 1979, 40). The major Christian advance into West Africa emanated from Sierra Leone (Hildebrant 1990, 97).

The first Protestant churches began with the arrival of the Loyalists from Nova Scotia, Canada, in 1792. These were the black slaves who fought gallantly on the side of the British during the American War of Independence and were sent to Nova Scotia with the promise of freedom and a better life (Fyle 1981, 35; Sanneh 1983, 60). They were disgruntled when the British did not keep to their promise of providing them freedom and land (Sanneh 1981, 35; 1983, 58). Contrary to British promises, they were made to work 'as farm labourers with no hope of ever owning land' (1983, 58). This led Thomas Peters, one of their own, to bring their grievance and predicament to the attention of the government in England. The authorities listened and decided to resettle them in Sierra Leone. Thus, in January 1792, under the leadership of John Clarkson, approximately 1,100[2] free Blacks left Nova Scotia and arrived in Sierra Leone (which subsequently became the first British Colony in Africa in 1808) three months later. The Settlers, as they would later be called, were Christians belonging to the Baptist, Countess of Huntingdon's Connexion, and Methodist denominations (Olson 1969, 67; Alie 1993, 64; cf. Yambasu 2000, 23–24). Fyfe narrated their momentous arrival in Freetown as follows:

> Their pastors led them ashore, singing a hymn of praise…Like the Children of Israel which were come out again out of the captivity they rejoiced before the Lord, who had brought them from bondage to the land of their forefathers. When all had arrived, the whole colony assembled in worship, to proclaim to the…continent whence they or their forbears had been carried in chains—'The day of Jubilee is come; Return ye ransomed sinners home'. (1962, 36–37)

With their respective preachers, 'each denomination continued in Sierra Leone without European supervision' (Olson 1969, 67).

The Baptist Missionary Society (BMS) sent two missionaries from England in December 1795 (Olson 1969, 67–68; Alie 1990, 102–103). Jacob Grigg, who went to Port Loko, was later expelled from Sierra Leone for meddling in politics. James Rodway, who was sent to Banana Islands, fell ill and returned to England.

In 1797 the Glasgow Missionary Society sent two missionaries to Rokon on the Rokel River, and in the same year, the London Missionary Society sent a team to Bullom, and Dr. Coke, the originator of Wesleyan missions, also sent missionaries to civilise the Fulani through community development. Later, in 1799, a joint effort was made by the London, Edinburgh, and Glasgow missionary societies. However, all of these endeavours to begin missionary work in Sierra Leone failed.

In 1800 the Maroons arrived in Sierra Leone (Olson 1969, 28; Fyle 1981, 37). The Maroons, who had been slaves in Jamaica, were mostly from the Ashanti in Ghana, West Africa. They rebelled and fled to the Jamaican mountains, where they formed their own government (Fyle 1981, 37). The Jamaican authorities eventually subdued them, promising that they would be allowed to stay in Jamaica, but broke this promise and sent them to Nova Scotia. Dissatisfied, they pleaded with the authorities and were sent to Sierra Leone. The Maroons, like the Blacks from Nova Scotia, were Christians belonging to the Wesleyan Methodist Church. They later built a church and rented it out to the Wesleyan missionaries. Both the Loyalists and the Maroons are referred to as 'the Settlers'.

In 1804 the first two Church Missionary Society (CMS) missionaries started an unsuccessful mission work among the Soso people in northern Sierra Leone on the Rio Pangos River (Olson 1969, 31; Alie 1990, 69; Sanneh 1983, 60–61).

After the abolition of the slave trade in 1807, Sierra Leone was found suitable to set up a British court that would try owners and crews of captured slave vessels (Fyle 1981, 38; Sanneh 1983, 72). Thus, slaves captured on board slave ships were emancipated in Freetown (Hildebrant

1990, 81–82). These slaves were called Recaptives on account of 'being captured the first time and enslaved, they had been recaptured and freed by the British Navy' (Fyle 1981, 38). They came from different parts in Africa and, in that regard, 'represented the concentrated potential of Africa's population resource' (Sanneh 1983, 73). In 1816 the CMS decided to set up a mission and administrative department for the Recaptives (Alie 1990, 69).

The colonial government also played a part in establishing and expanding Christianity in the colony, despite the presence of Islam, which constituted a powerful social force. With the help of the government, the foundation stone of Saint George's Cathedral was laid on January 1817, and the building was completed and opened in March 1828. It served as the colonial government church. In that regard, the government supported it with grants, which were withdrawn when the church became autonomous and changed its name to the Sierra Leone Church in 1898.

In 1818 Nylander, a CMS missionary, led a successful mission to the Bullom Shore, and later composed a Bullom grammar and vocabulary, and translated the Gospel of Matthew into that language, which became the first scriptural translation in Sierra Leone (Sanneh 1983, 61). In 1827 the CMS founded an institute for the training of teachers, catechists, and clergy, which was later relocated in the Fourah Bay area. Its first student was Samuel Ajayi Crowther. Later, the CMS opened two secondary schools: the Sierra Leone Grammar School, for boys, in 1845; and a female institute in 1849, which in 1877 was renamed the Annie Walsh Memorial School.

The Wesleyan Methodist Missionary Society came to Sierra Leone in 1811. It opened a training institute for ministers and missionaries at the Kingtom peninsula. The bearers of this society were mostly freed slaves of the Nova Scotians and Maroon migrations. The Nova Scotians built a Methodist Church at Rawdon Street. In 1874 the Methodist Boys High School was opened, followed, six years later, by the Methodist Girls High School.

The West African Methodist (WAM) Church began as a splinter from the Methodist Church on Rawdon Street (Olson 1969, 103–104).

When the Settlers in charge of the church refused to let liberated Africans preach from their pulpit, the liberated African preachers began their own church in 1844. In 1932 and 1933, some Krio churches that refused to join the English merger between the United Methodists and Wesleyan Methodists also joined the WAM church. This denomination was founded in Sierra Leone and has no foreign connection.

The Revs. W. T. Shirley, D. C. Kumber, and D. K. Fliekenger, the first United Brethren in Christ (now the United Methodist Church—UMC) missionaries, arrived in Freetown on 1 March 1855, and within a few days, travelled to the Good Hope station of the Mende mission, where they got temporary accommodation until they could establish themselves. The mission started its large-scale penetration of the hinterland of Sierra Leone at Rotifunk and Shenge with educational and religious ventures.

In 1859 a Roman Catholic bishop and several priests arrived in the colony to establish a mission. Five years later, Father Blanchet, of the Congregation of the Holy Ghost, successfully established the mission. He was later joined by the nuns of the order of Saint Joseph of Clunny (whose founder, the blessed Ann-Marie Javouhey, had visited the colony in Governor MacCarthy's time). This mission is credited for building the Sacred Heart of Jesus Cathedral, which is today the Roman Catholic Cathedral.

The American Wesleyan Church (AWC) entered Sierra Leone in 1889 and began work in the north (Olson 1969, 177–185). Their evangelistic approach was a combination of education, medical work, and outreach to as many villages as possible.

The African Methodist Episcopal (AME) Church came to Sierra Leone sometime in the late 1800s from the United States. The AME Church has small number of churches in Freetown and the hinterland (Olson 1969, 104).

The Seventh Day Adventists (SDA) started mission work in Sierra Leone in 1907 (Olson 1969, 186–188). Fifty-two years later, SDA membership had begun to grow rapidly. However, the mission has not yet grown to have churches in most of the major towns in the country.

Mission work by Assemblies of God (AOG) missionaries started in the early 1950s. The AOG is one of the strongest Evangelical churches in the country with churches in several major towns. Many of Sierra Leone's charismatic preachers have emanated from the AOG.

The Missionary Church Association (MCA) did not intend to start a new church in Sierra Leone. The first missionaries were intending to raise congregations and then turn them over to other churches. However, the existing churches in the hinterland were not ready to accept more staff or supervise new congregations and, as a result, the MCA began a new denomination in the north of the country.

The Church of the Lord (Aladura) came to Sierra Leone from Nigeria in 1947. It is has become one of the strongest African indigenous/independent churches (AIC) in Sierra Leone with quite a widespread influence. The intent of its founders was to establish an African indigenous church. The church is Pentecostal and syncretistic in nature. They combine elements of Christianity and African culture. Aladura churches are commonly referred to as spiritual churches for their emphasis on ecstatic experiences. Another AIC denomination is the God Is Our Light Church, which originated in Ghana.

At present, both separatist churches, most of which are interdenominational, and neotraditional charismatic movements are growing exponentially in Sierra Leone. Jules-Rosette has identified the following five factors responsible for the rise and growth of AIC, separatist churches, and neotraditional Christian movements that are applicable to the Sierra Leonean situation. The sixth factor is my own addition:

- The disappointment of local converts with the premises and outcomes of Christianity led to the growth of prophetic, messianic, and millenarian groups.
- The translation of the Bible into local African vernacular stimulated a reinterpretation of scripture and a spiritual renewal in Christian groups.
- The perceived divisions in denominational Christianity and its failure to meet local needs influenced the rise of separatist churches and community-based indigenous churches.

- The impotence of Western medicine in the face of personal problems, psychological disorders, epidemics, and natural disasters was a catalyst for concerns with spiritual healing in the new African religious movements.
- The failure of missionary Christianity to break down social and cultural barriers and generate a sense of community has led to the strengthening of social ties in small, sectarian groups. (Jules-Rosette 1991, 150–151)
- Mainline churches continue to painstakingly ape Western mannerisms and culture and are reluctant to blend African aspects into their worship.

Roman Catholicism and Protestantism are the two major streams of Christianity in Sierra Leone. Protestantism is further divided into what Sierra Leoneans call mainline/traditional (i.e., the Anglican and the various segments of Methodism), evangelical, Pentecostal, Baptist, charismatic, interdenominational, SDA, ecumenical, and AIC. It is hard in the present circumstances to keep an accurate record of all the Christian churches and movements in Sierra Leone.

BASIC BELIEFS AND PRACTICES OF CHRISTIANITY

Sources

The main source of Christian beliefs and practices in Christianity's three main streams (Roman Catholic, Orthodox, and Protestant) is the Bible, comprising the Old and New Testaments. On the basis of 2 Timothy 3:16–17, Christians believe that the Bible was written by men inspired by the Holy Spirit, at different times and places.

The Old Testament (OT) is a collection of books written over a thousand-year period ending in approximately 400 BCE. Most of the text was written in Hebrew, excepting five passages of Aramaic: Genesis 31:47; Jeremiah 10:11; Ezra 4:8–6, 18:7, 18:12–26; and Daniel 2:4b–7, 2:28. It is based on the covenant/agreement between God and the Hebrew people made on Mount Sinai (Exod. 19:3–6, 24:3–8) and consists of three parts: the Law, the Prophets, and the Writings.

The New Testament (NT) is a collection of books written in Greek during the first century CE. It consists of four Gospels, which record the life and work of Jesus of Nazareth (also called the Christ); the book of Acts, which records the history and expansion of the early church; a series of letters; and an apocalypse. The NT presents Christ as the fulfilment of the covenant presented in the OT and the institutor of a new covenant/agreement that was accomplished by Christ's death on the cross for the sins of humankind (Luke 22:20; 1 Cor. 11:25).

On account of the diversity and vastness of the Bible, Christians at various times have drawn different conclusions regarding the meaning and application of its contents. The first Christians, whose scripture was the Septuagint (LXX)—or Greek OT—had a disagreement about the interpretation and application of the teachings of Moses, which resulted in the first Christian council called at Jerusalem (Acts 15) about 49 CE. This was just the beginning of biblical and theological wrangling and disagreement in the church.

The patristic period (about 100–590 CE), which followed the apostolic period (about 30–100 CE), was full of theological controversies. Christians, both orthodox and unorthodox, were appealing to scriptures in support of their views, and there was no consensus on the proper interpretation of scripture (Klein et al. 1993, 36). This period saw the emergence of writings to instruct Christians in doctrinal issues and to defend Christianity against Jewish arguments. Prominent in all this was the Arian controversy, which was to break the church into warring factions (Gonzalez 1970, 261–271; Marthaler 1987, 79). Arius taught an absolute monotheism, which denied that Christ emanated from the Father, was part of the substance of the Father, or was similar in being with the Father, and taught instead that Jesus was a lesser god.

The ongoing Christian controversy did not sit well with the Roman emperor Constantine (Gonzalez 1970, 265–266). In his view, 'doctrinal disputes between the orthodox mainstream and its heretical tributaries threatened the empire's political stability', which led him to pressure 'the Church to settle differences and to standardise its disputed doctrines' (Klein et al. 1993, 36; Marthaler 1987, 80). In June 325, Constantine summoned a council of bishops to deal with Arian teaching and other problems confronting the church. This council, which met in Nicea, is known as the Council of Nicea.

This call for Christian peace and solidarity gave birth to the Nicene Creed, which was formulated on biblical teachings and became the basis of the ecumenical and universal Christian faith. Although it did explain the relationship of the Son to the Father (Marthaler 1987, 73–82; Gonzalez 1970, 261–271), the Nicene Creed did not put an end to Christianity's biblical and theological wrangling. However, it has helped to unify the faith statement of the church. The numerous denominations in Christianity, and the ever growing creedal statements of churches, indicate that the biblical and theological divergences will not soon come to an end. It is reasonable to say, then, that

> many Christians believe certain things, and most believe an even smaller number of core tenets, but to be intellectually faithful, it may not be possible to say that all Christians believe any one thing more than the opening statements of the tripartite form of the Nicene Creed. (Hughes 2005, 74)

Although the many denominations in the West have formulated various church creeds and statements/articles of faith, the generally accepted ecumenical creed and central statements of faith in the three main streams of Christianity are the Nicene and Apostles' Creeds. Apart from the growing AIC, most churches in Sierra Leone follow the teachings they have inherited from Euro-American missionaries.

I now discuss the tripartite form of the Nicene Creed. The discussion that follows is based on the contents of the Nicene Creed.

Beliefs
Belief in One God—Theology

> We believe in one God, the Father Almighty, maker of heaven and earth, of all that is, seen and unseen.

Christians believe in one God who is eternal and active in human life and history. The Bible is full of names and figures of speech that describe God. These figures give an understanding of God's intrinsic attributes and his activities. One of these figures that portray God's activity is the image of God as 'father'. The Christian image of God as father originated from the Hebrew tradition that associates God with the role of the father in the Jewish culture (Marthaler 1987, 33). In a patriarchal culture, the Jews looked to the father as an ultimate authority. The NT refers to God as father far more frequently than do the Hebrew Scriptures. Jesus frequently addresses God as father and, in the Lord's Prayer, uses this image to portray God's loving care and forgiveness. In Christianity, the image of God as father is based on the ideal qualities 'associated with fatherhood, the giving of life, love, faithfulness, continued care and protection, and the wisdom that guides and instructs' (34).

God's omnipotence is also evident in the Bible. In Genesis 17:1, God is called *El-Shaddi* ('God Almighty'). His omnipotence is seen in human life and personality (cf. Jer. 1:5; Gal. 1:15), in his ability to overcome apparently insurmountable problems (Jer. 32:15–17; Matt. 19: 26), and in his control of the course of human history (Acts 17:26). It is on the basis of God's almighty power that Christians can talk about the other intrinsic attributes and activities of God.

On account of his almighty power, the Christians believe God is the creator of all existence. The creative work of God plays a prominent role in the Bible. God created the heavens, the earth, and humankind (Gen. 1:1, 1:27; Deut. 4:32; Isa. 45:12). The biblical account of creation shows God creating *ex nihilo* ('out of nothing'). John 1:3 asserts that '[a]ll things came to being through' God. Thus, Christians teach that 'there are a connection and an affinity' among the creatures of God, and humankind is 'one with nature, for we are members of the same family' (Erickson 1992, 125). And further, on the basis of Genesis 1:26–30, humans should have concern for all of creation by preserving, guarding, and developing what God has made.

Belief in Jesus—Christology

> *We believe in one Lord, Jesus Christ, the only Son of God, eternally begotten of the Father, God from God, Light from Light, begotten, not made, of one Being with the Father. Through him*

all things were made. For us and for our salvation he came down from heaven, by the power of the Holy Spirit he became incarnate from the Virgin Mary, and was made man. For our sake he was crucified under Pontius Pilate; he suffered death and was buried. On the third day he rose again in accordance with the Scriptures; he ascended into heaven and is seated at the right hand of the Father. He will come again in glory to judge the living and the dead, and his kingdom will have no end.

Part two of the Nicene Creed outlines the beliefs about Jesus that are most significant in the Christian faith.

Jesus Is Lord

The NT ascribes the word *kyrios* ('lord', 'master') to Jesus (Luke 2:11; John 20:28; Acts 2:20–21, 10:36; Rom. 10:13; 1 Cor. 2:8, 8:6; Phil. 2:11; James 2:1; Rev. 19:16) to identify Jesus as both Lord and Messiah (Acts 2:36). The word *kyrios* had been used to refer to the gods and goddesses of the heathen religions of Asia Minor, Syria, and Egypt, and to Roman emperors in recognition of their political prowess (Marthaler 1987, 67). To Christians, the term 'lord' signifies the belief that Jesus is divine. It is a majestic epithet given to Christ 'in view of his resurrection and exaltation at the right hand of God' (68).

Jesus Is the Son of God

The NT is rich with references to Jesus as the Son of God (John 20:31; Acts 9:20; 2 Cor. 1:19; Heb. 4:14; 1 John 4:15, 5:5). The Gospel of John is noted for its references to the deity of Jesus, the book of Hebrews is noted for its emphasis on Jesus' divinity, and Paul frequently asserts a belief in the deity of Jesus (Erickson 1992, 210).

The title 'Son of God' is evidence of the Christian belief in Jesus' divinity.[3] Jesus' relationship to God as son was endorsed by a voice from heaven: 'You are my beloved Son' (Mark 1:11). The NT makes it clear that Jesus believed himself to be 'equal with the Father', with 'the right to do things which only God has the right to do' (Erickson 1992, 210). Although Christian believers are children of God (Rom. 8:16–17, 18:21; 1 John 3) by adoption through Christ (Eph. 1:5), the NT restricts the title of

'Son of God' to only Jesus in that regard. The title signifies that Jesus has a relationship to and with the Father distinct from that of any human being. Jesus alone is the Son of God in the divine sense that he can give believers the 'power to become God's children' (John 1:12).

Jesus the Incarnate
The NT teaches that Jesus is the Word who was with God (John 1:1), who became flesh through the Virgin Mary (Luke 1:26–31; Gal. 4:4), and who dwelt with humankind (John 1:14; Phil. 2:6–7).

Jesus Died for Humanity
The death of Christ for the salvation of the human race was predetermined (Matt 16:21–23; Mark 8:31–33; Luke 9:21–22). Adam was created perfect but sinned, and that action affected the entire human race. It is from this concept that the Christian teaching of original/universal sin emanated (Gen. 3:1–19; Rom. 5:12–21). Every human being is born a sinner (Ps. 51:5), a fact that should not be contested (1 John 1:8). However, God first took the initiative to remedy the taint of sin by giving his Son to die on the cross as the atoning sacrifice for the sin of the world (Isa. 53; Rom. 5:8–9; 1 John 2:2, 4:10). This action is known as prevenient grace. God took the initiative to reach out to humankind in order to reconcile humanity with himself. It is a manifestation of God's love for humankind (John 3:16) and a display of true love and friendship by Jesus (John 15:13; 1 John 3:16).

Jesus Is the Source of Salvation
The concept of salvation is complex. First, it is 'redemption of sin and from the dominion of Satan' (Asante 2001, 357) in order to regain fellowship with God, which will eventually lead to having a place in heaven. The Greek verb *sozo* ('to save') also carries the meaning 'preserve or rescue from natural dangers and afflictions', or to 'save or preserve from eternal death' (Bauer 1979, 798), and the 'deliverance from the evils of this life' (Ferdinando 1996, 125). Part of Jesus' mission was to preach the good news to the poor, 'to proclaim release to the captives and recovery of sight to the blind, to let the oppressed go free, and to proclaim the year of the Lord's

favor' (Luke 4:18–19). Christian salvation is based on both contemporary and eternal realities and can only be achieved through Jesus (Acts 4:12).

Jesus Rose From the Dead

The Resurrection of Christ is the core teaching of Christianity (1 Cor. 15:1–28; Matt. 28:1–10; Mark 16:1–8; Luke 24:1–12). This all-important teaching has provoked a great deal of controversy in Christian and non-Christian circles. Resurrection is the rising to life from death. It means 'a complete transformation of the human being in his or her psychosomatic totality' (Achtemeier 1996, 926). The Resurrection of Jesus is an act of God, who raised him from the dead according to 1 Corinthians 15:20 as the first fruits in anticipation of the general resurrection. There were no witnesses to the actual event of the Resurrection, since Jesus was the only one in the tomb when the event occurred. However, the same Jesus who was publicly crucified and whose death was witnessed by many people also appeared to many people, most of whom testified that they saw him alive (1 Cor. 15:3–8; Matt. 28:9–10). This evidence is further supported by the biblical evidence of the empty tomb, where Jesus' body was laid, and by the fact that his body was never found (Luke 24:1–3; Mark 16:6–7).

Jesus Ascended to Heaven to Be at God's Right Hand

The risen Jesus ascended into heaven after his appearances to his disciples. Luke 24:50–51 and Acts 1:6–11 describe the actual ascension of Jesus. On several occasions before his death, Jesus had talked about his return to the Father (John 6:62, 14:2, 14:12, 16:4, 16:10, 16:28, 20:17). The Epistles (Eph. 1:20, 4:8–10; 1 Tim. 3:16; Heb. 1:3, 4:14, 9:24) discuss the Ascension. The Ascension of Jesus means that he is now at the right hand of the Father. In other words, he is in a place of distinction and power.

Jesus Will Return to Judge

Jesus himself said that he will come again in glory to judge the nations (Matt. 25:31–46). The NT indicates that Jesus will return in glory at some point in the future (Matt. 24:29–31; Mark 13:24–27; Luke 21:25–28;

1 Thess. 4:13–18). The exact time is unknown (Matt. 24:36; Mark 13:32). The Second Coming of Christ is a vital teaching in most Pentecostal, evangelical, and charismatic movements.

Belief in the Holy Spirit—Pneumatology

> We believe in the Holy Spirit, the Lord, the giver of life, who proceeds from the Father and the Son. With the Father and the Son he is worshipped and glorified.

In the Hebrew Scriptures, the Spirit of God is revealed in three main capacities:

- As the agent of creation and the source of life.
- As the source of inspiration and power.
- As the presence of God in the covenant community. (Achtemeier 1996, 432; Marthaler 1987, 240)

Joel (3:1–5) proclaimed the messianic age by announcing that salvation would be accomplished with the outpouring of the Spirit on all people. The outpouring of the Spirit on Pentecost inaugurated the new era. In the NT, the Holy Spirit 'is the particular person of the Trinity through whom the entire Triune Godhead works' in the life of the Christian (Erickson 1992, 260).

The Spirit of the LORD/God and the Holy Spirit are one and the same (Acts 2:16–17) and represent God's mysterious power and presence, which he gives to individuals and communities to empower them with 'qualities they would not otherwise possess' (Achtemeier 1996, 432; see also Erickson 1992, 266–267). The Holy Spirit becomes personal to the Christian, residing within him/her and being active within his/her life. It is the Holy Spirit who endowed Jesus with the power to fulfill his mission (Matt. 3:13–17; Mark 1:9–11; Luke 3:21–22; see also Matt. 12, 28; Luke 4:16–21) and who empowered the apostles and the early church as seen in the book of Acts and the Pauline Epistles. Today it is believed that the Holy Spirit continues to sustain the church and individual believers. Jesus discusses the Holy Spirit extensively in John 14–16.

The Doctrine of the Trinity

The tripartite division of Nicene Creed just discussed portrays the belief in the Trinity—God the Father, Jesus the Son of God, and the Holy Sprit. The teaching of the Trinity—one God in three persons—is a revealed mystery that 'human language is never adequate to represent', because 'our experience—even when empowered by revelation—is too limited, too conditioned by time and space to permit us to get more than a hint of what the eternal, infinite Godhead is *really* like' (Marthaler 1987, 30). The Father, Son, and Holy Spirit are distinct entities but are one in that they share the same nature, intellect, and will. Although they are distinct from one another, they do not act separately. The Godhead acts as one.

Although the term 'Trinity' is not found in the Bible, the concept is based on a reasonable inference from Scripture (Matt. 28:19; 2 Cor. 13:13). There is only one God (Deut. 6:4; 1 Kings 8:60; Isa. 44:6, 45:5; Mark 12:29, 12:32; John 10:30), who exists in three distinct persons: God the Father (*hypostasis, subsitentia, persona, suppositum, intellectuale*— Gal. 1:1; Eph. 4:6), Jesus Christ the Son (John 1:1, 20:28), and the Holy Spirit (Acts 5:3–4).

The Trinity became a subject of intense debate in the third and fourth centuries as theologians attempted to develop reasonable explanations of the early Christian's beliefs and teachings (Marthaler 1987, 74–87; Gonzalez 1984, 158–167; 1970, 261–271). For the greater part of the third century, the debate over the relationship of the Father and Son preoccupied the clergy and laity (Marthaler 1987, 77). The debate of the third century set the stage for the great councils. The doctrine of the Trinity was initially formulated in the Nicene-Constantinopolitan Creed (381 CE).

Afterlife

Christians further teach about life after death. Humankind is created from the dust of the earth (Gen. 2:17, 3:19, 3:23) and is made up of soul/spirit and body/flesh (Matt. 10:28; Gen. 6:3; 2 Cor. 7:1; 1 Thess. 5:23; Col. 2:5). The soul is the breath of life that God breathed into Adam and he became a living being (Gen. 2:7; cf. 46:18). Similarly, according to Matthew 2:20, Mark 3:4, and Luke 12:20, the soul refers to one's life.

It is this soul/spirit that continues after death (Matt. 16:25–26), but there is no clear statement about the destiny of the body beyond the grave. In Genesis 3:19, at death, the body returns to the ground from whence it came, while in Matthew 10:28, it is inferred that the body may also experience the suffering of hell, or some will be raised (1 Thess. 4:13–18).

Practices
Christianity is both a historic and contemporary belief system, expressed in community and practised in the lives of individuals and institutions. This segment focuses on the practices of the two main streams of Christianity in Sierra Leone—Roman Catholicism and Protestantism.

Worship
Like all other religious faiths, worship is the most important aspect of Christian living. Although worship may take place on different days and at different times, the main day for Christian worship is the first day of the week (Sunday). This practice was adopted from the early Christians (Acts 20:7) because it was on the first day of the week that Jesus rose from the dead (Mark 16:9). One notable exception to this practice is the SDA, who meet on Saturday. Most evangelical, Baptist, AIC, Pentecostal, and charismatic movements hold morning and evening worship services. The Roman Catholics have morning and evening Mass, and the Anglicans have matins and evensong/vespers. Catholic and Anglican services are highly liturgical and have very similar liturgies.

The Sacraments
Many Christian denominations in Sierra Leone and elsewhere have certain rites that are referred to as sacraments. The meanings of sacraments—and which rites are considered sacraments—vary between the Protestant and Catholic churches. The word 'sacrament' has been

broadly defined as 'a sign or symbol of something which is sacred and mysterious' (Martos 1982, 12). Both the Protestant and Catholic streams acknowledge baptism and the Lord's Supper as sacraments instituted by Christ to be of perpetual obligation.

In view of this broader definition of the word 'sacrament', the Catholic Church teaches that all the religions of the world are full of sacraments (Martos 1982, 9–28). All religions have 'places and actions, objects, and even persons which are symbolic of some mysterious realities that are sacred' to these religions (12). This broader understanding of sacrament has led the Catholic Church to further acknowledge five additional sacraments: confirmation, confession/penance, extreme unction, orders, and matrimony (Liberia Editrice Vaticana [LEV] 1994, 265–358). The Catholics see the sacraments not merely as symbols of divine grace, but also as sources of divine grace. On account of their divine institution, it is believed that they cause that grace in the souls of people. In other words, the sacraments are not simply functions or ceremonies—they are outward signs instituted by Christ to impart grace to the soul.

All seven sacraments of the Catholic Church were developed during the nineteenth ecumenical council, which started at Trent on 13 December 1545 and ended there on 4 December 1563 (Martos 1982, 114). The council's main objective was the definitive determination of the doctrines of the church, in response to the Reformation of the Protestants, and the implementation of a thorough reform of the inner life of the church by removing the numerous abuses that had developed in it (114–124).

Some Protestant churches perform confirmation, and most perform matrimony, but these rites are not considered sacramental. In what follows, the two sacraments that are observed by both Protestants and Catholics will first be discussed, and I will very briefly discuss the additional sacraments of the Catholic Church.

THE LORD'S SUPPER. The Lord's Supper, also referred to as the Eucharist ('Thanksgiving') or Holy Communion, is one of the most important Christian rituals. The Lord's Supper is a version of what Jesus instituted and told his disciples to do in remembrance of his death (1 Cor. 11:23–26; Luke 22:14–23; Matt. 26:26–30; Mark 14:22–26). On the basis of Jesus' words, 'Do this is remembrance of me' (Luke 22:19b; 1 Cor. 11:24b), Christians have come to understand these words as a command applicable not only to the disciples and apostles, but to all Christians of all times. The 'bread', which represents Jesus' body, and the 'wine', which represents Jesus' blood, are the two special elements used to celebrate communion. While Protestants believe that this representation is symbolic, the Catholic Church teaches transubstantiation, the belief that the bread and wine, after being blessed, are changed into the actual body and blood of Christ, though their appearance does not change.

In Sierra Leone, most Catholic and mainline churches use wafers instead of bread and use specially made communion wine. On account of economic constraints—along with a change in theological perspective that recognises that Jesus did not use sophisticated elements when he instituted the Holy Communion, but rather local products—some churches, especially those in the hinterland, have resorted to the use of locally made bread and red juice/drink.

The frequency of taking the Eucharist varies from church to church. In general, the frequency depends on how a church interprets 'Do this is as often...', the first part of 1 Corinthians 11:25b. The Catholic and the Anglican churches take communion every Sunday and during most wedding and funeral services. Most Protestant denominations take communion once a month or as prescribed by their leaders. Some Methodist churches have a midweek communion service and also administer communion during weddings and funerals. Many Pentecostal, evangelical, and charismatic movements take the Lord's Supper less frequently.

Baptism. Baptism is another important Christian sacrament. A basic baptismal service involves either pouring/sprinkling water on the head of a person or immersing a person in water, with the simultaneous pronouncement, 'I baptise you in the name of the Father, the Son, and the Holy Spirit'. This is normally followed by a blessing.

The NT has many references to baptism in various contexts. It is only in Matthew 28:19 that baptism is recorded as a direct command of Jesus, and it is the only reference to baptism 'in the name of the Father, the son and the Holy Spirit'. Elsewhere in the NT, baptism is in the name of Jesus only (Acts 8:16, 19:5; Rom. 6:3; Gal. 3:27). Views of baptism vary, but common views of the rituals include the following: it offers or symbolises salvation (John 3:5), it commemorates Christ's death and resurrection (Rom. 6:3–5), it fulfils the command of Jesus to baptise (Matt. 28:19), it cleanses away sins (Acts 2:38), it confers grace, and it publicly expresses one's faith.

In the Pauline Epistles, baptism offers purification from sins, the putting off of the sinful body of the flesh, mortification of sin, renewal of life, regeneration, the power of the Holy Spirit, communion with the life of Christ, and incorporation into the mystical body of Christ, the church.

Throughout the NT, baptism appears to be represented as the means for obtaining real objective effects, with God as their cause, not just as a symbolic act. Baptism was usually performed immediately after the recognition of Jesus as the Messiah and the decision to join the messianic congregation.

Most mainline churches baptise both infants and adults by pouring/sprinkling. The churches see infant baptism as a ceremony initiating the child into the community of faith and indicating the community's commitment to raise him/her to be a faithful Christian. In other words, it is an initiation into Christ's Body.

Infant baptism is only the beginning of a child's Christian life and salvation. There is a need for instruction after baptism for the flowering of baptismal grace in the personal growth of the child, and for the child to understand the commitments that were taken by the godparents/sponsors or congregation on his/her behalf.

It has been argued that the act of infant baptism rests on prevenient grace. Baptism is 'a grace and a gift of God that does not presuppose any human merit; children are baptised in the faith of the Church' (LEV 1994, 277). All Christians come before God as no more than helpless infants, unable to do anything to save themselves, dependent upon the grace of a loving God.

The Baptist, Pentecostal, evangelical, and charismatic movements reject infant baptism. These Christians often dedicate infants, making commitments similar to those made in the mainline ceremonies, but, following a biblical model, they reserve baptism for individuals who are able to understand its meaning and consent to the sacrament. This practice, which follows the Protestant emphasis on justification by faith alone, is referred to as 'believer's baptism', and is usually done by full immersion in water.

In those churches that practise infant baptism, there are usually family members or friends that take on the role of godfather or godmother to the baptised child. The catechism of the Catholic Church describes their role this way:

> For the grace of Baptism to unfold, the parents' help is important. So too is the role of the godfather and godmother, who must be firm believers, able and ready to help the newly baptized—child or adult on the road of Christian life. Their task is a truly ecclesial function. The whole ecclesial community bears some responsibility for the development and safeguarding of the grace given at Baptism.

In Protestant churches, baptism and communion are two main sacraments of the church because they are based on biblical commandments, as already indicated.

Additional Sacraments of the Catholic Church
CONFIRMATION. Catholics believe that confirmation is a sacrament in which the Holy Spirit is given to those already baptised in order to make them strong and perfect Christians and witnesses of Jesus Christ. In Acts 8:14–17, after the Samaritan converts had been baptised by Philip the deacon, the apostles

> sent Peter and John to them. When they arrived, they prayed for them that they might receive the Holy Spirit, because the Holy Spirit had not yet come upon any of them; they had simply been baptised into the name of the Lord Jesus. Then Peter and John placed their hands on them, and they received the Holy Spirit.

Most Protestant denominations that practise infant baptism also practise confirmation, but with a different emphasis. In these churches, confirmation is seen as a believer's taking ownership of his/her faith and taking responsibility for the promises made on his/her behalf at baptism.

While churches that practise believer's baptism do not generally practise confirmation, most Pentecostal, charismatic, AIC, and 'spiritual' churches do not believe that the Holy Spirit is imparted at conversion, as is believed by most Baptists and evangelicals, or at baptism, as is believed by most mainline Protestant churches. Rather, they believe that the Holy Spirit is imparted in a (usually) separate event known as baptism of the Holy Spirit, which is evidenced by the believer speaking in tongues.

PENANCE. Penance is the Catholic sacrament in which forgiveness of sins committed after baptism is granted, through the absolution of the priest on the basis of John 20:22–23, to those who are truly repentant and sincerely confess their sins.

EXTREME UNCTION. Extreme unction is the sacrament (Mark 6:13; James 5:14–15) that offers spiritual aid, comfort, and perfect spiritual health—including, if need be, the remission of sins, as well as, conditionally, prayer to restore bodily health—to Christians who are seriously ill; it consists essentially in the unction by a priest of the body of the sick person, accompanied by suitable prayers. This sacrament, when performed just before death, is also known as last rites.

Most Protestant churches also have varying practices that resemble extreme unction. Most spiritual churches use specially consecrated 'holy water' for ablution and healing. Holy water symbolises faith in Jesus, the Living Water. Other groups also pray for healing and may anoint the sick with holy water and/or oil.

THE SACRAMENT OF HOLY ORDERS. The taking of holy orders is the sacrament by which the grace of God and spiritual power for the discharge of ecclesiastical offices are conferred. Orders are used to signify not only the ranks or general status of the clergy, but also the outward action by which they are raised to that status, and thus stand for ordination. Orders are what differentiate the various ranks of the clergy from each other and from the laity. Catholics find basis for the separation of ordered clergy in the biblical practice of the laying on of hands (2 Tim. 1:6; Acts 6:6; 1 Tim. 5:22).

THE SACRAMENT OF HOLY MATRIMONY. Ephesians 5:22–30 declares that the relationship between husband and wife should be as the relationship between Christ and his church. After this exhortation, Paul alludes to the divine institution of marriage in the prophetical words proclaimed by God through Adam (5:31). He then concludes with the significant words with which he characterises Christian marriage: 'This is a great mystery, but I am talking about Christ and the Church' (5:32).

Other important practices of the Catholic Church are canonisation and veneration of saints, devotion to Mary, praying the rosary, pilgrimages, stations of the cross, monastic life, the use of holy water, and exorcism.

CHRISTIANITY'S ENCOUNTER WITH TRADITIONAL BELIEFS AND PRACTICES

Christianity, like Islam, met Sierra Leoneans with the knowledge of God. As discussed in the section Advent and Expansion of Christianity, the mission of the church in Sierra Leone was to spread Christianity and Western civilisation. In order to achieve these goals, and because the Gospel cannot be disseminated in a vacuum, it was often necessary to come to grips with the culture of the societies involved. Some missionaries, in the process, became endeared to the people they worked among, while others became a nightmare. I now survey the church's encounter with Traditionalists from precolonial times to date.

Very little has been written about the work of the first Christian missionary to Sierra Leone. Father Barreira began working in Sierra Leone in 1605, but almost nothing is known about the approach or dialectical methods he employed to gain converts. However, we do know that he succeeded in baptising some rulers (Fyle 1981, 19; Alie 1990, 102), who gave him some of their sons to be instructed in Western education and religion (Alie 1990, 102). Nevertheless, many of the natives he encountered did not convert. Disappointed and frustrated, he returned home in 1610. Other priests that followed did not succeed either, as the people held tenaciously to their religion (Fyle 1981, 19).

Protestant efforts are somewhat better documented. Although the Recaptives in the Freetown settlement lived in a self-consciously Christian community, they preserved a great deal of their African religiosity and traditional practices (Sanneh 1983, 47). The Recaptives developed a strong stimulus for a reassertion of African religious practices and values. Their local communities became the screen behind which they practised their African traditional values. For instance, in 1833 two CMS missionaries in Freetown encountered a striking sacrosanct image in Kissy, east of Freetown, 'with bloodstained face, two horns, and a large bowl placed before it full of chicken blood' (1983, 83).

A CMS missionary, Rev. James Johnson, who later became a bishop, and Rev. Samuel Ajayi Crowther, an African CMS clergyman, who also later became a bishop, found very prominently among the Aku Recaptives the cult of *Shango*, the Yoruba god of thunder and lightning. The Aku also had the system of *Ifa* divination well preserved and widely patronised.

Rev. Johnson reported that every Friday there was a solemn ceremony of a large procession of *Shango* worshippers in Freetown singing and dancing in masquerade, in praise of *Shango*. Once, when Johnson tried to confront the devotees of the cult, an elderly devotee dismissed Johnson by telling him that his youth and status as a paid servant of the missionaries disqualified him from passing any judgment on the rites of *Shango*. Such encounters left an indelible mark on Johnson. Other missionaries also clashed with the natives concerning their traditional beliefs and practices that are incompatible with Christianity.

Rev. Crowther's attitude towards ATR and Islam in the nineteenth century is well documented (McKenzie 1976; Gordon 1957, 863–869; Sanneh 1983, 83–89). He grew up in a home that practised ATR and had many Muslim neighbours. Under the impulse of his newfound Christian faith, he attempted to transform the religious landscape over a vast area of West Africa (McKenzie 1976, 11). Throughout all of his encounters with ATR and Islam, Crowther continued to view these religions negatively. He considered the practitioners of these sects as being in need of transformation, and saw himself as the agent to bring about that change. Crowther's focus was set on gaining converts, because he believed that Christianity was the right path to a right relationship with God. In response to Crowther's persistent criticism of *Ifa* divination, an *Ifa* diviner told Crowther 'he could not give up his trade, that he could not consent to give his medicine to any applicant without consulting his god as to whether he should give it or not; as *Ifa* directed, so he would act' (Sanneh 1983, 84).

At that time, the village of Hastings, near Freetown, was reported to have the largest number of traditional religious worshippers, with four separate sacred Yoruba shrines, with a predominance of twin figures (*Ibeji*). Divination using kola nuts was widely practised, and funerals were deeply influenced by traditional religious customs. Hastings also promoted several prominent secret societies such as the *Egun*. The Methodist resident missionary at Hastings had regular confrontations with the leaders of these cults. Johnson and Crowther were strongly opposed to the religious practices of the Recaptives.

Later missionaries adopted a firmer stance. AOG missionaries that worked among the Kissi people in the hinterland and the Kru immigrants in Freetown required monogamy and abstention from alcohol, smoking, secret society membership, and Sunday marketing (Olson 1969, 190–194). The AOG enforced

> a complete break with the past through the burning of medicine and charms...a symbol of complete rejection of the old way and of complete dependence upon God through Christ and the Holy Spirit...members were prohibited from using charms or making sacrifices. (192)

The individualistic approach, brought to Sierra Leone by the first missionaries, alienated the indigenes from their families, communities, and cultures (Avery 1971, 8). Successive missionaries to Sierra Leone attacked African culture and required a complete abandonment of African culture and practices (Alie 1990, 110; Olson 1969, 192). Polygamy, slavery, magic, use of charms, and initiation ceremonies were vehemently condemned (Alie 1990, 110). Christian missionaries to Africa are still blamed for their cultural insensitivity to African values, which resulted in the transplantation of 'an ethnocentric form of Christianity' (Eitel 1988, 324). It was on account of the missionaries' insensitivity and condemnation that many Sierra Leone Traditionalists regarded Christianity as a disruptive force. As such, in the hinterland, many missionaries were murdered, and their churches destroyed during, the hut tax rebellion (Alie 1990, 110).

Insensitivity to African culture and worldview was not unique to Euro-American missionaries. They were not alone in their condemnation of traditional practices as heathenism or Satanism. Crowther is a prime example of an African who displayed such insensitivity, and the attitudes and practices he displayed in the nineteenth century still thrive today. Although most missionaries handed leadership over to the indigenes several decades ago as they left the continent, many churches still painstakingly follow the teachings and most of the practices of the missionaries. For example, the National Pentecostal Limba Church (in which I grew up and briefly ministered), like its forebears the AOG, continues the tradition of destroying by fire the charms possessed by Limba Christians. Indigenous leaders are still, as Kailing observed, 'espousing the same views and philosophy that the missionaries held' (1994, 492). In fact, most indigenous and mainline churches have adopted the use of Western liturgical vestments, songs, music, and musical instruments (cf. Taylor 1963, 15).

African leaders have been insensitive to the views and practices of Traditionalists and are reluctant to study ATR in an effort to understand it or create opportunities for positive dialogue. The stance of Christians in Sierra Leone in relation to charms and medicines varies 'from utter rejection as pagan idolatry, to acceptance as part of the traditional way of life' (Avery 1971, 10). This is also true in terms of some traditional practices. For example, the God Is Our Light Church, an AIC, prohibits secret society membership but approves of polygamy, calling it the lesser of two evils (Olson 1969, 198). Even the spiritual churches, whose aim was to create an indigenous church that bears the marks of African culture and practice, continue to criticise African spirits.

Even the involvement of traditional militia groups on the side of the government and the nation during the civil war did not sit well with many evangelical Christians. It was the opinion of the evangelicals that Christian prayers should never be mixed with devilish traditional spirituality.[4]

Over forty years ago, Bolaji Idowu made an observation about Christian Nigerians that, after many years of independent Christianity, the church has still been unable to develop a theology that bears the distinctive stamp of African thought and meditation. This observation remains true not only in Nigeria, but also in many places in Africa. The theology of these churches is 'book theology'; the church reads and accepts Euro-American theologies without critique. This approach demonstrates that some Christian Africans[5] 'have not yet begun to do their own thinking and to grapple spiritually and intellectually with questions relating to the Christian faith' (1965, 22). Most churches are still enslaved to Euro-American cosmology. It is right to say, then, that 'African Christians'[6] continue to 'struggle not so much against European domination as against that of Europeanised Africans' (Kraft 1978, 288).

In spite of the attacks on traditional religion and culture, staunch Traditionalists continue to offer strong resistance in order to keep their cultural heritage intact. To completely give up their God-given heritage in favour of a foreign culture, as the church requires, seems a very difficult task and is tantamount to losing their entire heritage, identity, and place—both spiritually and physically—within their religiocultural community. This is why African Traditionalists, even after conversion to Christianity, 'do not always adhere to religious and ritual demands that are formulated and expressed by the leaders of their churches' (Magesa 1997, 7).

CONCLUSION

When Christians entered Sierra Leone, the indigenes they met already knew God and had their own religious system. Wherever the Christians settled, they proclaimed their beliefs and established institutions for worship and learning. Several Christian missions opened schools, colleges, and medical facilities.

Christians are considered 'People of the Book', because they have scriptures, which claim to come from or be inspired by God, as the primary sources of their beliefs and teachings. Their faith is a way of life, which is expressed and practiced by believers through worship, prescribed duties, and actions.

Contrary to Islam, Christianity did not adapt as much to African society, but made heavy demands on its converts. Historically, missionaries were insensitive to African religion and culture, and even after many years of autonomy, this insensitivity is still being displayed by indigenous church leaders in Sierra Leone. Although in recent years Christianity has been making strides and growing, Muslims still significantly outnumber Christians.

The effects of Christianity on ATR and vice versa in Sierra Leone are evidently clear. Although ATR has been long marginalised in Sierra Leone, one would be naïve to think that it has not influenced the worldviews of Islam and Christianity.

ENDNOTES

1. Kato has argued that 'although missionaries from Europe and North America brought the gospel to Black Africa in modern times, they are not the first messengers of the gospel to our continent' (1980, 83). See also Mbiti (1986, 1–2) for a discussion on the advent of the Gospel into Africa way before Euro-American missionaries.

2. History books vary on the exact number of the Blacks who left Nova Scotia: Olson (1969, 28) puts it at 1,175; Fyle (1981, 35) puts it at 1,190; and Sanneh (1983, 58) puts it about 1,200.

3. The divinity of Christ has been a controversial matter among some Christians and non-Christians for many centuries now. The Gnostics applied their principle of dualism to Christology and created a problem for the church (Gonzalez 1970, 126–137). The controversy regarding Christ's relationship with the Father continues today. Some church leaders and Christians have openly challenged the divinity of Christ. They, as those who have challenged it before, have met with and received strong negative reaction from the church.

4. Although Sierra Leoneans are divided as to whether traditional spirituality or Christian or Muslim prayers brought the war to an end, one belief commonly held by all the faith groups is that the war was brought to an end through divine intervention.

5. This applies to Africans who reject ATR and believe that Christianity should supersede ATR.

6. This term refers to those who practise ATR and Christianity and believe that their African heritage supercedes Christianity.

PART II

MEETINGS AND PARTINGS

The three chapters that constitute part 1 have provided a basic understanding of the fundamental religious tenets and practices of SLIR, Islam, and Christianity. It is hoped that this has, to a greater extent, prepared the reader for part 2, which contains chapter 5, 'Comparative Analysis of ATR With Islam and With Christianity'—a discussion of the meeting and parting points of the fundamental tenets of ATR, the host religion, with each immigrant religion. This section provides a comparative analysis of SLIR with Christianity and with Islam, helps to draw contours for an understanding of the commonalities and differences between ATR and the two immigrant religions, and makes recommendations for better interfaith dialogue and cooperation later in our study.

CHAPTER 5

COMPARATIVE ANALYSIS
OF ATR WITH ISLAM
AND WITH CHRISTIANITY

The greatest challenge and condemnation of traditional spirituality and culture in Sierra Leone still comes from the Christians. Although the present Arab brand of Islam is attempting to purge the long-existing syncretistic brand of Islam, its opposition to ATR is much milder than that of Christianity.

The discussions on the fundamental tenets of SLIR and the basic beliefs of Islam and Christianity in the preceding chapters have provided a background for the analysis of traditional religion and its intersections with Islam and Christianity. This chapter tries to discover the affinities and differences between ATR and the two immigrant religions, as an attempt to hopefully map out possible strategies for mutual understanding and for the inclusion of ATR in interfaith dialogue and cooperation in Sierra Leone.

Although, in most cases, ancestral veneration, sacrifice, and charms and medicines are the three aspects of ATR that some Muslims and Christians most frequently dismiss as false religion, in what follows, I endeavour to discuss a variety of issues based on some of the fundamental tenets of ATR, as discussed in chapter 2.

THE SUPREME BEING

Which God Do Traditionalists Serve?

The Supreme Being holds the highest status in indigenous spirituality, which is also the case in Islam and Christianity, as seen in the previous chapters. God is the central focus of each of the three religions. They all accept the existence of God. Just six decades ago, Hargrave, an anthropologist writing about these three religions in Sierra Leone, said, '[T]he belief in God, the Creator, all powerful, invisible…is accepted by all religious groups' (1944, 63).

Most Traditionalists in Sierra Leone continue to make the claim that the God they serve is not different from the God the Muslims and Christians serve. This view resonates with the teaching of Islam that the Supreme Being is not just the God of the Muslims, nor the God of a particular race, religion, or nation, but the only God for all peoples.

At the first conference of African theologians in Ibadan, January 1966, on the theme, 'Biblical revelation and African beliefs', a consensus was reached 'that the God whom African religion acknowledges is the same God as in the Bible' (Mbiti 1989b, 61). This conviction was unanimously expressed by the participants in the following statement:

> We believe that the God and Father of our Lord and Saviour Jesus Christ…has been dealing with humankind at all times and in all parts of the world. It is with this conviction that we study the rich heritage of our African people and we have evidence that they know God and worship God. We recognize the radical quality of God's self-revelation in Jesus Christ…This knowledge of God is not totally discontinuous with our people's previous traditional knowledge of God. (Mbiti 1989b, 61)

Most Christians do not dispute the fact that Traditionalists have a belief in a God. However, Christians contend that the God served by Traditionalists is not the same one true God who has revealed himself as the eternally self-existent 'I AM', the creator of heaven and earth and the redeemer of humanity. Further, it is not the God who has revealed himself as embodying the principles of relationship and association as Father, Son, and Holy Ghost (Deut. 6:4; Isa. 43:10–11; Matt. 28:19; Luke 3:22). Thus, the Christians do not equate the God of ATR with their own. The following discussion will help readers make a decision if the God of ATR shares affinity with the God of Islam and, especially, with the God of Christianity.

God Above
In indigenous religion, the Supreme Being lives above in the skies; likewise, in the Qur'an, Allah is portrayed as living above, where he attends to humans on earth (7:26, 15:21, 39:6, 57:25). In the Bible, the transcendence of God is displayed in the concept that God dwells in the heaven/sky: *shamayim* ('heaven[s]/sky') or *ouranos* ('heaven/sky') is the abode of God (Deut. 4:39; Josh. 2:11; Matt. 3:17; Mark 1:11; Luke 2:14). Jesus taught his disciples to pray, 'Our Father in heaven' (Matt. 6:9; cf. Matt. 5:16, 5:45, 6:1, 7:11, 18:14). And like Traditionalists, Muslims and Christians balance their belief in God's transcendence with their belief in his immanence. In the Qur'an, Allah is nearer to humankind than the life vein (50:16, 2:186). Although God lives in heaven, for the Christian, the Supreme Being 'is not far from each of us' (Acts 17:27b).

The Bible makes reference to 'God in heaven above and on earth below' (Deut. 4:39; Josh. 2:11). This speaks not so much of a perceived residence, but of God's domain. God controls both 'heaven above' and the 'earth below' (Gen. 24:3; Luke 10:21; Isa. 66:1; Matt. 5:34–35; Acts 7:49).

While neither Muslims nor Christians acknowledge a 'God below', they do identify a single personal force responsible for much of the evil in the world. Both in the Qur'an and in the Bible, this force is called Satan. Muslims believe that Satan was a jinn who disobeyed God (Qur'an 15:26–42), and Christians, that he is an angel who fell from grace (Isa. 14:12–15). Jesus referred to Satan as the prince and ruler of this world (John 12:31, 12:14, 12:30). While ATR does not identify a single, personal 'big evil', the Limba belief in Kanu Wopothi ('God Below'), a general category used to describe any evil spirit, is somewhat similar to the Muslim belief in disobedient jinn and to the Christian belief in demons (Matt. 8:28–34; 1 Tim. 4:1–10).

Names of God
The names of God in ATR are highly significant. This concept is also found in Islam and Christianity. Although the proper and divine name of God in Islam is Allah, the Qur'an states that Allah has the best and most beautiful names (7:180, 17:110, 20:8, 59:24), which are referred to as the ninety-nine names (Baldock 2004, 213–221). Just as in ATR, these names express the excellent attributes, characteristics, and activities of God.

In biblical times, names were significant because 'they revealed character and identity and signified existence' (Achtemeier 1996, 736). Generally, names indicated who people were, their conduct, and the way they lived their lives. As such, great care and attention to significance were given in the choice of names (Erickson 1992, 83; Houtman 1993, 71). In the Bible, the revelation of God's name and its continued use were of great significance because it was the means by which God could be reached and known. Theophoric personal names are a valuable guide to qualities associated with God, and the personal names containing God's divine name *Yahweh* depict his nature, character, and peculiar qualities (Achtemeier 1996, 734).

The tradition and terminology of God's names in the NT was 'inherited from the OT and Judaism as mediated by the Septuagint (LXX)'. However, this inherited tradition was greatly modified both by the 'understanding of the teaching of Jesus' and by the 'understanding of the person of Jesus as the definitive expression of God' (Achtemeier 1996, 734). The names and titles of Jesus tell us about his character, peculiar qualities, rank, and power. For example, the name 'Jesus' (Heb. 'Joshua') means 'Saviour'. The instruction of the angel to Joseph was that the child Mary bore should be named 'Jesus, for he will save his people from their sins' (Matt. 1:21). The Hebrew name 'Emmanuel' means 'God is with us' (Matt. 1:23). The title the 'Christ' (Heb. 'Messiah') means the 'anointed'. Jesus was the long-awaited Saviour and Deliverer.

Although the vital Christian teaching of the Trinity is not present in indigenous religion, the Traditionalists continue to argue that the God of other religions is the same God they serve on the grounds that if it were not so, Christian missionaries in particular would not have adopted traditional names for the Christian God. A majority of 'Christian missionaries in their teachings and translations of scripture have adopted African names of God' (Smith 1950, 34).[1] They 'proclaimed the name of Jesus Christ. But they used the names of the God who was and is already known by African peoples' (Mbiti 1980, 818): Christian Mende use the name *Ngewo*, *Kuru Masaba* is the name used by Christian Temne, Christian Limba use the name *Kanu Masala*, and *Yaata* is the name used by Christian Kono.

Sanneh may have provided an answer to the Traditionalists' query as to the Christian adoption of traditional names for God when he wrote, 'The adoption by missionaries of African names for God was key to the effective transmission of the Gospel. It implied the abandonment of arguments of European ascendancy and, too, of the moral logic of permanent colonial and missionary tutelage' (2001, 114). Sanneh's argument was trying to portray the sensitivity of the missionaries in terms of superiority and status, which implies that the Christian adoption of African names has nothing to do with the religious conviction of the missionaries.

However, I believe that the missionary adoption of African names for God indicates recognition of the religiosity of the people—that they knew God. In fact, this practice reflects a Christian principle based on Acts 17:22–32, which records the apostle Paul's adoption of the Greek word *theos* to refer to the Christian God.

God Is Omnipotent
God, in ATR, is the one to whom absolute power and might are attributed. This belief is equally supported by Islam and Christianity. In the

Qur'an, absolute power over all things is attributed to God (2:20, 2:106, 2:284, 25:54). Allah is the only one who is powerful enough to give spiritual life (75:4), to chastise (6:65), to change things (70:40–41), and to control everything (4:85). As discussed earlier, there are many biblical references to God as the possessor and source of all power.

God Is Omnipresent
Traditionalists assume the presence of God in their daily lives and activities. Muslims and Christians teach about God's omnipresence in terms similar to those used by ATR. In the Qur'an, Allah is everywhere (57:4, 58:7) and in all directions (2:115), so that no one can hide from God (4:108). He is closer to humankind than the life vein (50:16). In Christianity, God is not subject to the limitations of time and space. God is found everywhere (Erickson 1992, 84). Christians, like traditionalists, also believe that God is especially present when they gather to worship him. Jesus said, 'For where two or three are gathered in my name, I am there among them' (Matt. 18:20), and later commissioned his disciples, saying, 'I am with you always, to the end of the age' (Matt. 28:20).

God Is Omniscient
God's omniscience is central to ATR, Islam, and Christianity. In Islam, Allah knows everything (2:29, 6:101, 24:35, 29:62, 42:12) and he comprehends everything (6:80, 7:89, 20:98). God's knowledge is described as covering heaven and earth (2:255, 29:52, 57:4), things visible and invisible (13:9, 32:6, 35:38, 49:18), every minute thing (10:61, 34:2–3), the content of human hearts and minds (2:235, 11:5, 29:10), human secret thoughts and open words (2:77, 6:3, 11:5), and every falling leaf (6:59).

In Christian theology, humankind is 'completely transparent before God…He sees and knows us totally' (Erickson 1992, 85). There is nothing that escapes God's knowledge. Humankind cannot hide from God (Pss. 139:7, 139:13; Jer. 23:24), and even what may be hidden from humankind is laid bare before God (Heb. 4:12–13).

God Is the Creator

ATR practitioners attribute creation to the Supreme Being, a view that resonates with Muslims and Christians. The creative power of Allah in Islam is similar to that in ATR and Christianity, as discussed earlier. Allah is referred to as the creator, maker, and fashioner (59:24), the creator who made all things (6:101, 13:16, 20:50), including the heavens and the earth (6:1, 14:32, 27:56–60) and humankind (55:3, 39:6). There is no one else with such power to have created the world, save Allah (13:16, 16:20, 31:11, 35:40), and he sustains his creation (11:6, 56:58–74).

Worship/Veneration—Sacrifice

Worship is a vital aspect in the practice of ATR. It is a way that God is accessible. Similarly, in Islam and Christianity, worship plays a crucial role in maintaining a close relationship with God. As already discussed, sacrifice is the primary method of indigenous worship. It should be noted here again, as above, that Traditionalists claim they neither make sacrifice to the spirits nor worship them. Offerings are made to spirits to appease or to return thanks.

There are at least four non-Islamic sacrifices that some Muslims in Sierra Leone reluctantly take part in:

- Heroes' sacrifice is offered for the inclusion of the deceased into the ancestral world.
- State sacrifice for appeasement or seeking the favour of the community's respected and feared pantheon. This sacrifice is offered in the place that is presumed to be the abode of said pantheon.
- Family sacrifice is usually made to the dead.
- Individual sacrifice is offered by an individual, usually through the help of a sacred specialist, for protection, prosperity, health, or safe delivery of a baby, or when seeking employment or going on a trip.

Most of these sacrifices are strongly opposed by strict Muslims as pagan rituals, especially the Ahmadiyyas and younger Muslim clerics who were trained in Arab institutions.

The generally accepted Muslim sacrifices are *Zakat* and *Fidahu*. In addition to how Muslims in general disburse *Zakat*, Sierra Leoneans offer sacrifice (*Zakat*) on the eighth day after the birth of a child, and *Fidahu*, a 'redemption' sacrifice, on the third, seventh, and fortieth days after the death of a person. *Fidahu* is an African traditional rite that Muslims have integrated into their practices.

Christian worship, while it does not offer physical sacrifices, remembers the sacrifice of Christ through the sacrament of the Eucharist. For some Sierra Leonean Traditionalists, the Christian teaching about the death of Christ as a sacrifice for the propitiation of sin seems strange and contradictory because missionaries have condemned human sacrifice as sinful and inhumane.[2] If human sacrifice has been condemned by God, how then could he, as a loving and faithful God, change his mind and become a savage by offering his own Son as a sacrifice? For Traditionalists, the teaching about Jesus' death as a sacrifice seems hypocritical.

Christians take part in traditional sacrificial rites such as the Krio *Awujoh* feast, a ceremony performed in honour of the dead. Libation, prayer, singing, chanting, dancing, postures, and signs are all symbols that serve as connecting links between the visible and the invisible, between the living and the supernatural. The pillars of Islam and the sacraments of Christianity are all symbols that represent spiritual realities.

ANGELS

Angels in ATR, according to this study, share affinity with those found in Islam and Christianity. It is probably that the concept of angels among the Limba is strongly influenced by Islam and Christianity. The Muslims I interviewed in Sierra Leone were largely unconcerned with the Traditionalist belief in angels, but the Christians I spoke with dismissed the Traditionalist's belief in angels, arguing that it has no affinity with the Christian belief, as Limba Traditionalists claim. Evangelical,

Pentecostal, and charismatic Christians believe that the angels known to Traditionalists are actually the fallen angels (Ezek. 28; 2 Pet. 2:4; Jude 6), which are also called 'demons' (Matt. 4:24, 7:22; Mark 1:32, 1:34; Luke 4:41).

In the Bible, as in ATR, angels are hylomorphic. They are portrayed as spiritual beings (Heb. 1:14), some of whom have wings (Isa. 6:2). They are also 'able to manifest themselves as active and effecting agents in the empirical world' (Lockyer 1995, 5). They appear in dreams (Matt. 1:20, 1:24, 2:13, 2:19; Acts 10:13; cf. Acts 12:9) to 'both Christians and some would-be-converts'. Dreams 'are vehicles of communication from God to people—to reveal, warn, and inform' (Mbiti 1997, 514). Angels sometimes appear in human likeness to visit people (Gen. 19:1; Judg. 13:16) and welcome hospitality (Gen. 19:2). For this reason, Hebrews 13:2 exhorts Christians not to 'neglect to show hospitality to strangers, for by doing that some have entertained angels without knowing it'. In their ability to assume human likeness, angels are able to affect material conditions and historical events (John 5:4; Acts 5:19, 12:7, 12:23).

Angels are endowed with proper names—for example, Gabriel (Dan. 8:16, 9:21; Luke 1:19, 1:26) and Michael (Dan 10:13, 10:21; Jude 9; Rev. 12:7)—which implies that they have personalities. Anytime reference to the gender of an angel is made in the Bible, it is always male.[3] This is contrary to Adelowo's (1982, 159) statement that the Bible does not make any serious attempt in associating gender with angels. Angels are also called children of God (Luke 20:36).

Angels in ATR and Christianity are not only similar in nature, but they are also similar in the roles they play. In the Bible, angels are portrayed 'as messengers or servants of God who are of unquestionable integrity, good will and obedience to Him' (Adelowo 1982, 158; cf. Locyer 1995, 3; Gen. 16:7–13, 21:17–20, 22:11–18; Judg. 6:11–23; 1 Sam. 29:9; 2 Sam. 14:17, 14:20). The Hebrew word *mal'akh* in the OT and the Greek word *angelos* in the NT mean simply 'messenger' (Lockyer 1995, 3). As messengers, angels are God's ambassadors and emissaries (1 Tim. 5:21), and as such, they simply follow whatever directive God gives them. They are ministering spirits (Heb. 1:14). As in Limba religion, their functions as 'God's messengers cannot be limited to specialised categories, but rather they are presented in broad and varied auxiliary functions', and as such, 'they appear as helpers and protectors to people in need, as proclaimers of news or mediators of revelations from God, and as guides and guardians' (Lockyer 1995, 4).

ANCESTOR VENERATION OR VENERATION OF THE DEAD

The issue of ancestral veneration has been dealt with in chapter 2. It was concluded that Traditionalists do not worship their ancestors or their dead, but venerate them. Muslims and Christians in Sierra Leone also venerate their ancestors/dead in prayers, festivals, and through sacrifice on the third, seventh, and fortieth day after the death of a relative or friend.

The words for ancestors in SLIR have the same meaning as Christianity's. Among the Mende, the ancestors are referred to as *kekeni* and *ndeblaa* ('our forefathers'), the Limba as *nbemben* ('forefathers', 'great grandfathers'), and the Kono as *Fuenu* ('great fathers') and *Mbimbanu* ('the great ancestral forefathers'). Similarly, in the Bible, the Hebrew word *'av* ('father') is also translated 'ancestor' (Gen. 10:21), 'forefather' (Gen. 15:15), and 'grandfather' (Gen. 28:13). In the NT, the Greek word *pater* ('father') is also translated 'forefather' and 'ancestor' (Mark 3:9; Luke 1:73, 16:24).

Although the Bible prohibits ancestor worship (Deut. 18:11–12) and Moses found it necessary to specify that such worship was not compatible with the worship of God (Deut. 26:14b), Saul, in desperation, solicited the help of the medium in Endor to help him contact the spirit of Samuel. When the medium succeeded in bringing up the spirit of Samuel, Saul 'bowed down and prostrated himself with his face to the ground' (1 Samuel 28:1–20). When Samuel enquired why Saul brought him up, Saul said, 'I am in great distress...The Philistines are fighting against me' (1 Samuel 28:15). This closely parallels the way the African Traditionalist speaks to the ancestor by revealing his/her problem and the cause of it.[4] There is archaeological evidence that shows that the ancient Israelites deposited food near the tombs of their venerated dead (De Vaux 1997, 61).

A similar custom continues among many Christians in Sierra Leone, especially among the Krio, who visit the graves of their departed relatives with food and gifts on New Year's Day, Easter, and Christmas; when going on local or overseas trips; when undertaking some responsible task; and for many more ventures. The deceased is also remembered in a memorial service in church called *berin choch* ('church after burial'). This is usually followed by a visit to the graveside and eventually by visits from time to time (Wyse 1989, 12).

Although Christians of other ethnic groups in Sierra Leone seldom go to the graveside of their dead relatives, much of their veneration of the dead is done at home. I was born into a Christian family where our parents led us in venerating our ancestors.

In many parts of Africa, Europe, and the Americas, Christians visit the graves of their deceased relatives and decorate them with flowers and paraphernalia. Mexicans hold

> picnics at the cemetery, and after eating a sumptuous meal they tell stories about the lives of the dead and leave special offerings. At an evening meal the family shares a loaf of bread called *pan de muerto* ('bread of death'). It is regarded as a sign of luck to be the one who bites into the plastic toy skeleton hidden inside. (Hale 2003, 85)

Major Christian denominations all over the world venerate the dead in special services/masses, prayers, and festivals. The Roman Catholic tradition makes provision for the veneration of departed Christian saints, and defines it in the doctrine of *Dulia*.

All Saints' Day (1 November) in many Christian traditions is a time to pray for and remember the dead. It is a time to recognise the common bond between the living and the dead, and the common bond between the church here on earth and the church triumphant in heaven. On All Saints' Day, the Catholic Church commemorates both canonised saints and others whose lives have been proven to be Christlike.

The night before All Saints' Day, originally known as All Hallows' Eve and now called Halloween, has its origin in the ancient Celtic day of the dead called *Samhain*. It was traditionally believed that the souls of the departed wandered the earth until All Saints' Day, and All Hallow's Eve provided one last chance for the dead to gain vengeance on their enemies before moving to the next world. In order to avoid being recognised by any soul that might be seeking such vengeance, people would don masks or costumes to disguise their identities. Today most North American and British children perpetuate the custom by dressing in costumes and going door to door in search of treats. Although many churches discourage any celebration of Halloween, it has become such a large part of secular North American culture that it is second only to Christmas in the production and sale of seasonal items such as decorations and costumes.

All Souls' Day (2 November), which emanated from the medieval worship of the dead, provides an opportunity to remember other Christians who have died. Some churches, including the United Church of Canada (UCC)—in which I minister—provide the opportunity for families and friends who have been bereaved during the year to remember their departed loved ones. Each year, my congregation remembers those of our members who have died since the previous All Saints' Day as I read a list of their names during the service.

In the medieval period, All Saints' Day and All Souls' Day were considered holy days ranking in importance after Christmas and Easter. During colonial rule in Mexico, 'Spanish missionary priests combined an indigenous pre-Hispanic religious festival of the dead with All Souls' Day to produce the "Mexican Day of the Dead"' (Hale 2003, 85).

The Greek Orthodox Church remembers the dead on the eve of Sexagesima (the second Sunday before Lent) or on the day before Pentecost. In the Armenian Orthodox Church, the feast of the dead is held on Easter Monday.

Christians who are involved in these practices (including myself), like Traditionalists, are careful to specify that their actions are not acts of 'worship' directed towards the dead. Rather, they indicate a feeling of affection for the dead and are regarded as an obligation that the living have to pay to the dead as an act of piety that is due them.

SPIRITS

The notion that there are myriads of spiritual forces in the world that manifest themselves in various ways is prevalent not only in ATR, but also in Islam and Christianity in Sierra Leone. There are a number of similarities between the pneumatology of ATR and of that of Islam and of Christianity. It seems that beliefs and discussions about spirits are influenced, to some extent, by traditionally held beliefs.

In addition to angels, the Qur'an also speaks of jinn, which are spirits created from the smokeless fire with free will (15:26–27). Some of these disobeyed Allah and became 'evil spirits' (72:1). They are believed to put low, selfish thoughts in the minds of people, misleading them and causing them to do evil (Aziz 1993, 14). In the Qur'an, the term 'jinn' has another distinct usage. In several instances (6:112, 34:12, 38:38, 46:30–31, 34:14), the word is used in reference to people because of their remoteness (Aziz 1993, 65).

Christians, on the basis of Ephesians 6:12, also maintain a strong belief in the existence of both good and evil spirits. The good spirits are allegiant and obedient to God. In this category, we have the Spirit of God—the Holy Spirit—and a great number of angels called ministering spirits. The Spirit of the LORD/God and the Holy Spirit are one and the same (Acts 2:16–17) and represent God's mysterious power or presence, which he gives to individuals and communities that empower them with 'qualities they would not otherwise possess' (Achtemeier 1996, 432; see also Erickson 1992, 266–267). Similarly, in Islam, God strengthens Muslim believers with his Spirit (58:22).

In the OT, leaders such as Moses, Joshua, the judges, David, Solomon, prophets, and kings receive their prowess from the presence of the Spirit of God. In the NT, it is God's Spirit that endows Jesus with power to fulfill his mission (Matt. 3:13–17; Mark 1:9–11; Luke 3:21–22; Matt. 12:28; Luke 4:16–21) and that empowers the apostles and the early church as seen in the book of Acts and the Pauline Epistles. Today it is believed that the Holy Spirit continues to sustain the church and believers.

In Christianity, evil spirits are believed to be disobedient to God and under the direction of Satan, who controls an organised host of wicked spirit beings. They are a formidable foe arrayed against God and his people. A close reading of the Gospels and the book of Acts reveals that Christ and his apostles accepted the reality of evil spirits and taught their followers to cast them out.

In the OT, there is evidence of a belief in malevolent spirits (Gen. 6:1–4; Lev. 16:6–10, 16:26; Job 6:4; Ps. 91:5–6; Isa. 34:14). Little was known about evil spirits. It was not until the late postexilic period that a cogent pneumatology of evil spirits developed in Hebrew thought. What developed during this time frame was a belief in 'numerous evil spirits or demons' (Achtemeier 1996, 236), who were led by an individual spirit whose most common designation was *ha Satan* ('the accuser'). This eventually came to function as a personal name 'Satan'. In the LXX, the title *ha diabolos* ('the slanderer/the devil') came to be used as the Greek equivalent (Job 2:1; Zech. 3:1; 1 Chron. 21:1). This was also used in the NT, for example, in Matthew 4 and Luke 4. The eventual understanding was of a hierarchy of demons, organised into armies, under the leadership of Satan, 'doing battle with God and God's allies'. These spirits were able to afflict and even possess humans in order to cause physical or mental illnesses. People even came to believe that 'demons could take control of nature and cause natural calamities and disasters' (Achtemeier 1996, 236). Jesus' earthly ministry included the exorcism of such demons (e.g., Matt. 8:28–34; Mark 5:1–20; Luke 8:26–39; Matt. 12:22–32; Mark 3:22–27; Luke 11:14–23), and the apostle Paul demonstrated an understanding of such a pneumatology (Rom. 8:38; cf. Col. 1:16, 2:15; Eph. 3:10; and also 1 Cor. 10:20).

Similar to Traditionalists, Muslims and Christians have, at least in part, attributed many of the completely inhuman and unnatural evils of society to the devil and his spirits. However, there are also instances in the Bible where God has sent evil spirits upon people (1 Sam. 16:14–16; 16:23, 18:10, 19:9; 2 Chron. 18:22).

Witchcraft
The views and discussions of witchcraft among Muslims and Christians in Sierra Leone are, like many issues, influenced by long-held traditional beliefs. Although both the Qur'an and the Bible acknowledge the existence of witchcraft, neither says much about it. However, on the basis of Leviticus 19:26b and Deuteronomy 18:10, Christians condemn witches and witchcraft. Parrinder has argued that the witchcraft discussed in the Bible is altogether different than anything known today and that it is therefore a mistake to use scripture to either condemn or justify witchcraft as we know it (1963, 117, 122): 'The plain fact is that the Bible knows scarcely anything of true witchcraft, certainly not the New Testament, and the few injunctions found in the Old Testament refer to something else' (118).

To buttress his argument, Parrinder gave a brief study on the Hebrew words that have been translated 'witch'/'witchcraft' (120–122). The Hebrew word most often used to denote a witch is *kashaph*. The meaning of the term is not clear, and its significance has to be judged from its usage (120; cf. Achtemeier 1996, 1217). *Kashaph*, in its various forms, is most often translated 'sorcery', 'sorcerer/sorceress', or 'diviner' (Holladay 1988, 166; Brown 1996, 506). Because so little is known about the meaning of this term or the practices it describes, it is almost impossible to prove any similarity or dissimilarity to the practice of witchcraft as described by practitioners of ATR. Despite their varying definitions of what exactly witchcraft is, practitioners of all three religions generally condemn its practice.

Ghosts
Although the Qur'an makes no mention of ghosts and Christian tradition says very little about the activities of ghosts, both Muslims and Christians strongly believe in the existence of ghosts. The belief in 'disembodied spirits' (Achtemeier 1996, 375) or 'shades' (Heb. *rephaim*) is found in the Hebrew Bible (Job 26:5; Ps. 88:10; Prov. 2:18, 9:18, 21:16; Isa. 14:9, 26:19; cf. Isa 29:4, 'a ghost [Heb. *ohb*] from the ground') (Achtemeier 1996, 375). Jesus' disciples, when they saw him walking

on water (Mark 6:49; Matt. 14:26), and later when they saw him risen, mistook him for a 'ghost' (Luke 24:37). However, as is the case with witchcraft, there is not enough information about ghosts in the Bible to adequately compare biblical ideas to those of ATR.

The 'Biblical perspectives on the spirit world are a good deal closer to traditional African thinking than to the skepticism and demythologising of much modern Western theology' (Ferdinando 1996, 120). There are a number of key similarities between African pneumatology and biblical pneumatology. Both biblical writers and African Traditionalists believe in the existence of individual personal spirit beings with identity, intelligence, will, and self-consciousness. These beings fall into some sort of hierarchy, which is not well understood by humans. These beings are powerful and sometimes use their powers to inflict misfortune on humans. This understanding helps to give meaning to suffering.

There are also a number of fundamental differences between the two pneumatologies. Biblical pneumatology is primarily theocentric and plays little attention to the roles of other spirits. Any attention that is given to these activities is always framed in the context of the sovereignty of God who sets limits on these beings (Ferdinando 1996, 130).

African pneumatology, on the other hand, is anthropocentric, and the spirits are defined morally by their relationship to man, whether they bring harm or good, and almost any spirit may move from one classification to another based on their actions. The chief harm inflicted by spirits is physical. 'In the event of misfortune it is an offending witch or spirit that is invariably sought out, which contrasts sharply with the theocentric reaction of Job or of the sufferers in the book of Psalms' (Ferdinando 1996, 123). God often appears to be silent in ATR pneumatology.

CHARMS AND MEDICINES

The previous chapter described how the Muslims who brought Islam into Sierra Leone adopted the Traditionalists' practice of making charms and medicines. Today, although the practice is often challenged by strict

Muslim clerics and believers, most of the manufacturers of these charms and medicines are still Muslims.

Many Christians continue to believe in the use of these charms and medicines. Staunch Christians, however, have condemned traditional charms as pathetic and useless, claiming that they offer no assurance and 'they evoke no voluntary self-surrender in those who trust in them' (Sawyerr 1968, 134).

Similar to Sierra Leone Traditionalists and Muslims, in the Bible, the Hebrews used charms in the form of amulets.[5] Hebrew women wore earrings (Gen. 35:4; Judg. 2:13, 8:24) and used amulets to ensure fertility (Packer et al. 1980, 442). Men wore pendants 'suspended from chains around the necks' and engraved with 'sacred words or the figure of a god' (481). To form another kind of amulet, scriptural texts were written on a papyrus or parchment scroll which was then rolled tightly and sewn up in linen (481).

Eventually, the practice of wearing amulets came to be considered idolatrous and was replaced by the wearing of phylacteries 'on the forehead between the eyebrows', and 'on the left arm' (Packer et al. 1980, 482). Moses' use of the image of the serpent (Exod. 4:3–5, 7:8–13), Naman's washing in the Jordan and eventual cure (2 Kings 5:1–19), and Christ's working of miracles in conjunction with natural objects (John 11:1–53) have been put forward as further evidence of the use of religious charms and objects in the Bible (Byaruhanga-Akiiki 1993, 192). The RCC continues to approve the use of statues, crucifixes, medals, and rosaries.

Sacred Places and Objects

Like Traditionalists, Muslims and Christians in Sierra Leone believe that some objects and places possess supernatural qualities. The Ka'ba, the cubic structure made of hewn stone in Mecca, has for many centuries received veneration by Muslims during Hajj, and all Muslims worldwide face the Ka'ba five times daily to pray.

The notion that nature and/or natural objects possess sacredness is attested to in the Bible. Jacob, after his dream at Bethel, remarked

'How awesome is this place!' (Gen. 28:17). At the burning bush, God told Moses to take the sandals off his feet, for he was standing on holy ground (Exod. 3:5). Because the Israelites and their ancestors were shepherds and peasants, they shared the Canaanite belief that there is a

> divine presence or action in the springs which made the earth fruitful, in the wells which provided water for flocks, in the tree which bore witness to this fertility, and in the high places where the clouds gathered to give their longed-for rain. (De Vaux 1997, 277)

At the wells of Beersheba, Abraham called upon the name of God (Gen. 21:31) and Isaac set up an altar to God, who appeared to him there (Gen. 26:23–25).

Trees had sacred associations in the Israelite religion. Trees served as memorial objects (Gen. 21:33), and 'they marked the open-air sanctuaries ("high places") honoured by the patriarchs (Gen. 12, 6–7) but condemned by the prophets for the illegitimate rites held there'—for example, Jeremiah 3:6 (Achtemeier 1996, 1174). The palm tree of the prophetess Deborah, between Ramah and Bethel (Jg. 4:5), where she settled 'disputes between Israelites, probably did have a religious significance' (De Vaux 1997, 278–279).

Despite the command against deifying mountains in the Hebrew religion (Ezek. 18:6, 18:11, 18:15; Jer. 3:2, 3:6; Hosea. 4:13), sacred mountains are attested in the Bible. Mount Sinai, or Horeb, and Mount Zion were associated with God (Achtemeier 1996, 710; De Vaux 1997, 281). Mount Sinai is called the 'mountain of God' (Exod. 3:1, 4:27, 18:5, 24:13). It was the place where the covenant between God and Israel was made (Exod. 19:24), the place where Moses spoke to God (Exod. 19:3, 19:10, 24:9), and the place where God's presence was revealed (Exod. 19:16, 19:18). Mount Zion is the 'holy mountain' of the Psalms (Pss. 2:6, 3:5, 15:1, 43:3, 99:9) and of the prophets (Isa. 27:13; Jer. 31:23; Ezek. 20:40; Dan. 9:16, 9:20).

In the NT, the worship of God was not restricted to any particular mountain (John 4:2–24). Mountains were significant in contexts of worship, prayer, and important religious events (Achtemeier 1996, 710).

For example, Jesus went to the mountains for the Sermon on the Mount (Matt. 5:1–7, 5:29), his temptation (Matt. 4:8), his Transfiguration (Mark 9:2), and for his own prayer and devotion (Matt. 14:23; Mark 6:46; Luke 6:12, 9:28; John 6:15). Further,

> the Mount of Olives was the setting for Jesus' entry into Jerusalem (Mark 11, 1; Luke 19, 29); his betrayal occurred on the slopes at Gethsemane (Matt. 26, 30–56; Mark 14, 26–50); and it is reported that the Mount of Olives was the site of his ascension (Luke 24, 50; Acts 1, 9–12). (Achtemeier 1996, 710)

However, in both the Israelite religion and in the NT, worship was not paid to these places: 'they merely mark the place of worship' (DeVaux 1997, 278).

Sin and Salvation

In ATR, Islam, and Christianity, sin is despised as antisocial, destructive, and an offence against God, and in all these belief systems, sin is believed to destroy the reputation and spirituality of the offender, and his/her relationship with the victim and with God. Islam teaches about *kabirah* (major) and *saghirah* (minor) sins. Muslims are exhorted to hate and denounce open and secret sins (Qur'an 6:120, 6:151).

Unlike ATR, Christianity teaches that every human is born a sinner due to original sin inherited from Adam. Also unlike traditional religion, the rules for the guidance of the socioreligious life for the Christian are sanctioned, not only by community and its traditions, but by God and Christ as contained in the Bible. I now look briefly into two issues that, among others, are considered sinful and abominable by Muslims and Christians alike.

Abortion is generally disapproved of by all three religious groups in Sierra Leone. Traditionalists, Muslims, and Christians all maintain that humans are formed by God in the womb, and that the foetus is a human being from conception onwards and therefore has the right to life from the moment conception takes place. For this reason, purely elective abortions are unquestionably immoral. Abortion that is deemed medically necessary, on the other hand, is regarded, with mixed feelings at best, as a necessary evil.

Homosexuality is denounced by Traditionalists, Muslims, and Christians. Chapter 2 discussed the Traditionalist beliefs about homosexuality. Muslims cite most of their teachings from Qur'anic passages about Lot's experience (7:80–81, 26:165–166, 27:54–55). Sierra Leone Christians also base their teachings about the outrage of homosexuality on Lot's stories (Gen. 19), on Leviticus 18:22, and mainly on Paul's teaching in 1 Corinthians 6:9. I did not receive a pleasant response when I suggested that my interviewees read and understand these passages in their context before applying them to contemporary situations.

The confession of sin and the seeking of forgiveness for a wrongful act is an accepted remedy by Traditionalists, Muslims, and Christians. However, Christians believe that God took the initiative to remedy humankind's sin through the death of Christ. Thus, it is only the shed blood of Christ that can take away sins, not the powerless sacrifices of the Traditionalists.

In all three religions, salvation is the state of being delivered from the evils of this life, both spiritually and physically. The difference, however, is that the Traditionalist's concept of salvation is based on contemporary realities, while the Muslim's and Christian's is based on both contemporary and eschatological realities. Unlike ATR, the Christians believe that the only source of salvation for every human being is through Jesus Christ, the Saviour of the world.

AFTERLIFE

All the three faiths believe that at death, the soul/spirit leaves the body. The difference is the destiny of the soul/spirit. For Sierra Leone Traditionalists, it seems life is only beyond the grave if the 'good' dead is accepted as an ancestor; otherwise, the 'bad' dead becomes a ghost. In Islam, the soul/spirit after leaving the body eventually ends in either the garden (paradise) or the fire (hell). Similarly, in Christianity, the soul/spirit continues after death (Matt. 16:25–26). In Genesis 3:19, at death, the body returns to the ground from whence it came, while in Matthew 10:28, it is inferred that the body may also experience the suffering of hell or be raised (1 Thess. 4:13–18).

CONCLUSION

While some staunch Muslims and, to a larger extent, Christians reject and condemn traditional practices like ancestral veneration, sacrifices, charms, and medicines, this chapter shows that liberal Muslims and Christians do take part in these practices. Although Muslims and Christians are 'People of the Book'—that is, people with scriptures—it appears that for some of them, their beliefs, thoughts, and practices are still influenced by the traditional culture they were born into and in which they were raised. The influence of traditional African ideas, beliefs, and practices on the modern versions of Islam and Christianity should not be underestimated.

This study further shows where the ATR worldview intersects with Islam and Christianity. As Muzadi noted,

> All religions believe in God but what makes the difference is who their God is. Every religion has their own ritual practices toward their God, practised in different forms and orders. Each religion wishes for a peaceful and united community with dignity, but how we achieve this is done through various strategies…Therefore, the differences should not be equalized, whereas the similarities should not be differentiated. (2006, 24)

In reference to Islam and Christianity, the IRCSL's Statement of Shared Moral Concerns (appendix B) states, 'We recognize that our religious and spiritual traditions hold many values in common, and that these shared values can provide an authentic basis for mutual esteem, cooperation, and free common living in Sierra Leone'. This chapter has proven that Islam and Christianity 'hold many values in common' with ATR, and these shared values of ATR, Islam, and Christianity 'can provide an authentic basis for mutual esteem, cooperation, and free common living' in the country.

Considering the extent to which ATR shares affinity with Islam and Christianity, it is reasonable to ask why ATR has not been included in interfaith cooperation in Sierra Leone. The reasons for the exclusion of ATR are dealt with in the closing section of the next chapter.

Endnotes

1. Missionaries to the Katonda and Banganda peoples adopted the local names for God (Parrinder 1962, 35). In the LXX, the often used word *theos* ('God') a translation of the Hebrew word *Elohim* ('God'), was also used for the gods of other nations, 'just as it was the standard word for the gods of the Greeks and Romans of NT times' (Achtemeier 1996, 735).

2. The challenge on the rationale behind the death of Christ, is not, however, confined to African traditionalists. Even in the West, many Christians have been challenging it. Many Western Christians in the mainline churches no longer believe that a loving God could have offered his son as a sacrifice for the sin of humankind. Africans are not alone: '[N]o people, ancient or modern, have found the whole of Christian thought congenial, or absorbed it painlessly into their own culture' (Fashole-Luke n.d., 2).

3. The masculine pronoun 'he' is used in reference to angels Gabriel and Michael, see Achtemeier (1996, 356, 682). In several other passages, strangers who are identified as angels are also referred to as 'men', for example, Genesis 19:1–12.

4. For example, see Conteh (2004, 136–138).

5. An amulet is 'a small object believed charged with divine potency and thus effective in warding off evil and inviting the protection of beneficial powers. Amulets were integral to belief in magic and derived their efficacy from close physical contact with a holy person or object' (Achtemeier 1996, 32).

PART III

THEN, NOW, AND WHY

The chapter in this segment, 'Historical and Contemporary Interreligious Dialogue and Cooperation, and Reasons for the Exclusion of ATR', examines interreligious debates and dialogues in Sierra Leone since the nineteenth century and discusses some of the causes given by Muslims and Christians during my 2006 fieldwork for the marginalisation of ATR.

CHAPTER 6

HISTORICAL AND CONTEMPORARY INTERRELIGIOUS DIALOGUE AND COOPERATION, AND REASONS FOR THE EXCLUSION OF ATR

Sierra Leonean Muslim and Christian leaders consider Sierra Leone a multireligious society (Foullah 2006), and the country has been described as unique for its high level of religious tolerance (Koroma 2003, 121).

I now look at the historical interreligious debates and contemporary attempts at interfaith dialogue and cooperation, and provide answers to our thesis questions, Why have the believers and traditional religious practices been long marginalised in interfaith dialogue and cooperation in Sierra Leone by Muslim and Christian leaders? What is lacking in ATR that continues to prevent practitioners of Christianity and Islam from officially involving Traditionalists in the socioreligious development of the country?

HISTORICAL INTERFAITH ENCOUNTER, DEBATE/DIALOGUE, AND COOPERATION

Samuel Ajayi Crowther

In chapters 1 and 3, this study briefly reviewed and discussed Crowther's evangelistic strategy and his encounters with practitioners of ATR in Sierra Leone. As already noted, Islam also came under Crowther's attack. He saw ATR and Islam as needing transformation and himself as the person to bring about that change. Crowther was intent on converting every non-Christian he encountered.

An incident between Crowther and a Muslim parent in Freetown, although unorganised, was one of the first historical interfaith debates between Christianity and Islam in Sierra Leone.

One day, before he became a priest, while Crowther was teaching at a school in Wellington village, Freetown, one of his Muslim pupils came to class with a protective amulet around his neck (McKenzie 1976, 15). Crowther became enraged, cut off the charm, and told the pupil to take it home. The boy's father came to the school and questioned Crowther's right to interfere with his child's beliefs. A long, heated debate about whose religion was superior ensued. The Muslim father held firmly to his ground and refused to be swayed by Crowther.

Throughout his ministry, Crowther's persistent criticism of *Ifa* divination ironically gave the diviners confidence in the face of the Christian challenge. In an attempt at reconciliation, one of the diviners called a meeting with the CMS missionaries, clergy, and other diviners to talk about his decision to incorporate Jesus Christ into the *Ifa* system. The diviner reported to the audience that he routinely told his Christian clients to first call upon the name of Jesus Christ before making any sacrifice to the *Ifa* gods. This bold syncretism put the missionaries on the defensive. The reason for this syncretistic action, the diviners argued, is that since *Ifa* gods exist for the good of humankind, devotion to these gods must necessarily be in concert 'with the worship of the God of Christianity'. The argument and debate of the diviners impressed Rev. Johnson and 'he took the lesson to heart' (Sanneh 1983, 84).

The Freetown Debate of 1888

The first organised public interreligious debate in Freetown, Sierra Leone, in 1888 was on the topic, 'Is Christianity or Islam best suited to promote the true interests of the Negro race?' (Sanneh 1996, 67–84). The debate was occasioned by Blyden's book, *Christianity, Islam and the Negro Race*, published the previous year. This masterpiece generated great public interest and attention. The debate was fully reported in the local newspaper, *The Artisan*. Unfortunately, *The Artisan* did not record exactly who the participants were, or from which background they came.

Blyden is considered the father of Pan-Africanism and the foremost African intellectual of the nineteenth century. Blyden, although himself a Christian, was also an astute student of Islam, the followers of which he considered to be more authentically African. Although he spent the majority of his career in Liberia, he was a greater intellectual influence in Sierra Leone.

The debate used a parliamentary style in an attempt to minimise 'the risk of the debate turning into a harangue or a one-sided tirade or degenerating into polemic or mutual recrimination' (Sanneh 1996, 68), to averted one-sidedness, and to preclude participants from interrupting the deliberations of the proceedings.

During the course of the debate, speakers dwelt upon the merits of Christianity and of Islam. Speakers in support of Islam emphasised 'the value of Islam as a religious system' and discussed 'its practical beneficial effects on African life' (Sanneh 1996, 70). The Islamic side of the debate made wide use of two authorities, both Christian—namely, Blyden, who had argued that Islam had contributed far more to the advancement of the African people and had made a far more lasting mark on Black culture than had its rival, Christianity, and Canon Isaac Taylor, who had argued that 'Islam was not an anti-Christian faith, but a republication of the faith of Abraham and Moses with Christian elements' (71).

Much was made of the Islamic focus on ethics and morality, as well as the transformative influence this had on African culture, and Islam's numerical successes in Black Africa.

The speakers for Christianity examined the theological claims of each religion and took advantage of the contemporary doctrinal prejudices against Islam. They also sought to discredit the arguments made by the Islamic side by dismissing Canon Taylor as a plagiarist who had quoted R. Bosworth Smith without giving him proper credit, and arguing that Blyden was disingenuous because, although he argued for Islam, he was a practising Christian who argued 'from expediency rather than from principle' (Sanneh 1996, 73). The Christian side also minimised the numerical successes of Islam as a matter of perspective in reading statistics.

CONTEMPORARY INTERRELIGIOUS COOPERATION AND DIALOGUE

Social Factors

Muslims and Christians have attributed the success of Sierra Leone's unique culture of religious tolerance and cooperation to several social factors. Sierra Leoneans share similar familial background. It is not unheard of to find Muslims and Christians in the same clan and family (cf. Foullah 2006, 17; Sesay 2006, 8). Muslims join their Christian relatives, friends, and neighbours in celebrating Christmas, Easter, and various church festivals. Christians also participate in the celebrations of major Muslim festivals, such as Ramadan, *Idul-Fitri*, *Idul-Adha*, and *Maulidu'l-Nabi*—the birthday of the Prophet Muhammad. Because they live together, they share resources.

Intermarriage is another factor that has contributed to the success of religious tolerance. For the Muslims, Islamic law makes provision for the marriage of a Muslim man to a Christian woman because Christians fall under the analytic category of 'People of the Scriptures' (Cole 1983, 3). For several decades, intermarriages between Christians and Muslims have been common practice in Sierra Leone. In most cases, couples make arrangements to have their wedding solemnised in both a church and a mosque on the same day. The ceremony takes place in the bride's place of worship first, followed by that of the groom with friends and relatives belonging to both faith traditions in attendance. Under Sierra Leone law, the first wedding that was solemnised and had the legal papers signed is the legal wedding.

Schools and colleges are composed of Muslim and Christian students. In the current educational system, Islam, Christianity, and ATR are taught under the subject, Religious and Moral Education (RME). Christians donated to the *Alimania* society for the building of the first Temne Islamic School in Freetown (Sesay 2006, 10). The Prince of Wales Secondary School, on their annual Thanksgiving service, students and staff first go to worship at the central mosque and later to the church.

In living memory, state functions normally begin with Muslim and Christian prayers. At opening ceremonies for the start of parliamentary sessions, Muslim and Christian prayers are always offered. Politicians and top government officials continue to participate in Muslim and Christian activities in the country. Religious feelings have never been exploited in Sierra Leone's politics. When I was in the National Pentecostal Limba Church (NPLC), the church openly supported two Muslim candidates who won their seats—one for parliamentary election and the other for ethnic election.

Religious Cooperation in War Camps
It was this long history and tradition of religious cooperation and harmony between Islam and Christianity that provided functional values to the Revolutionary United Front (RUF) rebels in the deep reserves of the fortified jungles of Sierra Leone during the civil war through maintaining religious life, rituals, and worship.

Daily life in the rebel camp began at 6:00 a.m. with compulsory prayers. Absentees were punished. Since every member of the camp was expected to be either Muslim or Christian, different members were appointed each day to lead prayers, which were concluded with a general recitation of the Lord's Prayer, followed by *Al-Fatihah*. Pictures received from the battlefront show most RUF fighters wearing crosses or carrying rosaries or talismans.

Christian and Muslim organisations in Freetown, which was considered relatively safe until the rebel invasion of 6 January 1996, encouraged their congregants to fast and pray. At Sunday worship services and at Friday prayers, sermons of hope and liberation were preached. The Council of Churches in Sierra Leone (CCSL) sent memos to churches instructing them to observe times of prayer. When Captain Valentine Strasser, the head of the military government that ousted the APC party, proclaimed a national week of fasting and prayer for the end of the war, and Muslim and Christian organisations again encouraged their members to support the call of the new head of state.

The Project for Christian-Muslim Relations in Africa (PROCMURA)

The Islam in Africa Project (IAP), which later became PROCMURA, was established in 1959 by churches in Africa, with the support of partner churches in Europe and North America, to foster a better relationship between Christians and Muslims. PROCMURA was established to promote, within the churches in Africa south of the Sahara, Christian witness in a spirit of mutual respect and love, rather than a spirit of confrontation and hostility. The project stressed the place of Islam in Africa and sought to help Christians understand Islam and reach out to their Muslim neighbours. In other words, the church, in its calling, should faithfully interpret the gospel of Christ in the Muslim world and endeavour to attain a deeper understanding of Muslims and Islam, which will ultimately foster a fruitful Christian-Muslim dialogue. Needless to say, practitioners of ATR were not included, even as 'neighbours'.

PROCMURA was introduced in Sierra Leone in the early 1970s (Khanu 2001, 56). It followed the aims and objectives of the wider body. In Sierra Leone, Muslims saw the project as an opportunity to meet and dialogue with their Christian neighbours referred to in the Holy Qur'an as 'People of the Book'. The excitement and reward of the project lasted several years. Conferences and thanksgiving services were held in Freetown and in the hinterland. Several of the conference papers on 'Islam and Christianity' were published by the *Bulletin on Islam and Christian-Muslim Relations in Africa (BICMURA)*. PROCMURA began to decline on account of the lethargy of the churches in owning the project, and the lack of a trained national to succeed the then adviser.

However, during the leadership of the late Bishop Michael Keili of the Anglican Diocese of Bo, the project was able to bring together Christian and Muslim leaders, and conducted several seminars for pastors in the south of the country.

Attempts to establish a national forum for Christian-Muslim dialogue did not materialise on account of fear and misgiving among some Christian leaders that a formal dialogue forum with Muslims was a betrayal of their Missions stance (Khanu 2001, 57). The Muslims, in turn, were suspicious that Christians would use such a dialogue as forum to pursue Muslim conversion.

The work of Bishop Keili did not go in vain. When he was brutalised in Bo, south of the country, by some military personnel of the then military government, Christians and Muslims came together in solidarity across the across the country to condemn the act. Muslims and Christians in Freetown protested to the government and asked for retribution. The officers who committed the act were reportedly disciplined (Khanu 2001, 57).

Although in Sierra Leone, PROCMURA did not thrive as expected and is still struggling to survive, its impact on Africa in general 'has shown impressive interfaith sensitivity among Africans, and nothing dramatises that fact better than the widespread attitude of Muslims and Christians supporting each other's faith, with donations, labour, personal visits, and participation in each other's feasts' (Sanneh 1996, 23). In Sierra Leone, PROCMURA laid the foundation and prepared the way for the realisation of the present IRCSL, which, ironically, is rendering PROCMURA redundant.

Inter-Religious Council of Sierra Leone (IRCSL)

In January 1997, the World Conference on Religion and Peace (WCRP) in New York brought together religious leaders for a consultative meeting that, among other things, introduced the idea of forming a forum for dialogue (Khanu 2001, 57). This resulted in subsequent meetings being held, and the proposal for a wider consultative forum was accepted in principle.

During the civil war, on 1 April 1997, at a one-day national con-ference convened in Freetown that attracted over two hundred Muslim and Christian delegates from areas that were not occupied by rebels in Sierra Leone, two statements were proposed, adopted, and presented to the head of state (Khanu 2001, 57). The two statements, entitled 'Shared Moral Concerns'[1] and 'Shared Values and Common Purpose',[2] were signed by a representative from each of the religious streams— Muslims, Roman Catholics, and Protestants. This officially launched IRCSL.

The objectives of IRCSL that were agreed upon in conjunction with WCRP were to equip and mobilise cooperative efforts among the religious communities in Sierra Leone and to take concrete steps in restoring stability, reconciliation, and renewal to Sierra Leone (Khanu 2001, 58). IRCSL promotes cooperation among the religious commu-nities of Sierra Leone for peace—while maintaining respect for reli-gious differences—works to identify common religious commitments and principles conducive to the peace of the human community, and undertakes actions for peace. The civil war in Sierra Leone brought a new awareness of the imperative to explore new and creative ways to reengage Sierra Leoneans in a meaningful relationship and dialogue. The formation of IRCSL was a step in the right direction.

Shortly after the inception of the IRCSL, the democratically elected Sierra Leone People's Party (SLPP) government was ousted in a military *coup d'état* on 25 May 1997. The IRCSL wasted no time in condemning the action of the military on international radio broadcasting stations, and demanded the return of power to the legitimate government. After nine months in power, the coup plotters were removed in a countercoup, and the SLPP government was reinstated in March 1998. The IRCSL held a joint Muslim-Christian service that was attended by thousands of people at the National Stadium in Freetown in thanksgiving to God for the restoration of the SLPP government.

After the 6 January 1999 'Day of Infamy', when the joint forces of the disbanded Sierra Leone Army and the RUF rebels entered Freetown and reined unfathomable atrocities on the city's people, once things eventually calmed down, the IRCSL called a consultative meeting that was attended by hundreds of leaders and dignitaries to seek a mandate to pursue peace mediation between the rebels and the government. The meeting unanimously mandated leaders of the IRCSL to pursue peace between the rebels and the government. The IRCSL succeeded not only in bringing together the head of state, rebel leaders, and all those who had a part in the conflict, but was able to persuade the warring factions to agree to talk and find a peaceful resolution to the conflict. Seeing the willingness of the warring groups to pursue peace, the Economic Organisation of West African States (ECOWAS), the African Union (AU), the Commonwealth, and the United Nations (UN) agreed to facilitate peace talks in Lome, Togo, West Africa.

These international facilitating groups and the sides in the conflict granted the IRCSL 'Track One' status in peace negotiations (Khanu 2001, 59). The IRCSL proceeded to formulate guidelines based on generally accepted moral principles and the relevant rules of law. The Lome Peace Accord was signed on 7 July 1999.

In January 2000, the IRCSL came up with a working proposal for the reconstruction and renewal in Sierra Leone to be implemented by Muslims and Christians. The proposal covered six areas in which the council intended to participate in the process of reconstruction and renewal:

- Disarmament and demobilisation of the estimated forty-five thousand ex-combatants.
- Unearthing and investigating human rights abuses during the war.
- Addressing the democratisation and special needs of ex-rebels.
- Integration, rehabilitation, and healing of ex–child soldiers.
- The provision of strategic human assistance for ex-soldiers in terms of skills training and reintegration into society.
- National campaign for confession, forgiveness, reconciliation, and renewal.

IRCSL has fully participated in these projects, and the national programme coordinator is proud to report that the council has successfully completed its assignment.

In his paper delivered at the International Congress of Dialogue on Civilizations, Religions and Cultures in West Africa, held at Abuja (Nigeria), 15–17 December 2003, Msgr. Denis Isizoh, of the Pontifical Council for Interreligious Dialogue (PCID) in the Vatican, acclaimed the mediatory role the IRCSL played between the government and the rebels as a successful step that continues to be considered a paradigm for peace initiatives and an inspiration to religious leaders and establishments in Africa to get involved in conflict resolution and become the voice of the marginalised and the voiceless (Isizoh 2005, 33).

Most importantly, interreligious dialogue and cooperation continue to take place between Muslims and Christians on the basis of a common humanity and unity through creation (Khanu 2001, 58). During and after the civil war, various Christian and Muslim organisations set up programmes to provide assistance and welfare to their members who were victims of the war.

Inter-Religious Publications (IRP) Series

The need for constant dialogue and cooperation, and the expression of views in support of harmony and interreligious unity for the common good of Muslims and Christians, gave birth to the launching of the IRP series by the CCSL. The first in the series, *Peaceful Co-Existence in a Multi-Religious Society* (2006), explored the historical and theological aspects of interfaith cooperation, and the affinities Islam and Christianity share as recorded in the Qur'an and the Bible. In the second publication, *War, Peace and Reconciliation* (2006), the authors from Christian and Muslim perspectives summarised their understanding of war, peace, and reconciliation based on the histories and holy scriptures of the two faiths.

The religious pluralistic ideology of PROCMURA and IRCSL can be described as a 'lazy pluralism', where the stances of each religion are obliterated for the sake of harmony. In the present national and global climate, this approach is a step in the right direction.

Challenges

Indeed, Muslims and Christians have had long relationships and cordial coexistence and cooperation in Sierra Leone. But this should not blind us to the fact that there is still prejudice and fanaticism on both sides that erupt occasionally. In 1966 a prominent Muslim politician threatened to turn all the churches into mosques, and likewise, a prominent Christian politician regretted the fact that new mosques were being built in the Christian city of Freetown. In 2000 the government banned a cassette tape recorded by a Muslim that was considered insulting to the Christian faith. In 2005 a conflict between a Muslim woman teaching at Saint Philips Primary School in the east of Freetown and the school's authority almost caused unrest when a large crowd of Muslim youths attempted to set Saint Philips Church on fire; but for the timely intervention of the police and of the IRCSL, the outcome would have been disastrous. These sudden eruptions, as seen in the latter case, have nearly always been kept in check.

As seen from the preceding discussions, African Traditionalists are not included in this unique culture of dialogue. This brings me to the discussion of the reasons given by Muslims and Christians why ATR is still excluded from interfaith cooperation in Sierra Leone.

REASONS FOR THE EXCLUSION OF ATR

Although the brand of Islam in Sierra Leone, as already noted, is syncretistic in nature and there are aspects of ATR that Christianity has adapted, a few Muslims and a majority of Christians hold strong reservations about ATR and do not support the idea of including it yet in Sierra Leone's interreligious dialogue and cooperation. This segment attempts to answer the following questions we identified at the beginning of this book:

- Why have Muslim and Christian leaders long marginalised ATR, its practices, and its practitioners from interfaith dialogue and cooperation in Sierra Leone?

- What is lacking in ATR that continues to prevent practitioners of Christianity and Islam from officially involving Traditionalists in the socioreligious development of the country?

The answers given by Muslims and Christians in Sierra Leone to these questions are not altogether new in African theological discussion. They are the classical responses. Here they are, along with my commentary,

Inherited Prejudices

Muslims and Christians have inherited prejudices from their conservative and insensitive forebears.[3] For many years, converts to Islam, and more so to Christianity, from ATR have been influenced by missionaries to abhor their traditional heritage. It seems that these inherited prejudices continue to hold the All Africa Conference of Churches (AACC) back from reaching out to or dialoguing with African Traditionalists. Islam and Christianity are considered monotheistic faiths and therefore superior to ATR. Although ATR practitioners are no longer labelled by most missionaries and scholars as 'heathens', polytheists', 'fetishists', or 'superstitious', some Muslim and Christian theologians and believers in Sierra Leone continue to use these derogatory epithets in reference to Traditionalists.

This contempt for ATR has been discussed at length by both African and Western scholars (e.g., Lucas 1948, 33; Parrinder 1962, 18; Mbiti 1989a, 8), who have strongly challenged the aforementioned terms as inadequate, derogatory, and prejudicial (Mbiti 1989a, 7; Parrinder 1962, 20–23; cf. Magesa 1997, 19–22). When closely studied, it is apparent that, while elements of each of these designations may be found in ATR, any one of these terms addresses only a minute fraction of African religious beliefs and should not, therefore, be considered singularly adequate to describe ATR.

ATR Lacks the Hallmarks of a True Religion
ATR Lacks Scriptures

Unlike Islam and Christianity, which are referred to as religions of 'the Book', and their followers as 'People of the Book',[4] ATR has no scriptures. In the words of a Sierra Leonean, 'there is a meeting point' between Islam and Christianity,

> a point of agreement to which Allah calls on the People of the Book to take advantage as in sura 3:64…in this verse Allah shows there is a common goal and destiny for both the Muslims and the People of the Book. (Sesay 2006, 4)

Regarding scripture as a hallmark of true religion, Magesa, arguing for a universal recognition of ATR, opposed liberal Western scholars who

> could neither conceive nor allow that a religion dependent on oral traditions, such as African Religion is, could be regarded as an equal…These scholars failed to consider that Judaism, for example, was an orally-based religion for many centuries before its oral story was codified in writing. The same is true for Christianity and Islam, although for a shorter period of time. Other things being equal, orality alone cannot disqualify a religious system from qualitative greatness. In fact, the existence of written scripture must be seen as only one criterion among many. (1997, 22)

This argument is relevant to the Sierra Leonean context. As revealed in Magesa's argument, Judaism, Christianity, and Islam were all accepted as religions before their tenets were written down. They did not attain religious status on account of their sacred writings. This raised the question of why ATR should be treated any differently. ATR theology is written on the hearts, minds, words, actions and symbols of the African people (1997, 3). This is one of the factors responsible for the survival of AR; as long as those who follow ATR are alive, it will never be extinct (Mbiti 1970a, xiv), and they are proud to discuss it, live it out, and pass it on to their children.

ATR Has No Founder or Leader

Unlike Islam and Christianity, ATR does not have an identifiable individual who may be credited with founding the religion, nor does it have a single identifiable leader. Although Islam and Christianity both have people they claim as founders and leaders of their faiths, one cannot help but wonder whether it is an identifiable founder that makes a religion authentic. Indeed, Hinduism, which is widely acknowledged as one of the world's great faiths, has no founder or prophet, and the same may be said of almost any truly organic religion.

ATR Is Not Organised or Institutionalised
Like Islam and Christianity

ATR is neither organised nor institutionalised in the way that Islam and Christianity are. There are no infrastructures such as worship buildings or schools.[5] However, again, one wonders if this is a legitimate hallmark of a true religion.

None of the faith traditions here considered alleges that God's presence is contained in a building. Is it then necessary to build a particular structure in which to worship God? Muslims everywhere in Sierra Leone, especially in the hinterland, pray outside in front of their homes, backyards, business places, and fields during festivals. Christians have open-air evangelical meetings and worship services on street corners and in stadiums. Both Muslims and Christians worship in public. These practices indicate that God is not subject to the limitations of time and space. As such, God is found everywhere. It is because of the belief in God's omnipresence that Muslims and Christians can worship God everywhere.

In Christianity, the church is not a 'building'. It is a body of believers. David's desire to build a 'house for God' was turned down by God who did not need such a dwelling place (2 Sam. 7:1–7). The 'house' his son would build for God would be for God's name (2 Sam. 7:13). At the dedication, Solomon declared that God cannot be contained by the new temple or anything in creation (1 Kings 8:27). God remains free to move as he chooses. Jesus did not refer to any particular place when he said, 'For where two or three are gathered in my name, I am there among them' (Matt. 18:20), and when he later commissioned his disciples, he promised them that he would be with them 'always, to the end of the age' (Matt. 28:20).

ATR practitioners, like Muslims and Christians, make use of God's omnipresence because God is not confined or restricted by time and space. Traditionalists usually pray or worship God directly and at any time and place as needs arise. That is why they take their religion everywhere they go.

One interviewee also mentioned the lack of schools or school buildings in ATR in Sierra Leone. While it is generally agreed that modern education is a good thing, it neither is innately religious nor was it provided by the church in many parts of the world for centuries after Christianity was recognised as a religion. Further, there are Sierra Leoneans who believe that the Western educational system is responsible for the heavy financial burden on families to send their children to school, and for the perpetration of postmodernism, which is gradually destroying African cultures.

ATR Is Primitive and Economically Weak

ATR is archaic, uncouth, and impervious to modern change and civilisation. Apart from the Krio Traditionalists, most ATR practitioners are nonliterate and do not understand modern trends or developments. A considerable number of ATR followers are poor and live in the lower echelons of society. In that regard, as one interviewee put it, 'for us young people coming up, it is a shame to identify one self with ATR practices'.[6] Again, one wonders how being poor or uncivilised diminishes the validity of ones religion. In the Qur'an and the Bible, the poor are held in high esteem by God, and believers are exhorted to take care of them.

Fear of Syncretism and Nominalism

Samartha has identified at least two kinds of syncretism, the one that 'is simply an indiscriminate patching up of incompatible beliefs', and another that centres 'around which elements in the cultural situation are integrated naturally' (1981, 27). Many Christians in Sierra Leone are opposed to both kinds of syncretism.

To guard against syncretism and nominalism, Christian leaders in the IRCSL and churches continue a policy of zero tolerance on the question of any cultural accommodation.[7] Christians think it is not right to mix elements of ATR into Christianity.[8] Therefore, as Schreiter put it, 'anything that would dilute or substantially alter the basic structures of Christianity' is strongly combated (1985, 144).

Kato, in his last lectures, called for a strong, biblically based Christianity in Africa and for a critique of syncretism in African churches. He asked, 'Should the revealed Christian faith be sacrificed at the altar of syncretistic universalism, in the guise of contextualisation?'[9] For the church, Kato's observation is still relevant: 'Just as syncretism plagued the church in the days of the apologists, so it challenges the historic faith in Africa today' (1987, 25). In view of this, the church enforces 'a complete break with the past' (Olson 1969, 192) as a preventive measure against 'syncretism and nominalism' (206).

Ariarajah has classified 'syncretism' as one of 'the three classical fears' of the missionary enterprise. The WCC Nairobi assembly in 1975 declared, 'We are all opposed to any forms of syncretism, incipient, nascent or developed, if we mean by syncretism conscious or unconscious human attempts to create a new religion composed of elements taken from different religions' (Ariarajah 1999, 102). As noted in the WCC's 'Guidelines on Dialogue with People of Living Faiths and Ideologies', the Nairobi assembly declaration clearly conveys a negative view of syncretism (Kinnamon and Cope 1997, 409). Syncretism has been used to warn against two major dangers:

- First, there is danger 'in attempting to "translate" the Christian message for a cultural setting or in approach to faiths and ideologies with which Christians are in dialogue partnership, they may go too far and compromise the authenticity of Christian faith and life. They have the Bible to guide them but there is always risk in seeking to express the Gospel in a new setting'.
- Second, there is danger in 'interpreting a living faith not in its own terms but in terms of another faith or ideology'. (Kinnamon and Cope 1997, 409)

It is ironic that Christians in Sierra Leone are concerned about syncretism when, as already noted, many of those same Christians blend ATR with Christian practices. Neither Islam nor Christianity can honestly claim complete immunity from syncretism. As they live in multicultural and multifaith communities, various elements of other religions have gone into their making. Historically, Islam and Christianity have both incorporated elements of other religions and cultures. For example, the form of Christianity that is most widely practiced today is a mixture of 'Hebrew-Hellenic-Graeco-Latin-Celtic-Gothic…' religiocultures (Samartha 1981, 29).

Does syncretism pose a danger to the integrity of Islam and Christianity? The words of Chenchiah, as quoted by Samartha (1981, 30) are helpful in answering this question: 'syncretism…is a bogey. Let us not turn it into a bugbear. Let us not be lured into a pursuit of shadows when far more urgent and decisive realities challenge our faith'. Islam and Christianity are 'in danger of being considered as the debris left behind by the receding tide of colonialism' (27) and missionary prejudices, if their fears of syncretism keep them from their neighbours.

The UCC provides a positive example by appropriately incorporating Aboriginal spirituality in worship when the opportunity arises during church functions. Aboriginal groups within the UCC have established a conference, called All Native Circle, which blends native spirituality and Christianity.

ATR Practitioners Are Already Muslims

Muslims feel that because of the prevalent dual religious practices in the country, most practitioners of ATR are at least nominally Muslims and, as such, they are already part of the ongoing interreligious cooperation in the country. The reason for this belief is that many ATR practitioners already participate in certain Muslim rituals and, in time of crisis, will turn to Islamic practice.

From the five reasons already given, one can conclude that 'it is the stock-in-trade' of Muslim and Christian leaders in Africa 'to put down Traditional African Religion, to look down on it, and not to accept it as a valid religion' (Abimbola 2005, 37).

In that regard, perhaps by defining religion, one can see if ATR meets the standard of a true religion. Tremmel, in trying to find a good working definition of 'religion', stated at the outset that 'a good definition of religion is hard to come by, mostly because it must incorporate an enormous array of beliefs and activities all the way from magic to mysticism, from private prayer to sacred community' (1983, 3). To remedy the situation, scholars of differing interests have come up with their own varying definitions of religion.[10]

Tremmel (1983, 4) identified two aspects that constitute religion, namely, the 'functional', which deals with the purpose, content, and benefits of religion, and the 'sacred', which deals with 'the experience of something mysterious and magnificent' that happens to religious practitioners. In other words,

> religion is both something that people do to deal with certain elements of their own finitude and something that happens to them that is mysterious, tremendous, and wonderfully renovating... a definition of religion must include both the functional and the sacred experience aspects of religion. (7)

Religion is something imperceptible and mysterious. All religions are based on faith and mystery. Because of these qualities, there are beliefs and practices in each religious system that deny human logic and understanding. That God allowed his son to die for the sins of the world is a mystery that Christians believe and accept by faith. Similarly, ATR belief in the power of the ancestors, in sacrifice, and in charms and medicines is a mystery that the practitioners have accepted by faith.

The expression of belief through practice and teaching makes ATR both sacred and functional. Religion can, of course, include a wide range of beliefs, practices, and cultural behaviours, and each religion, whether organised or organic, consists of different amounts of each of these elements. Although ATR, Islam, and Christianity are different in several ways, they share many of the same characteristics, as proven in this chapter.

Conclusion

ATR and its practitioners have long been marginalised in interreligious cooperation in Sierra Leone. Since the nineteenth century, there have been religious debates and cooperation between Muslims and Christians. This interreligious cooperation has benefited Sierra Leone immensely, and today the country is proud of the outstanding contribution the IRCSL made to bring the decade-long civil war to end, and to further help in the rehabilitation process. The international facilitating groups (ECOWAS, AU, and UN) for peace in Sierra Leone, and the warring factions, were right to grant the IRCSL 'Track One' status in peace negotiations for a job well done. Ariarajah is correct in noting that

> attempting to promote dialogue or inter-communal, interfaith harmony during or soon after a conflict…is a frustrating exercise. Communities by now are deeply polarized, confused and uncertain about who can be trusted. Solidarity across to the other community is often misunderstood as betrayal. Efforts to bring about peace and reconciliation do have their legitimate place in such situations, but they call for different methods and skills. (1999, 13)

There are several factors preventing Muslims and Christians from entertaining the idea of including Traditionalists in the ongoing interfaith cooperation in the country. Taking into consideration the discovery in the previous chapter that ATR shares affinity with Islam and Christianity, along with the issues addressed in this chapter, I do not deem plausible the reasons that Muslims and Christians give for the preclusion of ATR. It appears that some Muslims and Christians are not conversant with either their respective faith's development/tenets or with the basic teachings and beliefs of ATR to know that it shares many values in common with Islam and Christianity, and that ATR has the qualities of a true religion.

ENDNOTES

1. See appendix B for full statement.
2. See appendix C for full statement.
3. Rev. Moses Khanu, interviewed 18 May 2006 in Freetown.
4. Rev. Moses Khanu, interviewed 18 May 2006, in Freetown.
5. Mbompa Mansaray, interviewed 6 June 2006, in Makeni, Northern Province.
6. Sawudu Bangura, interviewed 15 June 2006, in Freetown.
7. Rev. Moses Khanu, interviewed 18 May 2006, in Freetown.
8. Rev. Tamba A. Koroma, interviewed 9 May 2006, and Rev. Olivia Wesley, interviewed 10 May 2006, in Freetown.
9. Kato (1987, 15).
10. For example, the eighteenth-century philosopher Immanuel Kant, the German theologian Friedrich Schleiermacher, and the sociologist of religion J. Milton Yinger (Tremmel 1983, 3,7), as well as the nineteenth- and early twentieth-century anthropologist Edward Taylor (Tremmel 1983, 3; Mbiti 1989a, 7).

PART IV

THE CHALLENGE

The following chapter, 'The Place and Recognition of ATR in Interreligious Cooperation', discusses the role and recognition of ATR both inside and outside of Africa, as a means for Islam and Christianity to give ATR its rightful place, and encourages these immigrant religions to face the challenge to put aside prejudice and to recognise and involve ATR in interfaith cooperation in Sierra Leone.

CHAPTER 7

THE PLACE
AND RECOGNITION OF ATR
IN INTERRELIGIOUS COOPERATION

This book has shown so far that Islam and Christianity are not yet prepared or do not have the expertise to include ATR practitioners in interfaith dialogue and cooperation in Sierra Leone. It appears that Muslims and Christians are reluctant even to acknowledge the contributions of Traditionalists in the socioreligious landscape of Sierra Leone. This tendency is not unique to Sierra Leone, as Muslims and Christians in many sub-Saharan African countries are struggling with the same issue.

I now discuss the place and recognition of ATR in contemporary Sierra Leone, in external secular and religious circles, and conclude with the necessity for dialogue and inclusion of Traditionalists in the ongoing interfaith dialogue and cooperation in the country.

THE PLACE AND RECOGNITION OF ATR IN SIERRA LEONE

The Place of ATR in Sierra Leone's National Politics

Over the past several decades, successive Sierra Leonean governments have recognised, encouraged, and promoted traditional religiosity in national politics. Like many other African politicians, Sierra Leonean politicians take their religion with them 'to the house of parliament' (Mbiti 1989a, 2). Sierra Leoneans have generally attributed the incorporation and promotion of ATR practices into national politics to two Limba heads of state from 1968–1992: Dr. Siaka P. Stevens and Maj. Gen. Joseph S. Momoh. It is believed that these two men, who were both leaders of the APC party,[1] popularised the idea of traditional religiosity as a way to achieve and maintain power. They made some government and political organisations see 'in traditional religion a potential source of reinforcement and legitimation for their activities' (Hackett 1991, 141). The supernatural became a very important element in politics, which encouraged many members of parliament to ally themselves with diviners or soothsayers.

Throughout the APC rule, both high-ranking politicians and those of lesser influence sought out the help of diviners and fortune-tellers to win and to keep their seats, or to gain favour with those in higher authority when seeking more lucrative political positions (Opala and Boillot 1996, 5).[2] The belief that it was not possible to attain political prominence without the help of these sacred specialists brought a great deal of deception into politics with sometimes disastrous results.[3] Political predators busied themselves trying to hunt down their supposed enemies/victims. It is believed that some politicians engaged the services of sacred specialists to kill their opponents through spiritual means.

Sacred specialists have taken advantage of the situation to make themselves rich by sending messages of concern to the politicians advising them on what traditional steps to take. These messages often warn politicians about their enemies who are trying to get rid of them; they predict coups and assassination attempts (Shaw 1996, 40).

The pouring of libation was reintroduced at public and state functions during the APC regime.[4] At these functions, libation is poured to seek God's guidance, blessing, and protection.

The Place of ATR in Finding and Maintaining Employment

ATR practices are also prominent when people are finding or applying for employment in either the private or government sectors. Because there is a high level of bureaucracy and political interference in these sectors, applicants who lack political backing often resort to traditional religious methods to secure a job.[5] The applicant approaches the sacred specialist with the belief that only God can make the impossible possible. This belief gives the applicant the faith that God is greater than the officials handling the application and has the power to touch their hearts to employ him/her.

For some applicants, visits to the sacred specialist do not end once they have gained employment. In a job culture where employers/supervisors may sack employees at will, employees are in a constant struggle to ensure that they keep their jobs. With the guidance and help of a sacred specialist, prayers and sacrifices for job security are offered to God through the ancestors, and the employee is given either a religious object or a potion to mystically make those in authority like him/her. It is wrongly believed that almost anyone who rises rapidly to a high ranking position is either dealing with a spirit or being helped by a sacred specialist.

The Place of ATR in the Judicial System

Another area that was/is prominent in traditional spirituality is the national judicial system. Sierra Leoneans who do not trust the national judiciary system, or who feel they will not receive a fair trial because of prejudice and injustice in high places through the constant interference of politicians and the government, solicit the help of sacred specialists for a favourable outcome. This is especially likely with high-profile matters such as treason, homicide, or the misappropriation and embezzlement of public funds. For this reason, the family and friends of the accused desperately search for renowned sacred specialists to offer sacrifice so that their loved ones might receive justice and be acquitted.[6]

The Role of Indigenous Religion in Sierra Leone's Civil War

Sierra Leone's ten-year civil war (1991–2002), commonly referred to as the 'rebel war', attracted great international attention. Its suggested causes, its cultural, political, and sociological dynamics, and its impacts are well documented.[7] In that regard, I will only discuss the role played by indigenous religion on the battlefield.

Sierra Leone's army had participated in the two world wars under the umbrella of the British, and had sent platoons on UN and regional military and peacekeeping missions; however, the army had been considered primarily 'ceremonial' and had never before fought a large-scale war on a home front. Several months after the 1991 outbreak of civil war, it became evident that the army was ill equipped and largely unprepared for combat. At the time the war broke out, there were approximately three thousand soldiers, and although that number was subsequently increased to sixteen thousand, there was still no strong military or police presence in the hinterland, and the people there were left vulnerable to the sporadic attacks by the RUF guerrilla fighters. On account of the lack of logistics and an unprepared army, the APC government came to believe that their only hope for victory was some form of supernatural intervention.[8] This led the government to make a public announcement on national radio encouraging all citizens, especially those in the hinterland, to use whatever traditional means or power they had to combat the rebels.

This call by the government gave birth to several ethnic defence groups in the hinterland. The *Tamaboro* group was formed by the Kuranko and Yalunka people in the north. This group was later joined by some Limba people who were said to have been recruited from the Warawara Bafodea Limba chiefdom, a place that is particularly noted for its attachment to traditional beliefs in Sierra Leone.[9] The *Gbeti* and *Kapra* groups were formed by the Temne in the north. The *Kamajoi* was formed by the Mende people in the south and the east, and the *Donsa* was formed by the Kono in the east. Members of these groups were mostly hunters who belonged to secret societies and were believed to be experts in traditional spirituality and medicine. On the battlefield, they used not only conventional arms and 'witch guns', but also, through spirituals means, used killer bees to attack and destabilise the rebels. It is believed that some rebels even died from the painful stings of the bees. The supernatural ability to turn daylight into darkness was another effective method used by these fighters to prevent the rebels from seeing where they were going. The traditional fighters could see the rebels but the rebels were unable to see the approaching traditional militia. It is also believed that many rebels were killed through these means. Although each ethnic defence group employed its own strategies, one thing that was common among all of them was the use of a protective traditional outfit called *huronko/ronko*.

The traditional militias were not the only ones to use African traditional means to fight. The rebels also made use of their own traditional religious powers to frustrate the efforts of the ethnic defence groups.

The Testimony of the TRC on the
Traditional Contributions and Values

It is through the SLPP government's TRC that the contribution of traditional religiosity and culture is appreciated and fully acknowledged. I here quote *in extenso* what the final report of the TRC on the subject 'Traditional values and methods informing reconciliation' stated:

> During the Interim phase of the Commission, the Office of the High Commissioner for Human Rights (OHCHR) contracted a local organisation…to conduct research on traditional methods of conflict resolution and reconciliation in Sierra Leone. While the report did not address all the issues the TRC had to deal with, it nonetheless provided a basis for the Commission's reconciliation policy. It covered the views of four ethnic groups on traditional practices on how to deal with conflict and reconciliation in relation to murder, burglary, arson, land, marital

conflict, assault and injury. The report confirmed that most Sierra Leoneans, irrespective of whether they follow the Muslim or Christian faith, still cling to traditional animist beliefs. It also confirmed that most of the ethnic groups have belief systems that promote truth telling and reconciliation. Truth telling, swearing or curse casting (or the threat of it) is an essential element of spiritual justice to encourage voluntary confession. The perpetrator can undergo cleansing or purification, or benefit directly from a pardon by society and thus be in peace with himself and with the community. All of the various ethnic groups have their own traditional mechanisms of conflict resolution, which can be used to deal with many of the violations committed during the conflict…However, given the amnesty established by the Lomé Agreement, traditional methods can be adjusted and applied to those violations too, as a condition for the integration of ex-combatants. Reunification ceremonies all over the country testify that such methods are already being widely applied. (*Report of the Truth and Reconciliation Commission of Sierra Leone* 2004, 3b: ch. 7, par. 32–36)

Caritas[10] Makeni applied such methods during reunification ceremonies for abducted children. When Caritas reunified child ex-combatants with their families, they allowed the families to use traditional methods to 'change the hearts' of their children through a combination of care, support, and ritual action. In most cases, the eldest member of the family prayed over a cup of water and rubbed it over the child's body (especially the head, feet, and chest), asking God and the ancestors to give the child a 'cool heart', a state of reconciliation and stability in which the child is settled in the home, a proper relationship with family and community, and the child is not troubled by nightmares and bad memories. Some parents would then drink the consecrated water that had washed their child. In this case, the consecrated water becomes the new physical bond between parent and child. In addition, some parents would offer kola nuts, and some would use liquid Qur'anic slate water; others would make a 'fol sara' ['chicken sacrifice'] to thank the ancestors and God, either dedicating a chicken and caring for it thereafter, or slaughtering and cooking it with rice as an offering to poor people or to a Muslim ritual specialist to eat (par. 37–38):

> Traditional methods of conflict resolution are not inert. They are dynamic and are capable of being adapted to deal with the kinds of violations committed during the war in Sierra Leone. Since reconciliation in Sierra Leone involves traditional values and beliefs, the reconciliation process cannot move forward without the participation of the religious and traditional leaders. (par. 39)

Article 7(2) of the TRC Act explicitly refers to the assistance from traditional and religious leaders in facilitating reconciliation as follows:

> The inter-faith community in Sierra Leone has played an important role in the negotiations for peace and is still one of the strongest support networks for people affected by the war. In view of the limited mandate of the TRC, partnerships with religious and traditional leaders have become all the more important. The dialogue that has started between various groups and the community can continue with the presence of these leaders. Traditional and religious leaders can help make reconciliation more sustainable. Traditional and religious leaders were involved in all the activities of the Commission, including truth telling and conflict resolution sessions, sensitisation activities, statement taking, the hearings and the reconciliation initiatives. They were consulted as to where monuments and memorials should be established. Community members assisted in identifying the sites of mass graves and torture chambers. They will continue the follow-up exercise with witnesses and implement the reconciliation programme funded by the UNDP.

From the Sierra Leone government's perspective, through this document, there is a place for traditional religious values and cultural practices. As seen from the preceding discussions, unlike Muslim and Christian organisations, successive governments have identified the place and importance of ATR in Sierra Leone.

I now give an overview of the progress and level of the recognition of ATR outside of Sierra Leone in an attempt to see how major regional and global secular and religious organisations have recognised and are recognising the place of ATR, which may serve as an inspiration to Muslims and Christians in Sierra Leone.

THE PROGRESS, PLACE, AND LEVEL OF THE RECOGNITION OF ATR OUTSIDE SIERRA LEONE

The Société Africaine de Culture (SAC) in France, which was borne out of the inspiration of the Négritude movement that was founded in 1934, was interested not only in the promotion of African literature and politics, but in African theology as well. It was partly on account of this interest that participants of the Congress of Black Writers and Artists meeting in Paris, France, in 1956 unanimously declared that ATR is the depot of African values and Black identity without which the construction of African theology would not be possible. Four years later, when the group was meeting in Rome, Italy, Pope John XXIII told participants that the RCC had been following with interest the impressive work of the congress, and endorsed the objectives of the group. These early African organisations in Europe undoubtedly contributed to the recognition of ATR and culture, especially by the RCC.

The AACC meeting in Ibadan in 1958 stated that,

> while the church cannot give a Christian content to every African custom, we believe that the church throughout Africa has a very rich contribution to make to the life of the world church. Under God's guidance she will be enriched by the wealth which African culture can bring to her life. (1958, 72)

The AACC later sponsored the first conference of African theologians in Ibadan, January 1966, on the theme, 'Biblical revelation and African beliefs' (Mbiti 1989b, 61). From that time, noted Mbiti, 'practically all African theologians say something more or less on the encounter between the two religions' (1996, 174). The AACC continues to promote dialogue between Christians and members of other faith communities. This dialogue, however, is promoted to a greater degree with Islam than with ATR.

Vatican II's monumental 'Declaration on the Relation of the Church to Non-Christian Religions' (*Nostra Aetate*), released on 28 October 1965, encouraged Christians to 'enter with prudence and charity into discussion and collaboration with members of other religions'. The document further states, 'Let Christians, while witnessing to their own faith and way of life, acknowledge, preserve and encourage the spiritual and moral truths found among non-Christians' (Flannery 1987, 739).

After Vatican II, the publication of Pope Paul VI's apostolic message *Africae Terrarum* in 1967 commended the value of ATR and culture, and went on to encourage Africans to cherish and maintain their spiritual heritage.

In 1968, in an effort to widen the knowledge of ATR, the then Vatican Secretariat for Non-Christians (later renamed Pontifical Council for Interreligious Dialogue—PCID—in 1988), published a booklet entitled *Meeting the African Religions*. PCID's first colloquium, entitled, 'L'Evangile de Jésus-Christ et la Rencontre des Religions Traditionnelles' met in Abidjan, West Africa, 29 July–3 August 1996. The acts of the colloquium are published in *Pro Dialogo* 94 (1997). PCID later held a second colloquium with the theme, 'Resources for peace in traditional religions', 12–15 January 2005, in Rome, Italy. The acts of this meeting are published in *Pro Manuscripto* (2006). The PCID has held a series of consultations and carried out several publications on ATR (Oborji 2002, 5). It continues to be convinced of the importance of paying greater attention to ATR.

In response to the recommendation of the Vatican II, *Ecclesiae Sanctae* 3, 6 August 1966, to set up study facilities for research (1987, 857–862), Vincent Mulago, an ordained Francophone cleric and scholar, established in 1967 Centre d'Etudes des Religions Africaines at the Catholic Faculties of Theology in Kinshasa, Zaire. This research centre for ATR has produced high-level research and publications of several books, and has organised several symposia on ATR and culture.

In recognition of the place of ATR in interfaith cooperation, Pope John Paul II in 1986 invited Togbui Assenou and Amegawi Attiwoto Klousse from Togo, and Okomfo Kodwo Akom from Ghana, practitioners of ATR, to participate in the day of prayer in Assisi, Italy.

In 1993, through the patronage of the government of Benin, West Africa, the Voodoo religion held an international Voodoo festival. When Pope John Paul II visited Benin later that year, he addressed Voodoo practitioners. These two incidents—the internal festival and the recognition by the pope—gave Voodoo religion an outstanding boost and recognition. The government has declared 10 January, the national day for the celebration of Voodoo festival, a public holiday in Benin. In fact, ATR is held as a quasi-state religion in the country. On 24 January 2004, when Pope John Paul II invited religious leaders for another day of prayer for world peace, among his invitees was a Voodoo priest from Benin.

The RCC's theological evaluation of other religions, including ATR, 'has gone all the way from the disregard and rejection which characterised much of Christian tradition, through a guarded acceptance and openness, to a positive assessment and recognition of salutary values' (Ryan 2004, 19).

In 1971 the Central Committee of the WCC that met in Addis Ababa, Ethiopia, recognised that the engagement of the WCC in dialogue is to be understood as a common undertaking of the Christian church. The church has a mandate to foster dialogue in a spirit of reconciliation and hope. Since the development of the 'Guidelines on Dialogue with People of Living Faiths and Ideologies' in Chiang Mai, China, in 1979, the WCC continues to take 'significant steps towards facilitating inter-religious relations and dialogue' (WCC 2003, 4).

A joint project for Africa was formed in 2000 by the Office on Inter-Religious Relations and Dialogue (OIRRD) of the WCC and the PCID to explore Africa's contributions to religious plurality. The main objective of OIRRD and PCID has been to 'provide space for various aspects of African religiosity and culture as a constructive and resourceful contribution to religious plurality' (Conteh 2005, 249). The organisers

> want to make available a forum that not only gives visibility to problems in Africa, but to the many deeply spiritual contributions which Africa provides to the manifold expression of the Christian faith, Islam, and ATR both on and off the continent. (249)

At its first meeting called to formulate strategies to carry out this joint project—which took place in Enugu, Nigeria, from 8–13 January 2001—participants came from various parts of Africa, Madagascar, the United Kingdom, Europe, the United States, and the Caribbean. In 2002 the project held a Francophone meeting in Dakar, Senegal, and another was held for Anglophones in Addis Ababa, Ethiopia, in 2004.

Twenty-seven delegates from Buddhist, Christian, Hindu, Muslim, Jewish, and Yoruba Religious traditions met 12–16 May 2006, for an interreligious consultation on 'Conversion—assessing the reality' at Lariano, Italy, organised by the PCID and the OIRRD (WCC, 2006, 46). The deliberations were described as 'intense, and took place in an atmosphere of cordiality, mutual respect and commitment to learn from one another's spiritual heritage, which together constitute the common inheritance of the entire humankind'. Although the consultation was unable to resolve the many differences and disagreements among the delegates, its deliberations helped the participants develop a convergent understanding of the aspects of religious conversion, and made them more aware of one another's concerns.

The consultations and workshops that have been held so far by the joint project have brought together Christians, Muslims, and followers of ATR from within Africa as well as representatives of some of the various religious communities of Africa in the diaspora. The project continues to make provision for the discussion of various aspects of African religiosity and culture.

At the Critical Movement conference in June 2005, which brought together 130 participants of different faiths, including indigenous religions, 'the WCC manifested its commitment to be involved in the present and future of Interreligious relations and dialogue' (Ukco 2005, 2).

THE NECESSITY OF DIALOGUE WITH, AND THE INCLUSION OF, ATR IN INTERFAITH COOPERATION IN SIERRA LEONE

The inclusion of ATR in interfaith dialogue and cooperation seems to be a difficult task for leaders of Islam and Christianity in Africa to undertake.

On account of the syncretistic brand of Islam practiced in Sierra Leone, Muslims do not see the rationale of coming together with Traditionalists for a dialogue. Christians talk about the intention to at least meet with Traditionalists for a discussion, but have never followed through on their intention. A wall of prejudice and other factors discussed in the previous chapter continue to hinder a possible dialogue among ATR, Islam, and Christianity.

The hope for a possible traditional dialogue and inclusion of ATR in Sierra Leone's interfaith cooperation now rests on the IRCSL. However, the IRCSL is not yet convinced that it is time to foster a dialogical relationship with Traditionalists, and apart from the reservations Muslims and Christians hold against ATR, leaders of Islam and Christianity are neither theologically nor methodologically equipped to begin dialogue with Traditionalists. These shortcomings do not, however, mean that there is no hope for a dialogue among ATR, Islam, and Christianity in Sierra Leone.

The Necessity for Dialogue With ATR

The traditional form of dialogue that brings parties together for a sensitive and respectfully discussion to foster a better relationship and recognition is a necessity. The differences in values and worldviews do not mean that dialogue will be futile or unproductive, because such a dialogue is not solely about accepting the opposite at all cost. Rather, it is about recognising 'the right of the opposite party to assert its own opinion in an atmosphere of freedom, mutual respect, sincerity and objectivity' (Bidmos 1993, 3).

On the basis of the Qur'anic verse that reads,

> Say, O people of the Book, come to an equitable word between us and you, that we shall serve none but Allah and that we shall not associate aught with Him, and that some of us shall not take others for lords besides Allah. But if they turn away, then say, Bear witness, we are Muslims (3:64),

some Muslim leaders in Sierra Leone assert that 'constructive dialogue is not only permitted, it is commendable' (Jah 1987, 1). And the methodology of such a dialogue is further explained in the Qur'an: 'Invite to the way of your Lord with wisdom and beautiful exhortation and argue with them in ways that are best' (16:125).

However, for most Sierra Leonean Muslims, this constructive dialogue is limited to the 'People of the Book'—Jews and Christians. A few Muslims in support of a dialogue between Islam and ATR have argued that sura 3:64 can equally be applied to religions other than Judaism and Christianity. Very little has been written or said about Islam's dialogue with ATR.

As for Christianity, although little has been done to dialogue with ATR, several initiatives have been taken and a lot has been written about Christianity's position on dialoguing with ATR. For a considerable portion of his papacy, Pope John Paul II was insistent in encouraging Christians to be committed to interfaith dialogue. On his visit to Belgium in 1986, the pope encouraged people of all religious backgrounds 'to come to know one another better, to engage in dialogue in order to find peaceful ways of living together and mutually enriching one another'. This process of mutual emulation, he believed, 'can benefit the whole society, especially those who find themselves most in need of justice, consolation and hope'. In his 1991 encyclical (*Redemptoris Missio*, 56), he stated, 'Each member of the faithful and all Christian communities are called to practice dialogue' (Gioia 2006, 110). This means that dialogue with the practitioners of other religions should be a vital component of the church's mission. It is a call to all Christian individuals, communities, and institutions to be involved in dialogue with non-Christians.

The Special Synod of Bishops of Africa (SSBA) came up with several reasons why the church must dialogue with practitioners of ATR:

- Irrespective of the religious difference, the church must dialogue with African Traditionalists since 'the living God, creator of heaven and earth and Lord of history, is the Father of one great human family to which we all belong'. In that regard, God wants Christians to bear witness to him through their 'respect for the values and religious traditions of each person, working together for human progress and development at all levels. (Gioia 2006, 119)

- Dialogue with ATR is crucial because it is still a force to reckon with in Africa. It is still strong and practised in most parts of Africa.

- Dialogue with ATR will reveal many shared values between Christianity and ATR that may serve as an indispensable tool for inculturation. However, the SSBA made it clear that, 'there can be no serious inculturation without dialogue with ATR where our religious values have their natural habitat'. (Gioia 2006, 119)

The Ninth Assembly of the WCC that met in Porto Alegre, Brazil, in February 2006 realised with interest how much the issue of inter-faith dialogue has impacted and influenced the WCC. The formulations of the institutional committees of the assembly stated, 'Interreligious dialogue is now more than ever an expression of the Council's essential identity engaging in the world, diffusing tensions, peacemaking, protecting human dignity and the rights of religious minorities' (Ukco 2006, 2).

Dialogue is necessary because it is a process of mutual empowerment, a cooperative and collaborative activity in which participants grow in faith, their faith is affirmed, and relations are nurtured (WCC 2003, 9–11). For people who live in mixed societies to understand one another and live in peace, there is need for dialogue.

If faith traditions are 'indeed committed to justice and peace, and are convinced of the need to struggle towards a reconciled human community, we seem to have no real alternative to dialogue…Where dialogue ends, the forces of darkness take over' (Ariarajah 1999, 21).

Dialogue of Life or in Community
Dialogue is not limited to people coming together and making pleasant, optimistic, carefully guarded statements, and showing sensitivity and respect to others. As evident in the actions of the Pope John Paul II, dialogue is more than mere talk and rhetoric. Again, in his 1991

encyclical (*Redemptoris Missio*, 56–57), on the issue of the necessity for interreligious dialogue, John Paul II stated that dialogue may not always be practised in the 'same degree or in the same way. For most, this will be through what is called the dialogue of life' (Gioia 2006, 110).

People living side by side meet and interact personally and communally on a regular basis. As such, they share common resources, communal benefits, and the joys, crises, and sorrows of life. The social and cultural interaction and cooperation involved in this dialogue of life are what compel people to fully understand the worldviews of their neighbours and to seek out better relationships with them.

As already indicated in this study, in most Sierra Leonean families and institutions, you will find people of various religious backgrounds. Humankind is born into relationships with other people. The communities to which people belong are held together with others by the cultures and values they share in common.

The question is whether Muslims and Christians in Sierra Leone are aware of the fact that they are sharing life with Traditionalists, and if so, when will something be done to get Traditionalists involved? The truth is, Muslims and Christians cannot exist without concern for and involvement with Traditionalists, with whom they share culture, history, and common humanity.

Dual Religiosity

As already noted, many Muslims and Christians in Sierra Leone are still influenced by their African heritage and spirituality. At various and critical times in their lives, many Muslims and Christians have resorted to ATR practices. For example, I was born into a Christian family in Freetown, and as in many other Limba Christian homes, the veneration of ancestral and nonancestral spirits was occasionally practised. Sacrifices and offerings to the supernatural were offered when necessary. Charms were hung on our doorpost for protection against witchcraft and evil spirits, and other traditional religious beliefs were practised to various degrees.

After completing secondary school, I got the opportunity to work as a helper in the NPLC. There I realised I was not the only one who emanated from a dual religionist family. For at the annual adult baptismal services, candidates were asked to give up their traditional charms and objects, and those who felt convicted of 'sin' brought them to be destroyed by fire before they were baptised. The leaders of the church did their best to discourage members from practising Limba traditional religion, but their efforts were to no avail. To date, candidates for baptism still bring their 'objects of worship' to the church for destruction.

Later on, as a minister in the Methodist Church, Sierra Leone (MCSL), in all the Freetown circuits I served, occasionally letters were received from church members belonging to hunters' societies asking for permission to use our churches for thanksgiving services. A considerable number of members in the MCSL are also members of various secret societies.

This situation of the persistence of ATR and culture in the church, and the refusal of African Christians to give it up completely in favour of Christianity, has created a tension between Christianity and ATR that has attracted the attention of scholars and religionists.

Some Christians have joined indigenous churches where they are free to experience certain elements of their African culture. Muslims and Christians should not be so naïve as to deny the strong influence ATR has on Islam and Christianity in Sierra Leone. This influence makes it crucial for Muslims and Christians to dialogue with ATR practitioners in an attempt to find out what is lacking in Islam and Christianity that prevents Muslims and Christians from making a full commitment to their new religions, and to identify the common ground and elements that could be adopted or adapted.

I now move on to offer a few practical considerations. Although these considerations may not be completely new in dialogical circles, in the context of the interfaith dialogue in Sierra Leone, they may prove to be helpful guidelines for mapping out possible strategies for a mutual understanding among the three religions, and an inclusion of ATR in interfaith dialogue and cooperation.

Some Practical Considerations
Respect and Tolerance

If Islam and Christianity are serious about dialoguing with ATR, it is vital for Muslim and Christian leaders to accept the validity of ATR (Abimbola 2005, 37). All the faiths of the world are valid. In the same vein, the SSBA held in Rome from 10 April to 8 May 1994 advised that ATR should be 'treated with great respect and esteem, and all inaccurate and disrespectful language should be avoided' (Gioia 2006, 120). Similarly, in almost identical words to that of the SSBA's, Pope John Paul II has urged all Christians to treat ATR practitioners with great respect and esteem (Gioia 2006, 115).

The Policy Reference Committee of the WCC appreciated the strong reaffirmation of dialogue by the council as outlined in the reports of the moderator and the general secretary. It supports that

> forming and deepening constructive, respectful, intentional relationships with others in this pluralistic world is one of the most important efforts the WCC can model for its ecumenical partners and for member churches at the international and grassroots levels. (Ukco 2006, 2)

Participants in dialogue should 'strive towards mutual respect', and 'it is important to respect the integrity of religious traditions in the variety of their structures and organisations' (WCC 2003, 10).

Christians and Muslims should endeavour to put into practice the tolerance and respect they preach by tolerating and respecting other religious faiths. Pope John Paul II was a good example in that regard.

Education

On the basis that valid discussion can only occur when both parties understand the subject matter, Muslim and Christian leaders must find ways and means to educate themselves about, and develop methods of relating their scriptures and teachings to, ATR values. Certain Muslim and Christian leaders have suggested similar concepts, at least in theory.

Adegbite, the secretary general of the Supreme Council for Islamic Affairs in Nigeria, proposed that in order to produce a better understanding of and regard for other religions, all practitioners 'must be taught the elements of their own religion as well as those of other faiths in their community' (2005, 36).

SSBA recommended that suitable courses in ATR 'should be given in houses of formation for priests and religion' (Gioia 2006, 120). The AACC, during its first assembly in Uganda, Kampala, made the following statement:

> The church should study traditional African beliefs. Traditional African culture is not all bad; neither was everything good. As in all cultures, there were positive factors that held the culture together; there were negative factors which degraded human personality. The churches should become involved in a serious dialogue between the traditional worldview and the continuing revelation of Jesus Christ through the scriptures. (1963, 48)

Religious practitioners need not only to know and appreciate their own religious heritage, but also to have an informed knowledge of the beliefs of other faiths, and of the similarities all religious groups share as human communities that struggle in different ways to deal with the basic issues of life (Ucko 2006, 37).

It is crucial 'to have a predisposition for understanding every person, analyzing every system and recognizing what is right; this does not at all mean losing certitude about one's own faith or weakening the principles of morality' (Gioia 2006, 93).

CONCLUSION

Nothing has yet been done by Islam and Christianity to recognise or acknowledge the place and contribution of ATR in Sierra Leone. In contrast, successive national governments have recognised and acknowledged the place and role of ATR in the country.

Through the agency of sacred specialists, traditional religious practices have long played a vital part in Sierra Leone's political system. Politicians have used traditional spirituality to gain and maintain political success, and the process has afforded them a sense of assurance and security. Politicians and persons in high positions sometimes use traditional means to get rid of their rivals or detractors. Sierra Leone governments have also encouraged the inclusion of ATR in state functions.

The use of traditional means in the job sector is also prominent. This is usually occasioned by the high level of bureaucracy and political interference by political and high level government authorities. A person who solicits the help of a sacred specialist to secure a job does so with the belief that the supernatural is more powerful than the efforts of politicians or any state hierarchy.

This understanding is also true of the judiciary. Most Sierra Leoneans consider the judicial system to be corrupt on account of the government and the persistent meddling and obstruction of justice by those in authority. Litigants solicit the help of sacred specialists to obtain favourable judgments.

ATR also contributed to ending the civil war through traditional fighters who used spiritual means to engage the rebels in combat. According to the SLPP government, traditional religious and community leaders played a vital role in the rehabilitation of war victims, and in the promotion of truth, healing, and reconciliation in the peace initiative of Sierra Leone.

Muslims and Christians would do well to learn from example: from the Sierra Leonean government, how to recognise and appreciate the contribution of ATR; and from international secular and religious organisations, how to recognise and dialogue with ATR.

The necessity for dialogue with ATR cannot be overemphasised. Muslims and Christians are called by their faith traditions, and are compelled by social factors, to dialogue with their neighbours. Very little is known about Islam's dialogical attempts with ATR. In Christianity, the

RCC and the WCC both recommend the recognition of and dialogue with ATR and its inclusion in interfaith cooperation.

If Islam and Christianity in Sierra Leone are serious about their intentions to dialogue with ATR and eventually include it in interfaith cooperation, Muslims and Christians must both tolerate and respect ATR as a genuine religion, and must educate themselves about ATR and about their own respective faiths.

ENDNOTES

1. Dr. Siaka P. Stevens ruled Sierra Leone from 1968 to 1985 as both prime minister and president. Upon his retirement in 1985, he personally chose Maj. Gen. Joseph S. Momoh, who was head of the army and a Limba himself, to succeed him. Momoh was overthrown in a military coup in 1992.

2. For a discussion on politics and divination in the APC party, see Shaw (1996, 30–55).

3. The failed so-called countercoup by the APC party was blamed on the false divination of an herbalist (Shaw 1996, 32). This attempt to overthrow the Military government and regain power resulted in the executions of seventeen alleged conspirators on 29 December 1992.

4. Pouring libations at state functions is also carried out in Nigeria (Hackett 1991, 141).

5. This is true of both literate qualified applicants and unqualified or nonliterate applicants.

6. When the NPRC military government seized power and charged many APC political appointees with the misuse of power and the misappropriation of funds, national newspapers ran stories every week of accused persons and their families visiting traditional spiritual leaders and offering expensive sacrifices to find favour in the justice system and hence escape the wrath of the military. Some of these traditional believers were not Limbas. They were, however, part of a system that encouraged traditional religion as the norm for over twenty years. See Shaw (1996, 30–55) for a discussion on politics and divination in Sierra Leone.

7. For a detailed study on these issues, see the works and bibliographies of Richards (1996) and Abdullah (2004).

8. See Richards (2005, 119–146).

9. Cf. Opala and Boillot (1993, 1, 5).

10. Caritas is a confederation of 162 Catholic relief development and social service organisations, one of which is found in Sierra Leone.

CHAPTER 8

CONCLUDING REMARKS

On account of the persistent marginalisation of ATR by Islam and Christianity in Sierra Leone, this book has investigated the place of ATR in interreligious encounters in the country since the advent of Islam and Christianity and has discussed possible ways in which ATR may be included in the present interfaith dialogue and cooperation between Islam and Christianity.

First, the tenets and practices of ATR, Islam, and Christianity were reviewed so that practitioners might become aware, or reaware, of their own values—social and religioculture—as well as those of the other religious traditions, and so engage in productive interreligious dialogue.

As in most of sub-Saharan Africa, ATR is the indigenous religion of Sierra Leone. When the early forebears and later progenitors of Islam and Christianity arrived, they met Sierra Leone indigenes with a remarkable knowledge of God and a structured religious system. Successive Muslim clerics, traders, and missionaries were respectful of and sensitive to the culture and religion of the indigenes who accommodated them and offered them hospitality. This approach resulted in a syncretistic brand of Islam.

In contrast, most Christian missionaries adopted an exclusive and insensitive approach to African culture and religiosity. Christianity, especially Protestantism, demanded a complete abandonment of African religioculture and a total dedication to Christianity. This attitude has continued by some indigenous clerics and religious leaders to the extent that SLIR and its practitioners continue to be marginalised in Sierra Leone's interreligious dialogue and cooperation.

Although the indigenes of Sierra Leone were and continue to be hospitable to Islam and Christianity, and in spite of the fact that SLIR shares affinity with Islam and Christianity in many theological and practical issues, and even though there are many Muslims and Christians who still hold on to traditional spirituality and culture, Muslim and Christian leaders of these immigrant religions are reluctant to include Traditionalists in interfaith issues in the country.

The formation and constitution of the IRCSL, which has local and international recognition, did not include ATR. These considerations, then, beg the questions,

- Why have Muslim and Christian leaders long marginalised ATR, its practices, and its practitioners from interfaith dialogue and cooperation in Sierra Leone?
- What is lacking in ATR that continues to prevent practitioners of Christianity and Islam from officially involving Traditionalists in the socioreligious development of the country?

Muslim and Christians have given several factors that are responsible for this exclusion:

- The prejudices that they inherited from their forebears.
- ATR lacks the hallmarks of a true religion.
- ATR is primitive and economically weak.
- The fear that the accommodation of ATR will result in syncretism and nominalism.

- Muslims see no need to dialogue with ATR practitioners, most of whom they consider to be already Muslims.

Considering the commonalities ATR shares with Islam and Christianity, and the number of Muslims and Christians who still hold on to traditional spirituality, these factors are not justifiable.

Although Islam and Christianity are finding it hard to recognise and include ATR in interfaith dialogue and cooperation in Sierra Leone, ATR continues to play a vital role in Sierra Leone's national politics, in the search and maintenance of employment, and in the judicial sector. ATR played a crucial part during and after the civil war. The national government in its TRC report acknowledged the importance and contribution of traditional culture and spirituality during and after the war.

Outside of Sierra Leone, the progress in the place and level of the recognition of ATR continues. At varying degrees, the SAC in France, the AACC, the Vatican, and the WCC have taken positive steps to recognise and find a place for ATR in their structures. Much about the necessity for dialogue and cooperation with ATR can be learnt in the works and efforts of these secular and religious bodies. The inclusion of ATR issues in the structure and deliberations of the Vatican and WCC shows that stereotypes and prejudices against ATR have been significantly diminished. The decision to include ATR was not made lightly. The suggestion was challenged and rejected several times, but after numerous meetings and consultations, the two largest Christian organisations of our time have African religioculture on their agenda. This should be a source of encouragement to the many churches in Africa that are still perpetuating the prejudice inherited from their forebears that the time for change and reconstruction has come.

If nothing else, there are two main reasons why Islam and Christianity in Sierra Leone must be in dialogue with ATR:

- Dialogue of life or in community. People living side by side meet and interact personally and communally on a regular basis. They share common resources and communal benefits. These factors compel people to be in dialogue.

- Dual religiosity. As many Muslims and Christians in Sierra Leone are still holding on to ATR practices, it is crucial for Muslims and Christians to dialogue with ATR practitioners.

If Muslims and Christians are serious about meeting and starting a process of dialogue with Traditionalists, certain practical issues have to be considered:

- Islam and Christianity have to validate and accept ATR as a true religion and a viable partner in the socioreligious landscape of Sierra Leone.
- Muslims and Christians must educate themselves about ATR, and the scriptures and teachings of their respective religious traditions, in order to relate well with Traditionalists.

These are starting points that can produce successful results. Although, at present, Muslims and Christians in Sierra Leone are finding it difficult to initiate dialogue and cooperation with Traditionalists, all hope is not lost. It is now the task of the established IRCSL to ensure the inclusion of ATR. Islam and Christianity must remember that when they came as strangers, ATR played host to them and continues to play a vital role in providing hospitality and allowing them to blossom on African soil.

FINAL THOUGHTS

Sierra Leoneans lived together as a peaceful and loving people for a very long time before the civil war. The war came and caused unwarranted and indescribable misery for ten long years. It is now over, and the people of Sierra Leone are working together to rebuild themselves and the country.

Religion was not responsible for the war, nor has it been a cause of civil unrest in the country. As the Sierra Leonean case shows, all three major religions played a vital role in helping the government restore peace and begin reconstruction. However, many people were hurt and some lost their lives on account of betrayals and of those seeking vengeance. It will take time to heal the wounds that resulted from the war and, even though the worst is now behind Sierra Leoneans, justice must still be pursued. Religious leaders in Sierra Leone are called to 'be vanguards of justice so that peace is sustained' (Temple 2006, i). Muslim and Christian leaders should endeavour to include Traditionalists in this process.

The establishment of a traditional form of dialogue with Traditionalists will not take place overnight. There is much reservation, distrust, and hurt to overcome. The burdens of our past can be an obstacle to overcome in building dialogue. Sierra Leoneans have to move beyond their sad stories. The work of IRCSL should not only include Muslims and Christians. Traditionalists are the hosts who welcomed Islam and Christianity and provided a peaceful atmosphere for them.

Serious dialogue with practitioners of ATR should take into consideration two groups and approaches:

- Dialogue with staunch ATR practitioners who do want to become either Muslims or Christians. In this regard, it should be understood from the perspective of encounter, respect, and mutual understanding of worldviews.
- Dialogue with dualists. Those who claim to be converted to Islam and Christianity but are still holding on to ATR should be approached from a pastoral perspective with a view to discussing the scriptures and theology.

Finally, in the words of Ariararjah (1999, 12–13), 'dialogue is not an ambulance service; it is a public health service!' Muslims and Christians should not wait until an outbreak of disaster before Traditionalists are taken seriously. Sierra Leoneans should not forget that Traditionalists have the capacity for deadly reactions when cornered. One is reminded of the hut (house) tax war of 1898, the rebellion of northerners led by the warrior Bai Bureh against the imposition of a hut tax by the colonial government.

Traditionalists all over Africa have proved that they are patient and accommodating. Apart from being marginalised, Traditionalists sit and watch Muslims and Christians perpetuate violence and unrest in their land. For decades now, most of the wars in Africa have been religious conflicts between Islam and Christianity. Sierra Leoneans should be grateful that this has never been a cause of violence in their country. This does not, however, mean that this possibility has passed. If the host religion continues to be trampled, the situation may yet escalate. It is, however, my hope that this book will contribute to peace in Africa by providing the information and tools necessary for the establishment of positive dialogue and interreligious cooperation among ATR, Islam, and Christianity.

Appendix A

Profile of Interviewees and Consultants

Solomon Koroma, Lahai Gbassama, and Mary Moseray—Mende Traditionalists.

Fatmata Turay, Amidu Sesay, and Bomporo Kalokoh—Temne Traditionalists.

Gbabon Samura, Alimamy Sesay, and Yainkaine Koroma—Limba Traditionalists.

Aiah Pessima, Kumba Pessima, and Tamba John—Kono Traditionalists.

Yvonne Spring, Beatrice Nicol, and Yvette Spring—Krio consultants.

Pastor Aske Bee Gbla, chair and lecturer, Sierra Leonean Languages department; lecturer, Religious Education and Temne Studies, Milton Margai College of Education and Technology, Goderich, Sierra Leone.

Rev. Moses Khanu, national programme coordinator, Inter-Religious Council of Sierra Leone (IRCSL).

Rev. Silas Nicol, national superintendent, Church of the First Elect, Maryland, USA.

Rev. Arnold Temple, circuit superintendent, Wesley circuit, Freetown, Sierra Leone.

Rev. Olivia Wesley, principal, Sierra Leone Theological College and Church Training Centre, Freetown, Sierra Leone.

Pastor Sahr Yiaba, graduate, Kono Culture and Studies, Bo Town, Sierra Leone.

Appendix B

IRCSL Statement of Shared Moral Concerns

Concerned for the physical and social reconstruction of Sierra Leone and for reconciliation among all peoples in our nation, the undersigned responsible representatives of the Christian Churches and the leaders of the Islamic Community have decided to issue the following common statement:

1. The people of Sierra Leone have undergone enormous suffering. But, thanks be to God, the peace accords have been signed. Our task now is to establish a durable peace based on truth, justice and common living, and to collaborate with all people of good will in the healing tasks of reconciliation, reconstruction, and rehabilitation for Sierra Leone.

2. We, the responsible representatives of the Christian Churches and the Islamic Community in Sierra Leone recognise that our Religious Communities differ from each other, and that each of them feels called to live true to its own faith. At the same time, we recognise that our religious and spiritual traditions hold many values in common, and that these shared values can provide an authentic basis for mutual esteem, cooperation, and free common living in Sierra Leone.

3. Each of our Religious Communities recognises that human dignity and human value is a gift of God. Our religions, each in its own way, call us to recognise the fundamental human rights of each person. Violence against persons or the violation of their basic rights are for us not only against man-made laws but also break God's law.

4. We jointly in mutual respectful recognition of our religious differences, condemn all violence against innocent persona and any form of abuse or violation of fundamental human rights. Specifically, we condemn,

    *   Acts of hatred based on political, ethnic or religious differences. We express our special concern at the burning of houses and property, and the destruction of religious buildings;
    *   The obstruction of the free right of return;
    *   Any acts of revenge;
    *   The abuse of any media by any agency or entity with the aim of spreading hatred.

5. Further, we call for respect for the fundamental human rights of all persons, regardless of political, religious or ethnic affiliation, which must include,

    *   The freedom of all responsible representatives or leaders of Religious Communities in Sierra Leone to fulfill their mission in every part of the country;
    *   Opportunities for the free performance of religious services and all forms of pastoral care by all Christian ministers and priests, and by all Sheikhs and Imams of the Islamic community;
    *   The right of every child to religious instruction in his or her own faith.

6. Finally, we call on people of good will to take responsibility for their own acts. Let us treat others as we would wish them to treat us.

7. With this statement we appeal to all believers of our Religious Communities, and to all citizens of Sierra Leone, and to H.E. Alhaji Dr. A.T. Kabbah, President of the Republic of Sierra Leone.

Signed on 1 April 1997 by,
Al-Sheikh Ahmad Tejan Sillah, Islamic Community in Sierra Leone
Rev. Moses Benson Khanu, Council of Churches in Sierra Leone
Archbishop Joseph Ganda, Roman Catholic Community in Sierra Leone

APPENDIX C

IRCSL STATEMENT OF SHARED VALUES AND COMMON PURPOSE

The following was the content of the Declaration of Shared Values and Common Purpose,

WHEREAS, we believe in God, and in the revealed law of God, and
WHEREAS, we believe in the natural law and the just law of man, and
WHEREAS, we believe in the equality of all people before God and the Law, and
WHEREAS, we recognise our common human destiny, and
WHEREAS, we recognise our common history with religious and cultural diversity, and
WHEREAS, we recognise our common benefit in unity with diversity, and
WHEREAS, we commit ourselves to truth, justice and common living, and
WHEREAS, we commit ourselves to the respect and protection of human rights, and
WHEREAS, we commit ourselves to peace in Sierra Leone and the world, and
WHEREAS, we trust the just Law of the land of Sierra Leone, and
WHEREAS, we feel responsible for the future of our nation, and the religious communities of Sierra Leone and beyond,

NOW, THEREFORE BE IT RESOLVED, that the Legitimate heads of the following religious communities of Sierra Leone,
The Islamic Community in Sierra Leone
The Council of Churches in Sierra Leone, and
The Roma Catholic Community in Sierra Leone have written their good will in the form of the Declaration for the establishment of an **Interreligious Council of Sierra Leone**.

Signed on 1 April 1997 by,
Al-Sheikh Ahmad Tejan Sillah, Islamic Community in Sierra Leone
Rev. Moses Benson Khanu, Council of Churches in Sierra Leone
Archbishop Joseph Ganda, Roman Catholic Community in Sierra Leone

BIBLIOGRAPHY

Abdullah, I., ed. 2004. *Between democracy and terror: The Sierra Leone civil war*. Dakar, Senegal, CODESRIA.

Abimbola, W. 1991. The place of African Traditional Religion in contemporary Africa. In *African Traditional Religions in contemporary society*, ed. J. K. Olupona, 51–58. St. Paul, MN: Paragon House.

———. 2005. How to improve the relationship between Islam, Christianity and Traditional African Religion. In *Proceedings of the International Congress of Dialogue on Civilizations, Religion and Cultures in West Africa*, ed. I. Oke, 37–38. Paris: UNESCO.

Achtemeier, P. J. 1996. *HarperCollins Bible Dictionary*. New York: HarperCollins Publishers.

Adegbite, L. 2005. The role of religious leaders in conflict resolution. In *Proceedings of the International Congress of Dialogue on Civilizations, Religion and Cultures in West Africa*, ed. I. Oke, 35–36. Paris: UNESCO.

Adelowo, E. D. 1982. A comparative study of angelology in the Bible and the Qur'an and the concepts of gods many and lords. *Africa Theological Journal* 11 (1): 151–167.

Ajayi, A. 2005. Promoting religious tolerance and co-operation in the West African region: The example of religious plurality and tolerance among the Yoruba of south-western Nigeria. In *Proceedings of the International Congress of Dialogue on Civilizations, Religion and Cultures in West Africa*, ed. I. Oke, 43–47. Paris: UNESCO.

Alharazim, M. S. D. 1939. The origin and progress of Islam in Sierra Leone. *Sierra Leone Studies*, o.s., 21:12–26.

Ali, M. M. 1992. *Introduction to the study of the Holy Qur'an*. St. Lambert, PQ, Canada: Payette & Simms.

————. 2002. *The Holy Qur'an, with English translation and commentary*. Dublin, OH: AAI Islam Lahore.

Alie, J. A. D. 1990. *A new history of Sierra Leone*. London: Macmillan.

All Africa Conference of Churches (AACC). 1958. *The church in changing Africa: Report of the AACC*, July 15–20, 1958. Ibadan, Nigeria: Ibidan University Microfilms. University Microfilms.

————. 1963. *Drumbeats from Kampala: Report of the first assembly of the All Africa Conference of Churches held at Kampala, April 20–30, 1963*. London: United Society for Christian Literature, Lutterworth Press.

Anderson, E. C. 1970. Early Muslim schools and British policy in Sierra Leone. *West African Journal of Education* 14:177–178.

Appiah-Kubi, K. 1993. Traditional African healing system versus Western medicine in southern Ghana: An encounter. In *Religious plurality in Africa: Essays in honour of John S. Mbiti*, ed. J. K. Olupona and S. S. Nyang, 95–107. New York: Mouton De Gruyter.

Ariarajah, S. W. 1999. *Not without my neighbour: Issues in interfaith relations*. Geneva, WCC Publications.

Asante, E. 2001. The Gospel in context: An African perspective. *Interpretation: A Journal of Bible and Theology* 55 (4): 355–366.

Avery, W. L. 1971. *Christianity in Sierra Leone*. Unpublished essay. Freetown, Sierra Leone: Fourah Bay College.

Awolalu, J. O. 1979. *Yoruba beliefs and sacrificial rites*. London, Longman.

————. 1991. The encounter between African Traditional Religion and other religions in Nigeria. In *African Traditional Religions in contemporary society*, ed. J. K. Olupona, 111–118. St. Paul, MN: Paragon House.

Aziz, Z. 1993. *Introduction to Islam*. Dublin, OH: AAI Islam Lahore.

Bah, M. A. 1991. The status of Muslims in Sierra Leone and Liberia. *Journal Institute of Muslim Minority Affairs* 12 (2): 464–481.

Baldock, J. 2004. *The essence of Sufism*. London: Arcturus Publishing Limited.

Bascom, W. R. 1973. *African arts in cultural perspective: An introduction*. New York: Norton.

Bidmos, M. A. *Inter-religious dialogue—The Nigerian experience*. Lagos, Nigeria: Islamic Publication Bureau.

Blyden, E. [1887] 1994. *Christianity, Islam and the Negro race*. Edinburgh, U.K.: Edinburgh University Press.

Booth, N., Jr. 1977. Islam in Africa. In *African religions: A symposium*, ed. N. Booth, Jr. Lagos, Nigeria: NOK Publishers, Ltd.

Bourdillon, M. F. C. 2000. Witchcraft and society. In *African spirituality: Forms, meanings and expressions*, ed. J. K. Olupona, 176–197. New York: Crossroad.

Byaruhanga-Akiiki, A. B. T. 1993. Africa and Christianity. In *Religious plurality in Africa: Essays in honour of John S. Mbiti*, ed. J. K. Olupona and S. S. Nyang, 179–196. New York: Mouton De Gruyter.

Conteh, P. S. 2004. *Fundamental concepts of Limba traditional religion and its effects on Limba Christianity and vice versa in Sierra Leone in the past three decades*. ThD diss., University of South Africa.

———. 2005. Discussing the Trinity with African traditionalists. *Mission* 12 (2): 245–263.

———. 2008. *The place of African Traditional Religion in inter-religious encounters in Sierra Leone since the advent of Islam and Christianity*. DLitt and DPhil diss., University of South Africa.

De Vaux, R. 1997. *Ancient Israel: Its life and institution*. Grand Rapids, MI: Eerdsman.

Dorjahn, V. R. 1982. The initiation and training of Temne Poro members. In *African religious groups and beliefs*, ed. S. Ottenberg, 35–62. Folklore Institute.

Downes, R. M. 1971. *Tiv religion*. Ibadan, Nigeria: Ibadan University Press.

Eitel, K. E. 1988. Contextualization, contrasting African voices. *Criswell Theological Review* 2 (2): 323–334.

Erickson, M. J. 1992. *Introducing Christian doctrine*. Grand Rapids, MI: Baker Book.

Evans-Pritchard, E. E. 1956. *The Nuer religion*. Oxford, U.K.: Clarendon Press.

Fanthorpe, R. 1998b. Limba 'deep rural' strategies. *Journal of African History* 39 (1): 15–38.

Fashole-Luke, E. W. 1974. Ancestor veneration and the communion of saints. In *New Testament Christianity for Africa and the world: Essays in honour of Harry Sawyerr*, ed. M. E. Glasswell and E. W. Fashole-Luke, 209–221. London: S.P.C.K.

Ferdinando, K. 1996. Screwtape revisited: Demonology, Western African, and biblical. In *The unseen world: Christian reflections on angels, demons and the heavenly realm*, ed. A. N. S. Lane, 103–132. Grand Rapids, MI: Paternoster Press & Baker Book House.

Finnegan, R. 1965. *Survey of the Limba people of northern Sierra Leone*. London: Her Majesty Stationery Office.

———. 1967. *Limba stories and story telling*. Oxford, U.K.: Clarendon Press.

Flannery, A., ed. 1987. *Vatican Council II: The conciliar and post conciliar documents*. Northport, NY: Costello Publishing Company.

Foullah, L. A. 2006. A Christian perspective of peaceful co-existence in a multi-religious society. In *Peaceful co-existence in a multi-religious society*, ed. S. Cooper, 12–19. Freetown, Sierra Leone: Council of Churches in Sierra Leone.

Fyfe, C. 1962. *A short history of Sierra Leone*. London: Longman.

Fyle, C. M. 1981. *The history of Sierra Leone: A concise introduction.* London: Evans.

Gbla, A. B. 1993. *African Traditional Religion: Short outline.* (Lecture notes.) Unpublished.

————. N.d. *An approach to Themne grammar.* (Lecture notes.) Unpublished.

Gioia, F., ed. 2006. *Interreligious dialogue: The official teaching of the Catholic Church from Second Vatican Council to John Paul II (1963–2005).* Boston: Pauline Books & Media.

Gittins, A. J. 1987. *Mende religion: Aspects of belief and thought in Sierra Leone.* Bahnhofstr, Nettenal: Verlag-Wort Und Werk.

Gonzalez, J. L. 1970. *A history of Christian thought: From the beginning to the Council of Chalcedon.* Nashville: Abingdon Press.

————. 1984. *The early church to the dawn of the Reformation.* Vol. 1 of *The story of Christianity.* San Francisco: HarperSanFrancisco.

Hackett, R. I. J. 1991. Revitalization in African Traditional Religion. In *African Traditional Religions in contemporary society*, ed. J. K. Olupona, 135–148. St. Paul, MN: Paragon House.

Hale, R. D. 2003. Christianity. In *The illustrated guide to world religions*, ed. M. D. Coogan, 52–87. New York: Oxford University Press.

Hargrave, C. G. 1944. *African primitive life: As I saw it in Sierra Leone British West Africa.* Wilmington, NC: Wilmington Printing Co.

Harris, W. T. 1950. The idea of God among the Mende. In *African ideas of God: A symposium*, ed. E. W. Smith, 277–300. London: Edinburgh House Press.

Harris, W. T., and H. Sawyerr. 1968. *The springs of Mende belief and conduct.* Freetown, Sierra Leone: Sierra Leone University Press.

Hastings, A. 1976. *A history of African Christianity 1950–1975.* Cambridge, U.K.: Cambridge University Press.

Hildebrant, J. 1990. *History of the Church in Africa: A survey.* Denver, CO: International Academic Publishers, Ltd.

Hocking, W. E. 1912. *The meaning of God in human experience.* New Haven: Yale University Press.

Hollenweger, W. J. 1993. Foreword to *Religious plurality in Africa: Essays in honour of John S. Mbiti*, ed. J. K. Olupona and S. S. Nyang, vi–xiii. New York: Mouton De Gruyter.

Houtman, C. 1993. *Exodus.* Vol. 1. Kampen, the Netherlands: KOK Publishing House.

Idowu, E. B. 1965. *Towards an indigenous church.* London: Oxford University Press.

———. 1973. *African Traditional Religion: A definition.* London: SCM Press.

———. 1977. *African Traditional Religion: A problem of definition.* London: SCM Press.

Ikenga-Metuh, E. 1981. *God and man in African religion.* London: Geoffrey Chapman.

———. 1987. *Comparative studies of African Traditional Religions.* Onitsha, Nigeria: IMICO Publishers.

Isizoh, D. 2005. Managing conflicts in the African context: The role of religious leaders. In *Proceedings of the International Congress of Dialogue on Civilizations, Religions and Cultures*, ed. I. Oke, 29–34. Paris: UNESCO.

Jah, al-Hajj U. N. S. 1987. Christian-Muslim relations: An Islamic point of view. *Bulletin on Islam and Christian-Muslim Relations in Africa* 5 (4): 1–6.

Jules-Rosette, B. W. 1991. Traditional and continuity in African religions. In *African Traditional Religions in contemporary society*, ed. J. K. Olupona, 149–165. St. Paul, MN: Paragon House.

Kailing, J. B. 1994. A new solution to the African Christian problem. *Missiology: An International Review* 22 (4): 489–506.

Karp, I., and D. A. Masolo, eds. 2000. *African philosophy as cultural inquiry*. Bloomington: Indiana University Press.

Kato, B. H. 1987. *Biblical Christianity in Africa: Theological perspectives in Africa*. Achimota, Ghana: African Christian Press.

Khanu, M. B. 2001. *The encounter of Islam and Christianity in Sierra Leone: A case study*. Diploma thesis, University of Hamburg.

King, F. J. 1994. Angels and ancestors: A basis for Christology. *Mission Studies* 11 (1): 10–26.

Kinnamon, M., and B. E. Cope, eds. 1997. *The ecumenical movement: An anthology of key texts and voices*. Geneva: WCC Publications.

Klein, W. W. et al. 1993. *Introduction to biblical interpretation*. Dallas, TX: Word Publishing.

Koech, K. 1977. African mythology: A key to understanding African religion. In *African religions: A symposium*, ed. N. S. Booth, Jr., 117–118. New York: NOK Publishers.

Koroma, A. 2003. A call to love for national development: The religious community responds. In *A call to love for national development*, ed. G. Williams, 121–124. Freetown, Sierra Leone: Ro-marong Ind., Ltd.

Kraft, C. H. 1978. *Biblical Christianity in Africa*. Achimota, Ghana: Africa Christian Press.

Liberia Editrice Vaticana (LEV). 1994. *Catechism of the Catholic Church*. Ottawa, Canada: Publications Service, Canadian Conference of Catholic Bishops.

Little, K. L. 1949. The role of the secret society in cultural specialization. *American Anthropologist* 51:199–212.

Lockyer, H. 1995. *All the angels in the Bible: A complete exploration of the nature and ministry of angels*. Peabody, MA: Hendrickson Publishers.

Lucas, J. O. 1948. *The religion of the Yorubas*. Lagos, Nigeria: C.M.S. Bookshop.

Magesa, L. 1997. *African religion: The moral traditions of abundant life*. Maryknoll, NY: Orbis Books.

Marthaler, B. L. 1987. *The creed*. Mystic, CT: Twenty-Third Publication.

Martos, J. 1982. *Doors to the sacred: A historical introduction to sacraments in the Catholic Church*. Garden City, NY: Doubleday & Co., Inc.

Mbiti, J. S. 1970a. *Concepts of God in Africa*. London: S.P.C.K.

————. 1970b. Christianity and traditional religions in Africa. *International Review of Mission* 59 (1): 430–440.

————. 1971. *The crisis of mission in Africa*. Mukono, Uganda: Uganda Church Press.

————. 1972. Some African concepts of Christology. In *Christ and the younger churches*, ed. G. Vicedom, 53–60. London: SPCK.

————. 1977. Christianity and African culture. *Journal of Theology for Southern Africa* 1 (September): 26–40.

————. 1980. Encounter of Christian faith and African religion. *Christian Century* 97 (1): 817–820.

————. 1986. *Bible and theology in African Christianity*. Nairobi, Kenya: Oxford University Press.

————. 1989a. *African religions and philosophy*. London: Heinemann.

————. 1989b. God, sin, and salvation in African religion. *Journal of the International Theological Centre* 16 (1): 59–68.

————. 1996. Challenge facing religious education and research in Africa: The case of dialogue between Christianity and African religions. *Religion and Theology* 3 (1): 170–179.

————. 1997. Dreams as a point of theological dialogue between Christianity and African religion. *Missionalia* 25 (1): 511–522.

Mbon, F. M. 1991. African traditional socio-religious ethics and national development: The Nigeria case. In *African Traditional Religions in contemporary society*, ed. J. K. Olupona, 101–109. St. Paul, MI: Paragon House.

McCulloch, M. 1950. *Peoples of Sierra Leone*. London: I.A.I.

McKenzie, P. R. 1976. *Inter-religious encounters in West Africa*. Leicester: University of Leicester Press.

Migeod, F. W. H. 1971. *The languages of West Africa*. London: Gregg International.

Mosley, A. G., ed. 1995. *African philosophy: Selected readings*. Englewood Cliffs, NJ: Prentice Hall.

Mugabe, H. J. 1999. Salvation from an African perspective. *Evangelical Review of Theology* 23 (3): 238–247.

Mulago, V. 1991. African Traditional Religion and Christianity. In *African Traditional Religions in contemporary society*, ed. J. K. Olupona, 119–134. St. Paul, MI: Paragon House.

Muzadi, A. H. 2006. Message to the assembly. *Current Dialogue* 47:24–25.

Nadel, S. F. 1954. *Nupe religion*. London: Routledge & Kegan Paul, Ltd.

National Curriculum Development Centre. 1993. *Source book for four Sierra Leone languages*. Freetown, Sierra Leone: Print Sundry and Stationers.

Nelson, A. 2005. The surrendering: An introduction to Islam. In *Five voices five faiths: An interfaith primer*, ed. A. M. Hughes, 93–116. Cambridge, MA: Cowley Publications.

Oborji, F. A. 2002. Revelation in African Traditional Religion. *Studies in Interreligious Dialogue* 12 (1): 5–22.

Oguejiofor, J. O. 2006. Resources for peace in African proverbs and myths. In *Resources for peace in traditional religions*. Vatican City: Pontifical Council for Interreligious Dialogue.

Oke, I., ed. 2005. *Proceedings of the International Congress of Dialogue on Civilizations, Religion and Cultures in West Africa.* Paris: UNESCO.

Okorocha, C. 1994. The meaning of salvation: An African perspective. In *Emerging voices in global Christian theology,* ed. W. A. Dryness, 59–92. Grand Rapids, MI: Zondervan.

Olson, G. W. 1969. *Church growth in Sierra Leone.* Grand Rapids, MI: Eerdmans.

Olupona, J. K., ed. 1991. *African Traditional Religions in contemporary society.* St. Paul, MI: Paragon House.

Olupona, J. K., and S. S. Nyang, eds. 1993. *Religious plurality in Africa: Essays in honour of John S. Mbiti.* New York: Mouton De Gruyter.

Oosthuizen, G. C. 1991. The place of traditional religion in contemporary South Africa. In *African Traditional Religions in contemporary society,* ed. J. K. Olupona, 35–50. St. Paul, MI: Paragon House.

Opala, J., and F. Boillot. 1996. Leprosy among the Limba: Illness and healing in the context of world view. *Social Science and Medicine* 42 (1): 3–19.

Opoku, K. A. 1993. African Traditional Religion: An enduring heritage. In *Religious plurality in Africa: Essays in honour of John S. Mbiti,* ed. J. K. Olupona and S. S. Nyang, 67–82. New York, Mouton De Gruyter.

Ottenberg, S. 1983. Artistic and sex roles in a Limba chiefdom. In *Female and male in West Africa,* ed. C. Oppong, 76–90. London: George Allan.

———. 1984. Two new religions, one analytic frame. *Cahiers d'Etudes Africaines* 24 (4): 437–54.

———. 1988a. Religion and ethnicity in the arts of a Limba chiefdom. *Africa* 58 (4): 437–465.

———. 1988b. The bride comes to the groom: Ritual and drama in Limba wedding. *The Drama Review* 32:42–64.

———. 1989. The dancing bride: Art and indigenous psychology in Limba weddings. *Man* 24:57–78.

———. 1994. Male and female secret societies among the Bafodea Limba of northern Sierra Leone. In *Religion in Africa: Experience and expressions*, ed. T. D. Blakeley, E. Walter, A. van Beek, and D. Thomson, 363–387. London: Heinemann.

———. 1996. *Seeing with music: The lives of three blind African musicians*. Seattle, WA: University of Washington Press.

———. 2004. Story and storytelling: The Limba. In *African folklore: An encyclopedia*, ed. P. M. Peek and K. Yankah, 141–142. London: Routledge.

Packer, J. I., M. C. Tenney, and W. White, Jr., eds. 1980. *The Bible almanac*. Nashville, TN: Thomas Nelson Publishers.

Parrat, John. 1995. *Reinventing Christianity, African Theology Today*. Grand Rapids, MI, Eerdmans.

Parrinder, E. G. 1962. *African Traditional Religion*. London: Sheldon.

———. 1963. *Witchcraft, European and African*. London: Faber and Faber.

———. 1967. *African mythology*. London: Paul Hamlyn.

———. 1969. *Africa's three religions*. London: Sheldon.

Parsons, R. T. 1950. The idea of God among the Kono of Sierra Leone. In *African ideas of God: A symposium*, ed. E. W. Smith, 260–276. London: Edinburgh House Press.

———. 1964. *Religion in an African society*. Leiden: E. J. Brill.

Peters, F. E. 2003. *Islam: A guide for Jews and Christians*. Princeton, NJ: Princeton University Press.

Pratt, D. 2005. *The challenge of Islam*. Hampshire, U.K.: Ashgate Publishing.

Report of the Truth and Reconciliation Commission of Sierra Leone. October 2004. Vol. 3b, ch. 7, par. 32–36.

Richards, P. 1996. *Fighting for the rain forest: War, youth and resources in Sierra Leone*. Oxford, U.K.: James Currey.

———. 2005. Green book millenarianism? The Sierra Leone war within the perspective of an anthropology of religion. In *Religion and African civil wars*, ed. Niel Kastfelt, 119–146. New York: Palgrave Macmillan.

Rieber, C. 1977. Traditional Christianity as an African religion. In *African religions: A symposium*, ed. Newell Booth, Jr., 222–255. Lagos, Nigeria: NOK Publishers, Ltd.

Ryan, T. 2004. Catholic perspectives on interreligious relations. *WCC Current Dialogue* 44:18–27.

Samartha, S. J. 1981. *Courage for dialogue: Ecumenical issues in inter-religious relationships*. Geneva: WCC Publications.

Sanneh, L. 1983. *West African Christianity: The religious impact*. Maryknoll, NY: Orbis Books.

———. 1996. *Piety and power: Muslim and Christians in West Africa*. Maryknoll, NY: Orbis Books.

———. 2001. A resurgent church in a troubled continent. Review of Bengt Sundkler's *History of the church in Africa*. *International Bulletin* 25 (3): 113–115.

Sawyerr, H. 1966. Ancestor worship II: The rationale. *The Sierra Leone Bulletin of Religion* 8 (2): 33–39.

———. 1967. A Sunday graveside libation in Freetown after a bereavement. *The Sierra Leone Bulletin of Religion* 8 (2): 41–49.

———. 1968. *Creative evangelism: Towards a new Christian encounter with Africa*. London: Lutterworth.

———. 1970. *God, ancestor or creator: Aspects of traditional belief in Ghana, Nigeria and Sierra Leone*. London: Longmans.

———. 1996. *The Practice of presence: Shorter writings of Harry Sawyerr*. Grand Rapids, MI: Eerdmans.

Schreiter, R. J. 1985. *Constructing local theologies*. Maryknoll, NY: Orbis Books.

Sesay, M. G. 2006. A Muslim perspective of peaceful co-existence in a multi-religious society. In *Peaceful co-existence in a multi-religious society*, ed. S. Cooper, 1–11. Freetown, Sierra Leone: Council of Churches in Sierra Leone.

Setiloane, G. M. 1978. How the traditional world-view persists in the Christianity of the Sotho-Tswana. In *Christianity in independent Africa*, ed. E. Fashole-Luke et al., 402–412. London: Rex Collings.

Shaw, R. 1985. Gender and the structuring of reality in Temne divination: An interactive study. *Africa* 55 (3): 286–303.

———. 1996. The politician and the diviner: Divination and the consumption of power in Sierra Leone. *Journal of Religion in Africa* 26 (1): 30–55.

Skinner, D. E. 1978. Mende settlement and the development of Islamic institutions in Sierra Leone. *International Journal of African Historical Studies* 11 (1): 32–62.

Smith, E. W., ed. 1966. *African ideas of God: A symposium*. London: Edinburgh House Press.

Steady, F. C. 1976. Protestant women's associations in an African city. In *Women in Africa: Studies in social and economic change*, ed. E. Bay and N. Hafkins, 213–237. Stanford, CA: Stanford University Press.

Taylor, J. V. 1963. *The primal vision: Christian presence amid African religion*. London: SCM Press.

Temple, A. C., ed. 2006. Editorial. *War, Peace and Reconciliation*. Freetown, Sierra Leone: CCSL.

Thomas, D. E. 2005. African Traditional Religion in the modern world. Jefferson, NC: McFarland and Company Publishers.

Tremmel, W. C. 1983. *Religion, what is it?* New York: Holt, Rinehart and Winston.

Trimingham, J. S., and C. Fyfe. 1960. The early expansion of Islam in Sierra Leone. *Sierra Leone Bulletin of Religion* 2 (1): 33–40.

Turay, A. K. 1967. Temne supernatural terminology. *The Sierra Leone Bulletin of Religion* 8 (2): 41–49.

Ucko, A. 2006. *Current Dialogue* 47:37–39.

Ucko, H. 2005. Editorial. *Current Dialogue* 45:2–3.

———. 2006. Editorial. *Current Dialogue* 47:2–5.

Westerlund, D. 1991. 'Insiders' and 'outsiders' in the study of African religions: Notes on some problems of theory and method. In *African Traditional Religions in contemporary society*, ed. J. K. Olupona, 15–24. St. Paul, MI: Paragon House.

———. 1993. The study of African religions in retrospect: From 'Westernization' to 'Africanization'. In *Religious plurality in Africa: Essays in honour of John S. Mbiti*, ed. J. K. Olupona and S. S. Nyang, 43–66. New York: Mouton De Gruyter.

Westermann, D. 1952. *Languages of West Africa*. London: Oxford University Press.

World Council of Churches (WCC). 2003. *Ecumenical considerations: For dialogue and relations with people of other religions*. Geneva: WCC Publications.

———. 2006. *Current dialogue* 47: 46–47.

Wyse, A. 1989. *The Krio of Sierra Leone: An interpretive history*. London: C. Hurst & Co.

Yambasu, S. J. 2002. *Dialectics of evangelization: A critical examination of Methodist evangelization of the Mende people in Sierra Leone*. Accra, Ghana: AOG Literature Centre.

Zuesse, E. M. 1991. Perseverance and transmutation in African Traditional Religions. In *African Traditional Religions in contemporary society*, ed. J. K. Olupona, 167–184. St. Paul, MI: Paragon House.

INDEX